The Shameful Years

The History of the Green Bay Packers

Larry D. Names

Eagan Hill Publishers

USA

THE SHAMEFUL YEARS

THE HISTORY OF THE GREEN BAY PACKERS

ISBN: 978-0-910937-73-3

Photographs courtesy of

The Green Bay Packer Hall of Fame

Pro Football Hall of Fame

Harold Elder cartoons – *Green Bay Press-Gazette*

Front cover photograph courtesy of Jeff Everson Collection

To

George Montejano

Packer Fan Extraordinaire!

One of the finest young men I ever had the honor

and privilege to coach

TABLE OF CONTENTS

§§§

Acknowledgments

The first person I wish to thank is my wife Peggy who isn't a football fan. She has displayed the patience of a saint for these many years as I have bombarded her with every little bit of information about the Green Bay Packers I gleaned from the various sources used to re-create each portion of Packer history. Also, she was an invaluable research assistant. I couldn't have done this book or any of the previous three volumes without her.

This series may never have gotten off the ground if my close friend and confidant Fr. Joseph Schlaefer hadn't given me the confidence to write it. He knows how grateful I am for this opportunity, but I would like the whole world to know what a truly remarkable man he is. It's a great honor to be his friend.

My friend Greg Scott provided some invaluable editorial assistance. His suggestions and prodding kept me digging for the facts.

Staffers at the Wisconsin Historical Society in Madison put me on the right track in researching the old newspapers. They include Craig Cramer, Lori Bessler, and Mary Jo Norton, who were especially helpful to me on one volume or another over the years.

The librarians at the Brown County Library in Green Bay and the Berlin (Wis.) Public Library were very kind and helpful when called on for assistance.

Abe Abrohams was a fountain of information about Nate Abrams and his family's contribution to Packer history.

Many thanks to Pat O'Connell at the Green Bay Packer Hall of Fame. Same for Joe Horrigan and Sandy Self at the Pro Football Hall of Fame in Canton, Ohio. Joe gave me some incredible insights into the overall history of the NFL, and Sandy made my visit to the Hall's library just about perfect.

Of course, I can never say enough about my good friend, the late Jim K. Ford, for his research assistance, advice, encouragement, and compliments on the first three books in the series. So often Jim pointed me in the right direction to find some detail or he confirmed information I had uncovered through another source. Jim also spoke to several people who provided answers to a myriad of questions about the Packers and Curly Lambeau in the early years and about the Packers and their coaches of the 1950s for this volume. Without Jim and his contacts, this series would not have been possible. Jim was a great guy, and I sorely miss him.

In the third volume's *Acknowledgements,* I gave thanks to Judge William J. Duffy for his valuable contribution to this work. I reiterate my gratitude here.

Part I in this series was dedicated to the memory of John Torinus. How greatly I miss him as well!

In Part III, I presented an explanation for my criticism of Art Daley's work, and to reinforce that explanation.

§§§

Introduction

Fate! An amazing concept. Defined by the dictionary as a force viewed as unalterably determining in advance the way things happen. In another word, destiny.

Not everybody believes in fate or destiny or even predestination or whatever. That fictional time-traveler, Dr. Emmett Brown in the very popular film trilogy, *Back to the Future,* said in the third episode: "Your future hasn't been written yet. No one's has. Your future is whatever you make it, so make it a good one..."

Maybe Dr. Brown was right. Maybe the future hasn't been written yet but maybe the professor was wrong. Call it fate. Call it destiny. Call it predestination. Call it coincidence, if you will. Call it whatever. Incidents do happen that do seem out of our control as human beings. As my wife Peggy said to me very early in our relationship. "If it's meant to be, it will happen. I guess that's fate or destiny or whatever. Right."

All right, whatever.

All I know is, on December 8, 1949,[*] the Green Bay Packers stood at the bottom of a giant hill looking up at the rest of the professional football world; the Packers head coach and corporate

[*] For more details on this time period, read *The History of the Green Bay Packers, The Lambeau Years: Part Three.*

vice-president Earl L. "Curly" Lambeau appeared to be walking on thin ice with the Packers executive committee; and the financial cupboard in Green Bay was bare. Talk about gloom and doom. The Packers looked like a drowning man going down for the third time.

Then Fate stepped in.

As usual, I'm getting ahead of the story here. Let's back up for a moment and briefly review the whole picture for the Green Bay Packers on that fateful December day.

For four straight seasons, the Green Bay Packers had been a crummy football team that was getting crummier by the game, and the Green Bay Packers, Inc., was a crumbling organization that was on the verge of toppling into a sports trivia question: What small town in the Upper Midwest's tundra country had the audacity to think that it could support a franchise in the National Football League? Or something like that. On the field, the team's record had gone from NFL champs at 8-2 in '44, to 6-4 in '45, to 6-5 in '46, to 6-5-1 in '47, to 3-9 in '48, to 2-10 in '49. At the cash register, matters were just as bad, if not worse. The only rays of hope in the whole organization beamed from two men: Emil Fischer, the corporation's president, and Gerald Clifford, the legal genius who was also a member of the executive committee.

The wolves were growling and howling at the gates to City Stadium. Starvation and death for the Green Bay Packers seemed imminent.

The National Football League and the All-America Conference had been fighting each other for those same four years, and one of the bones of contention between the two circuits was the Green Bay franchise. Why should a backwater burg in Wisconsin have a team in the NFL and fine cities—real cities—such as Cleveland, Dallas, Baltimore, and San Francisco, shouldn't? This question wasn't being voiced only by the football moguls from those places; owners in NFL cities such as New York, Washington, Philadelphia, Pittsburgh, and Detroit were also saying it. Only a few good men were gasping and replying: "Professional football in America without a team in Green,

Bay is sacrilege! It's worse than doing away with motherhood!" Well maybe they weren't going to that extreme, but you get the idea.

On the home front, Curly Lambeau, the man who believed that he had singlehandedly founded the Green Bay Packers back in 1919, the man who believed that he was the team's first and only head coach, the man who believed that the Green Bay Packers would never have ever existed without him, the man who believed that the team couldn't possibly exist in the future without him, this man, Curly Lambeau, decided it was time to take back what he believed belonged to him and him alone: the franchise to field an NFL team in Green Bay, Wisconsin. Rumor had it that he planned to move the franchise to one of the real cities that had been home to one of the failing AAC teams.

Then two things happened. Emil Fischer and Gerald Clifford stopped Lambeau and his co-conspirators from absconding with the franchise, and George Halas, Bert Bell, and George Marshall made peace with the AAC. Both of these events directly affected the other.

The NFL's powers were hoping that Lambeau and company could steal the Packers from the stockholders in Green Bay. If Curly was successful and he could move his team to San Francisco where the AAC had a strong franchise, the NFL could keep up its fight with the upstart loop for one more year and probably win the war. When Curly failed, Halas and the boys were left with no other choice except to settle matters with the AAC.

With Green Bay's place in the NFL confirmed, Fischer and Clifford could then move ahead with their problems. The first of these was to force Lambeau into resigning from the executive committee by stripping him of his powers as a corporation vice-president. Following that move, they had to make him mad enough to resign as head coach. Fischer played all the right cards, and Lambeau finally obliged them on the last day of January 1950.

The *Associated Press* reporter who covered the Packers' last game of 1949, a 21-7 defeat at the hands of the Lions in Detroit, probably had no idea how prophetic he was being when he wrote:

> "For Green Bay a new era of professional football begins today [December 11, 1949] as a note is made of another [era] that

died here Sunday. In the gathering blackness and bleakness of a rain periled brief December afternoon."[Author's italics.]

He could have written about several other changes that were about to befall the Packers, but his job was to report how the Packers put a fitting finish to what to date was their worst season in the team's 29 years in the NFL.

Nobody really knew what the future held for the Packers in the last days of 1949. Everybody did sense that some drastic changes were being made and that the Packers, Green Bay, and the NFL would never be the same again.

Oh, yes, Fate did intervene one other time in 1949, but that's where this portion of the history of the Green Bay Packers really begins.

§§§

THE
SHAMEFUL
YEARS

1

On a Windswept
Hill in Michigan

John Torinus loved to ski. He was quite proficient at it. He even
taught others.

The weekend before Christmas 1949 he went up to Iron Mountain,
Michigan. for an outing on the slopes. While there, he bumped into one of
the natives, Gene Ronzani, the former two-sport star for Marquette
University, a former player and current assistant coach of the Chicago
Bears. Torinus knew all this about Ronzani, but Ronzani only knew
that Torinus was from Green Bay and that he wrote outdoor sports
for the *Green Bay Press-Gazette*. Ronzani didn't know that Torinus was a
member of the executive committee of the Green Bay Packers.

Their conversation gravitated from skiing conditions to football
in general and the situation of the Packers in particular. Gradually, they
went from speaking in polite generalities to making hypotheses to
outlining full-blown scenarios. Their dialogue, as this writer was told
by Torinus, went something like this:

> "Gene. What's wrong with the Packers?"
> "Their style of play is outdated. Curly's still trying to win games
> with the offenses and defenses that he used back in the '30s.

The game has changed a lot since then, and I don't think Curly has kept up with all the new innovations..."

"Like what?"

"The Bears proved that the T-formation with a man in motion is the best offense, and nobody uses a six-man line on defense these days. There's too many good quarterbacks and ends now. Everybody's passing the ball a lot more..."

"Do you think the Packers need a new coach?"

"They need a new coach and a lot of new players. Most of the players they've got in Green Bay are mediocre at best, and the stars there are all past their prime. I'm surprised that Curly got as much out of those boys that he did."

"If Curly did such a good job with the players that he had, then why should the Packers get a new coach?"

"There's been too much water under the bridge now for Curly to stay with the Packers. I understand the players are real unhappy with him, and I've heard stories about him and the front office not getting along now. The Packers need a clean slate if they ever want to get back on top like they were in the '30s."

"A clean slate?"

"New blood. A new coach. A new coaching staff. New players. The Packers need to rebuild from the ground up."

"Who would you hire as the Packers' new coach?"

"I'd hire a man who knows the passing game real well. You can't compete in this league if you don't have a passing game.

"Would you be interested in coaching the Packers if the job was offered to you?"

"Sure. Who wouldn't? Just about every assistant coach in the league is interested in becoming a head coach with some team. I don't see Mr. Halas retiring any time soon, so why not the Packers?"

By evening's end, after a few toddies at the lodge, Torinus curled up in his warm bed thinking that he had just drawn an ace in the executive committee's poker game with Curly Lambeau, which was just beginning to get really hot.*

On Saturday, January 28, 1950, the *Green Bay Press-Gazette* placed a minor item in the middle of an *Associated Press* story about the coaching search being conducted by Ray C. Benuigsen, president of the Chicago Cardinals. The single paragraph mentioned the forthcoming meeting of the stockholders of the Green Bay Packers, Inc., to be held on Monday evening, February 6 at the Brown County Courthouse in Green Bay.

The stockholders will take action on the board of directors' recommendation to sell $200,000 in Packer stock. [Author's italics]

Conspicuously absent from this note and the story that it interrupted was any mention of Curly Lambeau and his status with the organization.

The next day the Chicago newspapers weren't so remiss. They listed Curly as one of the four candidates for the Cardinals' post.

Of course, Art Daley denied the Chicago tale in the *Green Bay Press-Gazette*. After ruling out the other three men as potential head mentors

for the Cardinals, Daley went to work on Lambeau's candidacy, citing the Packer board of director's resolution "to rename Lambeau for two more years" as head coach of the Packers. Oh, he mentioned that Lambeau hadn't signed a contract yet, but he discounted that bit by stating "that the Cardinals would be violating the league rule on tampering if they cast "ogling eyes" at (Clark) Shaughnessy (the head coach of the Los Angeles Rams) or Lambeau."

Two days later Bennigsen announced his choice: Lambeau. Wisconsin went into mourning.

Contacted in Miami Beach, Florida, where he was vacationing, Emil Fischer, president of the Packers, said that Lambeau's resignation "was not entirely unexpected." He also said a search for a replacement would begin immediately.

Unidentified Packer officials said: The move would considerably step up work on plans for the reorganization of the club for the coming season.

---

[*] For more details, read *The History of the Green Bay Packers, The Lambeau Years: Part Three*

Translation: Lambeau had been in the way.

Frank Jonet, the secretary-treasurer of the corporation, said:

> "'The one thing I would like to say is that this does not mean the end of the Packers. The Packers will definitely continue in Green Bay."

Translation: The threat of the Packers moving elsewhere had been very real as long as Lambeau was in the picture.

Other unidentified directors voiced the opinion that *"the way was now cleared for everyone* [Author's italics] to get in and pitch and put the Packers back on top of the pro football heap."

The next day Daley wrote:

> "It's possible that some "feelers" have already been put out by the Packers in view of Fischer's statement yesterday that "this was not entirely unexpected."

Daley went on to list some of the potential candidates: Cecil Isbell, the former star passer for the Packers and coach of the Baltimore Colts in the AAC; Bob Snyder, the current backfield coach of the Packers; Tom Stidham, current line coach; Lou Brock. current defensive coach; Sid Luckman, the All-Pro quarterback of the Bears; Luke Johnsos, the former great lineman of the Bears; Gene Ronzani, the Bears backfield coach; Jimmy Conzelman, former Cardinals mentor; Ray Flaherty, former head coach of the Washington Redskins. New York Yankees, and Chicago Hornets of the AAC; Red Smith, former Packer player and assistant coach under Lambeau, now line coach for the New York Giants: Bud Wilkinson, the head coach at Oklahoma University; and Ivy Williamson. the head coach at the University of Wisconsin. Curiously, the only one of these who received his own paragraph of ink was Ronzani.

> Ronzani, the Bears backfield coach, was quoted earlier this winter as being interested in a Packer coaching job if it should open up. That was before Lambeau was offered a two-year contract.

Wrong, Mr. Daley. Lambeau was offered a contract on November 30, 1949, when the board of directors passed the resolution that you had stated only a few days before was the reason why Lambeau would never be named as head coach of the Cardinals. This was long before the December 28, 1949, story where Ronzani was quoted about being interested in the head coaching job in Green Bay.

On February 3, the *Milwaukee Journal* reported that Ronzani had declared himself a candidate for the head coach's job of the Packers. The article went on to state that Ronzani would "formally" apply for the post in a day or two.

On the same day, Emil Fischer returned from his vacation in Florida in order "to organize the coach-hunting campaign. The first of several applications were to be looked over today. In addition, plans for the stockholders' meeting Monday night were to be outlined."

Torinus wrote in his book *The Packer Legend: An Inside Look*:

> Once again, the old warhorse, Lee Joannes, played a key role in the revival of Packer fortunes. He told the Executive Committee on February 6, 1950, that he had talked with Gene Ronzani. When several members of the committee questioned Joannes on whether any other prospective coaches were available, Joannes retorted in his typical Belgian style, "We're not taking a chance on Ronzani, he's taking a chance on us. Hell, he doesn't even know if he is going to get paid."

That day Ronzani signed a contract to coach the Packers for the next three years.

All of the other so-called applicants were only a smoke screen for the truth. Ever since meeting with Torinus in Iron Mountain just before Christmas, the executive committee hadn't seriously considered anybody else for the job except Ronzani. He was the only logical choice for them. With only two minor exceptions, none of the other alleged candidates came close to the one qualification that made Ronzani the right choice. Cecil Isbell and Lou Brock had played for the Packers, and Brock had been one of Lambeau's many coaching assistants over the years. Tom Stidham and Bob Snyder had also been assistants, but they hadn't spent enough time in Green Bay to develop a real connection to the Packers. Isbell and, more so, Brock had. Admittedly, Ronzani had spent all of his professional career as a player and an assistant coach with the Bears, but he possessed the one factor that all the other candidates were missing. Gene Ronzani was a native. His roots were planted deep in the frozen earth of the North. He came from a small town where people looked at Green Bay as a big city. Gene Ronzani was no stranger to the region. The only thing that made him different from the folks of northeastern Wisconsin was the state line that declared the Upper Peninsula to be a part of Michigan. Art Daley made it clear in his article on Ronzani's hiring that this was the one qualification that made the former Marquette University back the best man for the job.

In making their selection, the Packers investigated all angles concerning Ronzani. His appointment will mean *the return of the vast Northeastern Wisconsin and Upper Michigan following. In addition, Ronzani has a following in Milwaukee* [Author's italics] where he cavorted as one of Marquette's all-time backs.

In other words, Ronzani would be a name attraction for the Packers. Isbell might have filled that billing, if he hadn't made so many disparaging remarks about Green Bay being a bush league town when he was coaching the Baltimore Colts in the AAC. Brock might have made the grade here, too, except that he wasn't the head coach type. For certain, he had been a tenacious, intelligent player, but he was no authority figure. Also going against him was his association with Lambeau and his familiarity with the current players.

Ronzani was the only logical choice. At the time, he was considered to be the greatest athlete ever to come out of Iron Mountain. He led his high school team to its only Michigan state basketball title, and he earned eight varsity letters in football, basketball, and track. At Marquette, he earned nine varsity letters in the same three sports, and he captained the football team in his senior year. He signed with the Chicago Bears in 1933 and played the next six years with them. In 1937, George Halas switched him from halfback to quarterback, and Ronzani developed into an able field general. In 1939, he was appointed head coach of the Newark Bears, a Chicago farm team, and the following year, his eleven won their league's title. He coached one year at Wichita, another Chicago affiliate, then he returned to Chicago in '43 when World War II drew off many of the best players in the NFL. He played and coached for two years, filling in for Sid Luckman who was doing duty for the Coast Guard. After the war, Ronzani served on Hugh Devore's staff at Notre Dame in '45, then he was again a head coach for a Chicago farm team; this one in Akron where he developed the great Bears running back, George Gulyanics. In '47, he was back in Chicago as the quarterback's coach. Among his early pupils were three future Pro Football Hall of Famers: Johnny Lujack, Bobby Layne, and George Blanda.

Daley reported that the Bears were calling Ronzani "one of the most promising young coaches in the game. With the Packers, Ronzani will get every opportunity to prove himself. And his first National-American Football league opponent likely will be the Bears—and Halas."

While Ronzani was accepting the Packer post, Isbell signed on to be Lambeau's backfield coach in Chicago.

Lee Remmel reported that Ronzani was "the people's choice" to become the Packers head mentor. He quoted several local businessmen, including former Packer Charley Mathys, who said:

> "The only name that stuck in my mind—during the days that everyone was mentioning candidates for the job—as the right man for the job was Ronzani. He's the logical choice."

And that was the general consensus as well. Ronzani was the only logical choice.

§§§

2
To Build a Firm Foundation

The same night that the stockholders of the Green Bay Packers, Inc. met to discuss the future of the corporation at the Brown County Courthouse new head coach Gene Ronzani was introduced to them. After all the glad-handing was over, the stockholders got down to business.

Former corporation president Lee Joannes made a motion to increase the corporation's stock from 500 authorized shares to 10,000 shares. The motion carried unanimously. The 9,500 new shares were to be sold for $25.00 each in order to raise sufficient working capital to see the Packers into the next decade. When one of the stockholders wanted an amendment to the articles of incorporation that would prevent the Packers from ever leaving Green Bay, Jerry Clifford reminded everyone that the Packers couldn't move as long as the organization continued to be a non-profit business. As an extra measure, though, they voted to amend the articles in such a way as to prevent any small group of stockholders from gaining control of the corporation and thus make changes in the articles that would do away with the non-profit status that Clifford and others had guarded so jealously over the years. The amendment forbade the sale of more than

200 shares of stock to any one person or group of persons. This motion also carried with unanimous enthusiasm.

In order to prevent the abuses that Curly Lambeau had committed over the years, the executive committee voted to keep separate the posts of head coach and general manager. Ronzani would be allowed a free rein in coaching matters, including the hiring and firing of players and assistant coaches, but the contracts and other business matters would be placed in the hands of an expert. The first suggested candidate for the job was former corporation president Lee Joannes.

In another front office move of significance, the Packers fired George Strickler* and hired former player Francis I. Earpe, better known as Jug Earpe, the great lineman from the '20s. After his playing days. Earpe entered the automobile business with the Brown County Motor Company. During World War II, he served with the civil Government, and after the war, he joined Don Hutson's automobile business.

Packer President Emil Fischer appointed Lee Joannes to chair the stock sales committee. Included in that committee were Green Bay Mayor Dominic Olejniczak, Jack Paeps, Savior Canadeo, Emmett Platten, Walter Scherf, William Servotte, Frederick J. Lenfesty, and Verne Lewellen. This group included representatives from the Green Bay Packers, Inc., the city government, the Quarterback Club, the Alumni Club, the American Legion, the Association of Commerce, and the public at-large. Joannes selected insurance agent Max Murphy to head up the drive in the city of Green Bay, and he gave Jug Earpe the task of organizing stock sales committees in other communities. Murphy divided the chore between five teams that were headed by Ben Rosenberg, Russ Bogda, Emmett Evans, Al Rose, and Gene Leicht. By the time the stock drive was set to begin, over 400 workers were set to make the sale a success.

Next, the committee held a contest for a slogan for the stock sale.

The winner of the contest was Donald D. Krawczyk who offered:

---

* For more details about George Strickler's involvement with the Packers, read *The Green Bay Packers, The Lambeau Years: Part Three.*

"Back the drive with twenty-five."

The corporation made a major push to sell the new stock, beginning in March 1950. As always, the *Green Bay Press-Gazette* co-operated completely. The newspaper ran a series of articles answering questions that potential stockholders might have about the stock.

The first question asked: Why do the Packers need the money? **The answer:** To give the franchise some financial stability.

Question #2: Will the money be used to pay off old debts?

Answer: No, the corporation was debt-free.

Question #3: What will stockholders get for their money?

Answer: A pretty stock certificate suitable for framing, a vote for something positive for the community. The *Press-Gazette* tried to convince its readers that buying the new stock would mean

new blood on the board of directors of the Green Bay Packers, Inc. For sure, some changes would be made in the board, but realistically, the old guard wasn't about to give up the control that it had exercised for the past three decades. The fourth and fifth "answers" had no questions.

In the fourth article, the *Press-Gazette* tried to make its readers think that the success of the stock sale would have a direct bearing on the forthcoming season's schedule by insinuating that having four games in Green Bay and only two in Milwaukee was dependent on the support given by the people of northeastern Wisconsin and Upper Michigan. In reality, the Packers had determined some months prior to this that the team would play four games in Green Bay and only two in Milwaukee. The sale of the stock had nothing to do with the scheduling.

In the fifth story, the newspaper related how the sale of the stock would give Green Bay the appearance of a "Big League" city. This was a very real appeal to the pride of Green Bayer's. In some really well written words, the unbylined article stated how unique Green Bay was in the world of professional sports in that the Packers had survived on the field and at the box office when every other city of less than a half million people had slipped into minor league status. Green Bayer's, the people of northeast Wisconsin, and the people of Upper Michigan had a right to crow because they had overcome incredible odds and had maintained a major league professional football franchise through the best of times and through the worst of times.

A public rally was held at the Central Catholic High School auditorium on the second Tuesday in April. Verne Lewellen, the newly elected Chief Quarterback of the Quarterback Club, acted as master of ceremonies.

In connection with the drive, a scoreboard that would register the progress of the sale was erected on the lawn of the Brown County courthouse. The sign depicted a halfback racing up a football field toward a goal of $200,000.

To set the proper tone for the stock sale, the *Press-Gazette* set the best example by purchasing $5,000 worth of stock. The newspaper announced the move with an editorial on April 11, 1950:

> Packer Stock
>
> The *Press-Gazette* has made an offer to the Packer Corporation to buy the maximum permissable [sic] amount of stock in the forthcoming drive, $5,000 worth.
>
> It is impossible to place a monetary figure on the value of the Packers to Green Bay and to all of Packerland. There is no method of computing the worth to a community, its people and its institutions of a great athletic institution like the Packers. But those who are in close touch with the pulse of this vast area are quite uniform in their conviction that materially and spiritually the Packers are a healthy and helpful ingredient. We must have bread. But we cannot live by bread alone. We need lively interests and rugged, cheering contests to make life sparkle.
>
> Perhaps a better way to assess the value of the Packers is by asking oneself: How would I feel if the Packers were giving up the ghost and going to Dallas or Houston?

Chance brought the Packers to Green Bay over 30 years ago. Enthusiasm fostered their development. Spirit and toil and the fervent support of hundreds of thousands of people so inspired them that during those three decades they captured leadership on so many occasions and secured an all-time undisputed title to second place, competing with the fastest, smartest, roughest and most durable teams it has been possible to find in the whole country.

The future offers the Packers an even break at the nation's talent. There is no good reason why in a reasonable time they should not be elbowing others out of the way for the top. They know that we cannot win tomorrow's game with yesterday's touchdown. Miracles are neither asked nor expected.

We feel certain that the public will never let the fighting Packers down.

The sales campaign started off on the right foot when Max Murphy announced the sale of 1,000 shares on the morning after the rally at Central Catholic High School. Within a week, the sales total had reached $62,850, almost a third of the way toward the goal. Two weeks later the total amounted to $77,050 in the Green Bay area. In three weeks, the goal of $100,000 from the Green Bay area was within reach as the total sale came to $90,275 on May 2. Week four saw the figure climb to $93.425. By the fifth week, sales had only gone up another $1,800 to $95,225, thanks largely to a group of Appleton supporters who raised $1,025 on their own.

Other communities now wanted to join in the drive. Heading up the outlying cities were Dan Steinberg, Harold Sherry, and William Pifer, Appleton: Gordon Steinberg, New London: Art Tiedeman, Kimberly: George Vander Loop, Little Chute: Carl Hansen, Kaukauna: C.J. Overweiser, Menasha: William Sample, Neenah: Elmer Collar. Hortonville: and George Kaufman, Dale.

Fred Miller, president of the Miller Brewing Company of Milwaukee, the radio sponsor for Packer games, backed up his rhetoric with a $5,000 purchase of stock.

All through this drive a sense of urgency pervaded the stories in the *Press-Gazette*. Why? Was there some sort of deadline to be met? And if a deadline did exist, why? Nobody asked those questions back in 1950. In fact, nobody questioned anything publicly until May 18. That was the day NFL Commissioner Bert Bell replied to a May 17 story in the *Chicago Tribune* that stated Green Bay's status in the NFL would be reviewed at the league meeting to be held June 2-3. He called the report "ridiculous." If it was ridiculous, why did he bother to respond to it?

Art Daley used all of his column of May 19 to dispute the claims in the *Tribune* of May 17 that the Green Bay franchise was on the ropes with the NFL. He complained about the *Tribune* "crying wolf" the year before when that newspaper announced that the Packers-Bears game. Usually slated for Green Bay, would be played in Milwaukee. Daley had his nerve complaining about this minor item, especially after all the times that he had made some sensational announcement that turned out to be nothing more than an attempt to draw attention away from the real news. He also attacked the Milwaukee papers for similar reasons.

The bottom line to all this ink was the frightening truth: The Green Bay Packers were on the verge of becoming a footnote in professional football history. Why? How? The corporation had no debts whatsoever, and it was far from penniless because it had money in the bank from the insurance settlement over the fire at Rockwood Lodge. So why were the Packers in trouble?[*]

The previous winter when the AAC and NFL agreed to a merger George Preston Marshall, the owner of the Washington Redskins, stated that it took $500,000 to operate a franchise in the NFL, and the Buffalo Bills were told that they would have to raise that kind of money if they wished to be included in the merger of the two circuits. After raising the money, the Bills were still denied a place in the new league, and they raised a howl, saying that the Packers didn't have the money that they had; so why should Green Bay be allowed to stay in the NFL and they should be kept out?

(The howl died when Buffalo's owner, Arthur McBride, was allowed to buy 25% of the Cleveland Browns.)

[*] Part of the answer to that question has already been detailed somewhat in the third volume in this series, *The History of the Green Bay Packers: The Lambeau Years, Part III.*

Unofficially, the Packers were told the same thing, although not in terms so stiff. The Packers had to raise only $120,000 which was the total amount of the guarantees for their six home games in 1950. Since the corporation already had about $40,000 in the bank from the settlement of the insurance claim on the Rockwood Lodge fire, they had to raise a mere $80,000 to make the total. There was a catch, however. The Packers had to be funded by the June 2-3 dispersal draft meeting of the NFL. Why that date? That was as late as the owners could allow before they had to make a concrete schedule for the coming season.

Why would the NFL owners place this burden on the Packers? The Packers were potentially the weakest franchise in the National

Football League; financially, that is. The Packers played in the smallest stadium and had the cheapest tickets in the NFL. Since the league was built on revenue-sharing (i.e., visiting teams were guaranteed a minimum amount of money or a portion of the gate receipts, whichever was larger, just for showing up), NFL teams couldn't make as much money visiting Green Bay or Milwaukee

as they could make by playing in larger cities with larger stadiums. This wasn't bad because as long as the Packers were a winning, exciting football team, they drew well on the road, and being a good draw in the other fellow's stadium made up for a smaller paycheck in Green Bay or Milwaukee. All this changed once the Packers became the doormat of the NFL in '48 and '49 and their road attendance faded dramatically. That is when the grumbling began around the league.

Fortunately, Green Bay had friends in high places like Chicago, New York, and Washington. Men like George Halas, George Marshall, and Tim Mara supported Green Bay at league meetings, fighting to keep the Packers in the NFL and in Green Bay. That worked well when the league consisted of 10 teams and any four of them could band together to stop any legislation placed before the league. Now that the NFL numbered 13 franchises it took five owners to band together to put a halt to anything. Again, the Packers found a friend in Art Rooney, the owner of the Pittsburgh Steelers.

LARRY NAMES

Divided eight-to-five over the issue of the Packers, the owners placed the unofficial stipulation on the table that put the Packers on the proverbial bubble. To make matters even tougher, Green Bay had to become competitive on the field again and draw well on the road as well as draw better in Milwaukee and at home. Thus, $150,000 wasn't enough; they needed $250,000. The extra $100,000 was for player salaries. The Packers needed new players, better players, if they were to compete in the NFL and draw well on the road.

Simply put: If the Packers couldn't make money for the other teams, then the other teams would throw the Packers out of the NFL.

For that reason, the executive committee busted its collective butt to make the stock drive a success, and that success was attained at a banquet held May 22 at the Beaumont Hotel where Chairman Max Murphy announced that the drive had netted $105,825 so far. Daley wrote:

The Greater Green Bay phase of the Packers' stock drive came to a glorious close at the Beaumont Hotel with these heart-warming revelations:

(1) A total of $105,825 has been collected for the purchase of non-profit sharing stock in the area—$5,825 over the goal of $100,000.

(2) A total of $89,800 already is money in the bank, the rest being in due-soon pledges.

(3) The spirit shown in the campaign is the kind of spirit that *justifies the Packers remaining in Green Bay.* [Author's italics]

Strange, Mr. Daley, if the story in the *Chicago Tribune* concerning the Packers' future was so false, why did you make such a statement as "justifies the Packers remaining in Green Bay"?

The Packers were secure for the moment; they had the money now to meet the guarantees that their opponents needed for the coming season. Now to raise additional revenue for player salaries.

At the summer stockholders meeting, the corporation made a few changes in its structure.

16

The first of these was the addition of 15 new directors on the board, giving it a total of 30 now. Each director would serve a three-year term, and one-third of the board would be elected annually.

A new position was added: chairman of the board of directors. Lee Joannes was elected to this post, and the articles of incorporation were amended so that future chairmen would also have to be past presidents of the corporation.

The annual meeting date was changed from July to the first Monday after January 20 each year. This was done so the board of directors and operating officers could be elected at the beginning of the business year instead of in the middle.

With one exception, all the officers were retained. Emil Fischer

was president, and Frank Jonet was again elected to be secretary and treasurer. The newcomer was, of course, Gene Ronzani who was elected vice-president to replace Curly Lambeau.

With that business done, everybody looked forward to the coming season with renewed enthusiasm.

§§§

3

A Bear at the Helm

Gene Ronzani's first task as head coach of the Packers was to hire a staff of assistant coaches. This wasn't as easy as it sounds.

Lambeau's last staff included Lou Brock, Bob Snyder, and Tom Stidham. Snyder, who coached the backfield, took the head coaching job at the University of Toledo, and Tom Stidham took the line coaching job with Lambeau in Chicago. Only Lou Brock, the former All-Pro lineman who was already under contract to the Packers, was retained to handle the defense for Ronzani just as he had under Lambeau, but by the beginning of training camp, Brock was also released.

Ronzani wanted his old friend from their Bear days, Jumbo Joe Stydahar, to be his line coach, but Stydahar, Clark Shaughnessy's line coach with the Rams in '49, was hired to replace Shaughnessy who had a falling out with Los Angeles Rams owner Dan Reeves. Oddly, Ronzani considered hiring Shaughnessy for the post of backfield coach for the Packers, but Shaughnessy decided against it, choosing to retire from coaching for the time being and tend to his shoe store business.

In March, Ronzani chose John L. "Tarzan" Taylor as his line coach. Born in Superior, Wisconsin, Taylor played guard and tackle at Central High School in Duluth, Minnesota, then he played his collegiate ball for Ohio State, graduating in 1920. He played for the Chicago Staleys (1921), Chicago Bears (1922), and Canton Bulldogs (1923). He coached the lines of Michigan State (1924-26), Ohio University (1927), and Ohio State (1928) before joining Marquette University's staff. He stayed there until 1942 when he joined the Navy during the war. After the war, he took a position with the Briggs & Stratton Corporation of Milwaukee. He returned to coaching in 1947 with the Baltimore Colts of the AAC.

Almost two months later Ronzani finally completed his staff by hiring Ray Nolting to coach the backfield and Dick Plasman to coach the ends.

Nolting was the backfield coach with the New York Bulldogs in '49. Before that he was a star halfback with the Chicago Bears for nine years, then he was head coach of his alma mater, the University of Cincinnati, for four years, where he compiled a winning record of 23-14. He was born and raised in Cincinnati.

Plasman was a famous end with both the Chicago Bears and Chicago Cardinals, and he was on the Cardinal coaching staff for four years, leaving in the shake-up which came at the end of the '49 season.

As one extra item to the coaching staff, Ronzani was able to convince Shaughnessy to come out of his self-imposed retirement to act as an advisor during training camp and the exhibition season. Shaughnessy was hired to help Ronzani develop the offensive and defensive strategy.

That summer the National-American Football League changed its name back to the National Football League and established two conferences: the National and the American. The National Conference consisted of the Green Bay Packers, Chicago Bears, Detroit Lions, Los Angeles Rams, New York Yanks, San Francisco 49ers, and Baltimore Colts. The American Conference was made up of the New York Giants, Chicago Cardinals, Pittsburgh Steelers, Philadelphia Eagles, Washington Redskins, and Cleveland Browns.

The 1950 schedule was released in early May, and it contained something new for the Packers: an open date. Beginning with a home game with the Lions on September 17, the Packers were set to play in succession: Washington in Milwaukee, Bears in Green Bay, Yanks in New York, Bears in Chicago, Yanks in Green Bay, week off, Colts in Baltimore, Rams in Milwaukee, Lions in Detroit, 49ers in Green Bay, Rams in LA, and 49ers in San Francisco.

A major step for the Packers was the signing of a new radio agreement with Milwaukee station WTMJ. The key to the pact was the Miller Brewing Company which agreed to sponsor all 12 broadcasts on the network of stations that WTMJ was establishing throughout Wisconsin and Upper Michigan. Frederick C. Miller, president of the beer firm, made the announcement, and Ronzani responded by naming Miller the team's honorary line coach.

Curly Lambeau's last official act as Green Bay's head coach was to choose players at the College Draft in January. Those draftees included future Packers Clayton Tonnemaker, C, Minnesota, in the first round; Tobin Rote, QB, Rice; Larry Coutre, HB, Notre Dame; Jack Cloud, FB, William & Mary; Leon Manley, G, Oklahoma; and Carleton Elliott, E, Virginia.

Ronzani's first signees from the College Draft were Frank Kuzma, fullback, and Robert W. "Buster" Mealey, tackle, both from Minnesota; neither ever played for the Packers. Lew Ferry became the first '49 Packer to sign a contract for '50. Those were the only contracts that carne into the Packers' office while the stock drive was in full gear that spring of 1950. Most of the Packer players from '49 and the team's draft choices held off signing until it was determined whether their playing rights would still be Green Bay's property or if their names would be thrown into the dispersal draft set for June 2-3 in Philadelphia.

After the announcement that the Packers were secure in Green Bay, the contracts started coming regularly to Ronzani's office. Rookies signing were Jack Cloud; Rebel Roy Steiner, end, Alabama, who was taken as a future choice in the '48 Draft; Tobin Rote; Clayton Tonnemaker; Carlton Batt "Stretch" Elliott; Willie Leon Manley; Fred Leon; Clarence "Clink" McGeary, tackle, North Dakota; and Al Cannava, halfback, Boston College. Other Packer veterans signing were Steve Pritko, end; Jug Girard, halfback; Glen Johnson, tackle; Dan Orlich, end; Buddy Burris, guard; Ted Fritsch, fullback; Red Vogds, guard; Walt Schlinkman, fullback; Bob Forte, halfback; Stan Heath, quarterback; Bill Kelley, end; and Ed Neal, guard. Free-agent signings included Ray DiPierro, guard, whose last team was the Bears; and Ed Ecker, center, Bears.

Jim Clark and Jim Thomas, a pair of rookies from Ohio State, were the first descendants of slaves ever to sign with the Packers.

At the dispersal draft in Philadelphia, the Packers and Baltimore Colts were given five extra choices each, but Commissioner Bell spread them out over the entire draft. The Packers had the third choice overall, and Ronzani picked Billy Grimes, a halfback who had played his college ball at Oklahoma A&M and most recently had played for the Los Angeles Dons. Following Grimes, Ronzani chose Al Baldwin, end, Arkansas, Buffalo Bills; Homer Paine, tackle, Oklahoma, Chicago Hornets; Abner Wimberly, end, LSU, LA Dons; Jim Lukens, end, Washington & Lee, Buffalo Bills; John E "Moose" Kerns, tackle, Ohio U., Buffalo Bills; James Bailey, guard-tackle, West Virginia State, Chicago Hornets; Wilbur Volz, halfback, Missouri, Buffalo Bills; Ziggie Czarobski, tackle, Notre Dame; Charley Schuette, tackle, Marquette; Denver Crawford, tackle, Tennessee; Paul Duke, center, Georgia Tech; R.M. Patterson, tackle, McMurry; Vic Schleich, tackle, Nebraska; and former Packer Ted Cook. Only Grimes, Baldwin, Wimberly, Schuette, and Cook signed with the Packers.

Ronzani opened camp on July 22 with 42 players reporting. In the succeeding days, more men arrived, but two who were missing early were All-Pro Tony Canadeo and tackle Dick Wildung. The Grey Ghost of Gonzaga signed a contract and reported to camp two weeks later and Wildung did likewise a few days after that.

Like all football coaches, Ronzani's first concern was finding a topnotch quarterback. He started with seven names on paper, but four of those were erased before the first day of camp. Draft choice Arnold Galiffa graduated from the Military Academy at West Point and went into the Army. Jack Jacobs, the veteran of three campaigns under Lambeau, decided to go north of the border to play for the Winnipeg

Blue Bombers of the Canadian League. Ray Malloul, the rookie from SMU, decided against playing for the Packers. Rookie free agent Pandel Savic from Ohio State decided against playing pro football in favor of a regular job at a glass factory. That left rookie Tobin Rote, Stan Heath, and Jug Girard.

Neither Heath nor Girard had ever played quarterback in a T-formation. Rote had in college, but this was the pro game. He remarked:

> "This is so much harder than college. Here, I even have to call the signals for the linemen."

Ronzani said early on, "Green, aren't they?" He referred to the number of rookies in camp—18—and the fact that not one of the key performers had ever played under Ronzani's style of offense.

During the second week of camp, Stan Heath asked to be released from his contract. The Milwaukee native said: "It was better for both parties that I left the Packers." Ronzani agreed and put Heath on waivers. Heath was subsequently signed by the Bears.

The first casualties of training camp were Bill Osborne and Fred Leon. Osborne had an old injury that refused to improve, and thus, it forced him to hang up his cleats. Leon broke a leg during the first practice.

Tackle Glen Johnson walked out of camp without saying why, but it was soon learned that he was headed to Canada to play for Jacobs who became the head coach of the Blue Bombers. The next day end Bill Kelley followed Johnson to Canada to play for Winnipeg.

Tackle Paul Lipscomb decided against playing for the Packers again, so Ronzani traded his rights to Washington for tackle Len Szafaryn. In another personnel move, the Packers picked up Alex Wizbicki on waivers from the Cleveland Browns who had gotten him as part of the merger deal that kept the Buffalo Bills from making a fuss about being excluded from the new league. Just before the first pre-season game, tackle Bob Mealey left the team for a coaching job in Minnesota. This last defection reduced the roster to 40 players, not including four players, Gordon Soltau, Clayton Tonnemaker, Willie Leon Manley, and Larry Coutre (unsigned), who were practicing with the College All-Stars in Chicago for their bout with the NFL champion Philadelphia Eagles.

An indication that the major pro football circuit was beginning a new era came with the announcement that the Packers would play their first exhibition game on August 12 and the opponent would be the Cleveland Browns, one of the new kids on the block. Prior to this arrangement, the Packers had only played scrimmages that early in the season. They should have stuck to playing against themselves that early because the Browns smashed Green Bay in Ronzani's first ever game as head coach, 38-7.

After the game, Ronzani traded rookie Gordy Soltau to the Browns for tackle Joe Spencer, and he released rookie fullback Frank Kuzma. Veteran guard Joe Etheridge received his draft papers, and thus, he became the first Green Bay loss to the Korean War. On a positive note, veteran Bob Summerhays signed his contract and reported for practice.

The Packers also scheduled an exhibition game with Curly Lambeau's Cardinals to be played at City Stadium on August 16. Lambeau spiced up this contest. Allegedly, after watching the Packers being humiliated by the Browns, he remarked to his former backfield coach Bob Snyder: "Just like 1949—no effort." The *Press-Gazette* played this up, of course, in order to drum up ticket sales. The ploy worked because over 20,000 fans showed up to watch the Packers slip past the Cards, 17-14. Art Daley started his report of the game with:

> Unleashing a tremendous wave of fight, fire and tenacity, the 1950 Green Bay Packers—once again the pro team with the college spirit—opened a new era in professional football/lore [Author's italics.] by defeating Curly Lambeau and his Chicago Cardinals before 20,136 almost hysterical fans at City Stadium Wednesday night.

Daley was so right. The Packers were beginning a new era in pro football lore. It was a slow starting time, and it would take a long time to get to the really exciting chapters; but this was the only beginning to another of the greatest episodes ever told and retold about a professional sports team. Lambeau was gone, and the new era was

24

begun. Green Bay and Wisconsin were shedding the quaint rural image and were taking on a new aspect; something akin to a farm kid trying on his first pair of store-bought shoes. The fit wasn't perfect, however.

When the Cardinals lost to the Packers, some Green Bay fans displayed poor sportsmanship and a lack of class by taunting Lambeau. Lee Remmel reported:

> But he [Lambeau] was shortly dismayed when the Packers stopped the Cards' drive and shortly scored. And the fans, who were 'on' him most of the night, didn't permit the touchdown to pass without acrid comment. "What's the matter, Curly?" and "You sorry now, Curly?" they hooted.
> Packer players also had some remarks about Lambeau after the game. Ed Neal chuckled to nobody in particular, " he'd like to see Lambeau's face now." And Ted Fritsch hooted, "That's the way to welcome Lambeau home, boys!"

These two little sentences said a lot about the feelings of his players toward Lambeau. He was not missed.

Over the next two weeks, Ronzani made a few minor roster moves, and he finally signed halfback Larry Coutre to a contract. He picked up halfback Wally Dreyer on waivers from the Bears, and he traded a draft choice to the Browns for the services of quarterback Tom O'Malley.

The Packers played an intrasquad game in Ronzani's hometown of Iron Mountain, Michigan, and over 4,000 fans showed up for the affair.

A second intrasquad game was played in Elkhart, Indiana, the following week as the Packers worked their way to Boston to play the New York Giants in an exhibition contest. The Packers shut down the New Yorkers, 10-0, and optimism about the regular season reigned supreme in Wisconsin.

Ronzani started making roster cuts before the final pre-season game with the Baltimore Colts. He dropped both of Green Bay's African American players, Jim Clark and Jim Thomas; ends Frank Ellis and Claude Radtke; guard John Cahill; and backs Lee Pete and Mike

Graham. At the same time, he acquired halfback Billy Boedeker from the Cleveland Browns for yet another draft pick.

The contest against the Colts was the First Annual Midwest Shrine Game to be played in Milwaukee. Shriners throughout Wisconsin pitched in to sell tickets, and they were mildly successful with an attendance of 17,191. This was the largest crowd to watch the Packers play in Milwaukee since the Cardinals beat the Packers there in '48. The moderate crowd was treated to another Green Bay pre-season victory, 16-14.

With three wins and a single loss behind them now, the Packers headed into the 1950 regular season with "oodles of optimism" that they would win a fair share of their games during the campaign. First things first, however. The roster had to be cut down to 32 players. Three veterans were cut adrift: guards Evan "Red" Vogds and Joe Etheridge and recently hired halfback Ed Smith. The others were center Gene Huebner; tackles Dan Bradach, George Hekkers, and Fred Leon; ends George Benigni and Carleton Elliott; and halfback Harry Szulborski. Later in the week veteran tackle Lew Ferry was placed on waivers, and rookie tackle Don Stansauk was picked up on waivers from the Lions.

A minor item of little note at the time but which would loom large in the future was the hiring of Jack Vainisi to the front office staff of the Packers. Vainisi, 23 and a native of Chicago, played tackle for Notre Dame. He was hired to keep records on college players, handle statistical information, etc. Nobody gave Vainisi a second thought in 1950, but that would all change in the future.

Ronzani's first season as head coach of the Green Bay Packers opened with the Detroit Lions invading aging City Stadium. The Packers dazzled their 22,096 fans on game day by coming out of the locker room wearing new uniforms. Both the jerseys and pants were kelly green with gold numbers on the tops, two gold stripes around the upper sleeves, and a one-inch gold stripe down the side of each leg. The new threads didn't help much after the kickoff as the Lions showed why they were 14-point favorites, demolishing the Pack, 45-7. To add insult to injury, literally, Tobin Rote suffered a shoulder bruise and had to be removed from the game in the second quarter, and his backup, Tom O'Malley, had to be taken out because of a back injury in the fourth period. This was not a good start for the young Packers.

The mauling by the Lions was quickly forgotten the following week, thanks to a controversy stirred up by George Halas. It all started on September 9 when Halas traded five players to the Colts for Dick Bergegan, an All-Pro guard in the defunct AAC. Included in the transaction was quarterback George Blanda and a certain stipulation that the Colts couldn't trade any of the five Bears to any of the other teams in the National Conference. Commissioner Bert Bell put the skids on the deal unless the stipulation was removed. Halas complied. Baltimore coach Clem Crowe put Blanda on waivers after the first game of the season, and the Packers claimed him. Halas then prevailed upon Crowe to withdraw the waivers on Blanda, and he immediately purchased Blanda's contract for $500.

That was on the surface. Under cover, the Colts put Blanda on waivers. As soon as he heard that the New York Yanks had passed on claiming the quarterback, Ronzani put in a claim for the Packers. Blanda got the word that he'd been claimed by the Packers, so he packed a bag and headed for Green Bay. Halas didn't want the Packers or any other conference rival to have Blanda. He offered to buy Blanda from the Packers, but Ronzani refused to sell. Halas then turned to Baltimore to talk them into rescinding the waivers on Blanda. Crowe agreed to do it. Blanda arrived in Green Bay, and Ronzani immediately put him up at a hotel. Feeling that the 24-hour period to recall waivers on a player had run out on Baltimore, Ronzani argued that Blanda was a free agent and he could negotiate with any club in the league. Working under this premise, the Green Bay coach hid Blanda in the basement of his house to keep him away from the press and everybody else, especially the Bears. Halas disagreed with Ronzani's argument, and so did Commissioner Bert Bell who upheld the new deal between the Bears and the Colts. Defeated, Ronzani relayed the bad news to Blanda, and the quarterback took the next train to Chicago.

On the roster front, Ronzani picked up guard Chuck Drulis and halfback Floyd "Breezy" Reid off the waiver wires from the Bears.

Also, Ronzani made a deal with the Cardinals for veteran quarterback Paul Christman. Dropped from the team were halfbacks Walt Schlinkman and Al Cannava.

On Sunday, the Packers were set to face Washington in Milwaukee. The Redskins had always been a reflection of the Packers. When the Pack did well, so did George Marshall's boys. The Packers were now at the bottom of their division, and the Redskins were at the bottom of theirs. An even match was expected, and it would have been, too, if not for seven Washington turnovers—four intercepted passes and three fumbles—that gave big breaks to the Packers. The result was a 35-21 Green Bay win, and all Packerdom was elated as the fans figured that their Pack was back. The crowd was small at 14,109 paid admissions.

Fresh from a pair of victories on the West Coast, the Bears came to Green Bay the following Sunday sitting atop the National Conference with the Detroit Lions at 2-0 each. When they left Sunday night, the Bruins found themselves in a five-way tie for first with the Packers, the Lions, Yanks, and Rams. Using an alert defense that picked off four Bear passes and returning two of the them for touchdowns, the Packers pulled off a major upset, 31-21, over the highly touted Monsters of the Midway in front of 24,893 fans.

Ronzani remarked to George Halas as they were leaving the field: "I'd rather be lucky than good." Both men knew that the Packers had been very fortunate that day, that the Bears were actually the superior team, that the Bears had beaten themselves, that the second game in Chicago would more than likely prove this to be so.

The New York Yankees won the American League baseball pennant in 1950, and their appearance in the World Series forced the New York Yanks of the NFL to change their home schedule. The first victim of this switch was Green Bay. The contest between the Yanks and Packers that had been scheduled for New York on October 9 was changed to Green Bay, and their second game, which had been slated to be played in Green Bay on October 22 was changed to Thursday, October 19, in New York. These changes were good and bad. Bad because the Packers would have to face the Yanks in Green Bay, the

Bears in Chicago, and the Yanks again within 12 days, and good because the Packers would have 16 days off after the second game with the Yanks.

The Packers went into the New York game as 10-point underdogs, and they came out of it 44-31 losers before 23,891 fans. Turnovers made the difference as the Packers fumbled once inside New York's 10 and had three passes picked off at inopportune times. Trailing 24-3 early in the third period, the Packers showed that they weren't quitters, storming back into the game with two quick touchdowns to cut the lead to 24-17, then 30-24, then 37-31 before finally succumbing to the vaunted Yank passing attack.

The NFL conference races were shaping up now. The Lions, Bears and Yanks (all 3-1) were tied for the top spot in the National, and the Giants (3-0) stood a half-game ahead of Cleveland (3-1) and a full game ahead of Philadelphia (2-1) in the American.

Next up for the Packers was a visit to Wrigley Field in Chicago to face the Bears. Green Bay hadn't beaten the Bears twice in one season since Don Hutson's rookie year of 1935, and over the ensuing years, the Pack had only defeated the Bruins four times in the Windy City, the last time being in 1941 in their regular season matchup, while the Bears won a playoff game for the divisional title to start a streak of nine straight wins against Green Bay at home. The Bears entered the game as 14-point favorites, and they emerged as victors by that very margin, 28-14, before a record crowd of 51,065 screaming fans. Once again turnovers did in the Packers as they scored first and last, but in between the Bears scored all their points with the help of a pair recovered fumbles and an intercepted pass.

The National Conference was led now by the Yanks and Bears (both 4-1) with the Lions and Rams (both 3-2) a game back. The Giants (3-1) suffered their first loss as they slipped into a second-place tie with Philadelphia in the American Conference a half-game behind Cleveland (4-1).

The Packers flew out of Chicago on Monday morning for New York and a date with the Yanks on the following Thursday. They encamped at Bear Mountain for their stay, and Ronzani prepared his troops for the coming contest. He complained that they could have practiced at 42nd and Broadway and had more privacy and secrecy. The Yanks were installed as 17-point favorites, and they responded by winning the game by 18 points, 35-17, before a meager showing of 13,661 fans. Again, the Packers did more to beat themselves with turnovers than the opposition did.

After allowing their opponents 194 points in just six games, it was rapidly becoming apparent to Ronzani and his staff that the staunch defense that the Packers had shown during the exhibition season had been a fluke. On the plus side, the offense that had been almost totally absent in the pre-season campaign was beginning to show signs of life as the Pack had put 135 points of their own on the board, 128 in the last five games. Still, the turnovers were killing them, and that was something Ronzani had to work on.

While the Packers took a two-week vacation from the NFL wars, the rest of the league went at it head-to-head. The Giants (4-1) recaptured first place in the American Conference by dumping the Browns (4-2), and the Eagles (4-1) joined New York in the top spot by slipping by the Steelers (2-4). In the National Conference, the surly Bears (4-1) were idle, allowing the Yanks (5-1) to move ahead of them in the standings. The Rams (4-2) kept pace with the Yanks by slaughtering the Colts (0-5), 70-27, in Baltimore. The Packers (2-4) were now in fifth place behind the Lions (3-3) in fourth.

On the second Sunday that the Packers sat idle, the Yanks (6-1) pounded the Bears (4-2) in New York, and the Rams (5-2) annihilated the Lions (3-4), 65-24, in LA. The American Conference race had a shakeup as the Giants (4-2) were dropped out of first by Curly Lambeau's Cardinals (3-3), and the Eagles (5-1) moved on top a half-game ahead of the Browns (5-2).

Ronzani expressed a pair of fears before the next game in Baltimore. He was afraid that the 16-day layoff had made his team rusty, and the Colts' passing attack had him shaking in his shoes, especially after his own passers ran the Baltimore offense quite effectively in practice against his first-string defense. Although the oddsmakers installed the Packers as 14-point favorites, the coach's fears proved out as the Packers were once again their own worst enemies. A mere 12,971 fans showed up to watch their Colts break a 14-game losing streak, 41-21. Leading 21-20 with five minutes left in the game, the Packers fell apart. Paul Christman threw an interception that was returned for a TD to give Baltimore the lead. On the ensuing possession, the Packers fumbled the ball away at midfield. Green Bay got another shot, but the Pack ran out of downs. Still trailing by a 27-21 score, the Packers received a third opportunity to score in the last minute, but this one was thwarted by an interception of a Tobin Rote pass that was returned for six points. To add insult to injury, Rote's next pass was also intercepted and brought back for a TD.

For all practical purposes, Green Bay's season was over. The Pack's record stood at 2-5, while first-place New York, idle that Sunday, remained at 6-1. The Rams (6-2) and Chicago Bears (5-2) were winners that week, making the task of passing up all three leaders impossible for the Pack. In the American Conference, the Browns (6-2) moved on top by nipping the Cardinals (3-4), while the Eagles (5-2) were upset by the Steelers (3-5). The Giants (5-2) kept pace by beating cellar-dwelling Washington (1-6).

Clark Shaughnessy predicted the Rams would beat the Packers in Milwaukee by four or five touchdowns. He was right. With the temperature around freezing, the Rams took advantage of several Green Bay miscues to down the Packers, 45-14, in front of the largest crowd, 20,456 fans, to see a Packer game in the Cream City in over two years.

The win put the Rams (7-2) atop the National Conference, a half-game ahead of the Yanks and Bears (both 6-2). Cleveland (7-2) remained on top of the American, a half-game ahead of the Giants and Eagles (both 6-2).

The Packers traveled to Detroit for their 10th contest of the year, and to a man, they wanted to avenge their earlier defeat to the Lions. The game turned out to be a case of "coulda been-shoulda been" for the Packers. Twice in the first half, Ronzani eschewed the field goal inside the 10-yard line and went for all the marbles on fourth down. Ted Fritsch missed a 31-yarder on another occasion. A drive to the

Detroit 22 was stopped in the first quarter by a Jack Cloud fumble, and another was halted on the Detroit 14. The final drive of the game was stopped by an interception in the end zone of a Tobin Rote pass, and the Packers lost for the seventh time in 1950, 24-21.

With another high-scoring victory over the Yanks (6-3), Los Angeles (8-2) moved a little closer to the division title, leading the stubborn Bears (7-2) by a mere half-game. The Browns (8-2) had the exact same situation in the American Conference, leading the sagging Giants (7-2) by a half-game and the Eagles (6-3) by a game and a half.

Ronzani had shown some courage in the pre-season by signing African-Americans Jim Thomas and Jim Clark to Packer contracts, but he took the easy way out when the time came to trim the roster for the regular season. After watching his team get its collective butt whipped on several occasions and attributing their poor showing to the glaring fact that the Packers were one of the two teams in the 13-team league without a player of African ancestry (the other being the Washington Redskins), the coach picked Bob Mann off the waiver wires just before the home finale in Green Bay against the 49ers. Mann had played for the Lions in '49 and was the NFL's second leading pass-catcher. He was traded to the Yanks during the off-season, but New York released him. When he stepped onto the field at City Stadium on November 26, 1950, Bob Mann became the first African-American to play in a regular season game for the Green Bay Packers.

With the aid of a biting blizzard, the Packers came from behind to defeat the 49ers in their first-ever meeting, 25-21, in front of 13,196 loyal, enthusiastic fans at "homecoming" for nearly 100 former Packers and their wives. Trailing 21-13 as they entered the final period of play, Green Bay mounted what looked like a scoring drive, but it fell short when Ted Fritsch missed a 21-yard field goal attempt. The Green Bay defense held, and the 49ers were forced to punt. The weather intervened. and Frankie Albert's punt from the seven went out of bounds on the 14. Four plays later Jack Cloud bolted over the line from the two. The defense held again, and the wind held up another Albert punt. Starting on San Francisco's 44, Christman led the Pack down the field in four plays, finishing the drive with a scoring strike to Breezy Reid.

The win guaranteed the Packers (3-7) a better record than the year before, and that was all Ronzani and Packer fans expected or wanted from the team in 1950. All knew that the road back to the top would be long and arduous, that rebuilding a team and organization wouldn't happen in a year or even in two years. Considering that Ronzani began the season with only 10 holdovers from Lambeau's last team and that none of them—and very few of the rookies and the veterans picked up in the dispersal draft and off the waiver wires—had ever been part of a Chicago-style T-formation, the kid from Iron Mountain had done a very credible job. With a little more luck, the Packers could have been a 5-5 team with two games to go on the West Coast, but Dame Fortune had not smiled on them in 1950.

As it was, the Packers were out of the National Conference race, but the Bears (8-2) weren't, as they bounced the Rams (8-3) to take over the top spot again. The Yanks (6-4), upset the victims of the improving Lions (5-5), were virtually out of the chase; while in the American Conference, the Giants and Browns (both 8-2) were two full games ahead of Philadelphia (6-4).

The Packers lost their last two games on the West Coast, 51-14 to the Rams and 30-14 to the 49ers. The only bright spot came in the final two plays of the season when Tony Canadeo gained 20 yards to put him atop the all-time rushing list for the Packers. Gaining 35 yards that day put him at 3,875, 15 yards ahead of Clarke Hinkle's old mark.

All things considered Ronzani's first campaign as head coach of the Packers could be called a mild success. He achieved two goals: (1) Improvement on the 1949 won-lost record, and (2) bringing the fans back to watch the Packers play exciting football. A total of 118,621 fans bought tickets for Packer games in Green Bay and Milwaukee, an improvement of 32,000 over 1949's attendance. The Packers finished tied for fifth place in the National Conference, but better than that, they finished in the black in the ledger where it really counted.

The Pack appeared to be on its way back to the top.

§§§

Packers Present Four-Game Ticket Gift Plan

4

The Rumors Persist

Both 1950 conference races ended in ties. The Bears and Rams sat atop the National Conference standings at 9-3, while the Browns and Giants shared the American Conference title at 10-2. Playoffs were necessary, and National Football League Commissioner Bert Bell couldn't have been happier. The two extra big games meant lots of windfall money for the four teams involved and the NFL overall.

The Bears defeated the Rams twice during the regular season, and the Giants did the same to the Browns. The old cliché about beating a team three times in a season suddenly appeared in the press, and George Halas in Chicago and Steve Owen in New York fretted about it. The oddsmakers were familiar with the old adage, and they made Cleveland and Los Angeles seven-point favorites to meet in the championship game to be played Christmas Eve. The old saying proved out as the Rams downed the Bears and the Browns slipped by the Giants. Cleveland won the NFL title by defeating the Rams, 30-28, in what Bert Bell termed as "the greatest game I ever saw."

On the business front, Bell stated that 1950 had been "the greatest season in National Football League history." He was right. On the field and at the box office, the NFL did have its greatest season to date in 1950. Much of the success was due to the end of the war between the

NFL and AAC. Of the 10 NFL teams in the merger, the New York Giants and Los Angeles Rams lost a little money from football operations, but they made up for it with television and radio contracts. The New York Yanks weren't that lucky, however. Of the AAC teams in the merger, the 49ers lost a little money, but their red ink was nothing like it had been when they were in the old circuit. The only big loser was Baltimore where fans refused to support a loser—at home as well as on the road. All of the other franchises made clear profits.

When questioned by news writers about the future of the loop, Bell refused to comment. His tight-lipped response gave rise to rumors that Baltimore and/or Green Bay would be surrendering their franchises in order to make room for new teams in Buffalo and/or Houston.

Emil Fischer, president of the Green Bay Packers, Inc., didn't hesitate to reply to the rumors. He said:

> *"They don't have to worry about us when they start talking about trimming off the 13th member of our league.* [Author's italics] They don't have to worry about us…We've been around this league a lot longer than most of the other clubs and we'll be in it next year and a good many more."

He then declared that the Packers were in the "best financial condition in our history" and that the club was in the "best shape it's ever been."

Still, the rumors persisted. Art Daley of the *Green Bay Press-Gazette* wrote that a television announcer in Baltimore had started the latest round of gossip because his own Colts were in jeopardy of losing their franchise. John Torinus, a member of the Packer executive committee, speaking in the absence of Fischer, stated:

> "The only reason for our folding would be finances, and we don't have any financial problems at all. We're busy now on season tickets and player plans for next year. We're in the league to stay. We have more than $100,000 in cash from our fund drive last year still not touched. We'll not only pay all

expenses out of this year's gate receipts, but we'll have a little left over."

Well, this certainly was good news. Almost. Fischer said:

"...when they start talking about trimming off the 13th member of our league."

What did he mean by that? Simple answer. The NFL moguls were planning to reduce the circuit to 12 teams in the near future. The question remained: Which franchise would be dumped?

Ideally, the owners and commissioner wouldn't have to make that decision. It would be made for them by one team deciding that it couldn't sustain any more losses and would fold up on its own accord. But if that didn't happen, then what? Then somebody would have to be axed out of the loop. But who? Logically, the team that was dragging down the rest of the league. That would be either Baltimore or Green Bay. Baltimore because of its poor showing at the box office, because of its finances, and because of its close proximity to Washington and thus its infringement on George Preston Marshall's territorial rights. And Green Bay because it was the smallest city with the smallest drawing area in the NFL.

Baltimore's problems bore an odd resemblance to the Packers problems of a year earlier. The Colts had 200 stockholders and they had a president, Abe Watner, who wanted to make the franchise his personal property. The stockholders opposed this idea, of course.

As part of the plan to admit the Colts to the NFL when the senior circuit merged with the AAC, Baltimore's management agreed to pay George Marshall $150,000 over three years as compensation for playing in his back yard. The first payment, $50,000 was due within 30 days of the completion of the 1950 season.

The Colts lost $83,078.71 in 1950. Watner agreed to pay the organization's losses when he took the president's post. If the stockholders paid the bills, he would step aside. He paid them, but now another $50,000—the first payment to Marshall—was due. The stockholders wanted Watner to pay the Washington owner. Watner told the stockholders that he wouldn't pay Marshall unless he was given a free rein with the team. The board of directors balked, saying Watner would have to pay Marshall and then step aside. Watner laughed at them.

Marshall tried to help the situation by giving the Colts an additional week to make their payment to him. Bert Bell stepped in and said Marshall couldn't do that without approval from the league and that required positive votes from 11 owners. The owners would vote on the question at the winter meetings in Chicago during the third week of January 1951. "If they disapprove," said Bell, "everything would be over..." Meaning, Baltimore would be out of the league. Period.

Watner paid the $50,000 to Marshall before the original due date, and Bell declared that this act made Watner the recognized owner of the Baltimore Colts. The board of directors of the Colts had a different idea about that. They contested Bell's declaration, but they were so meek about it that Bell ignored them. Watner was the official owner of the Baltimore Colts.

The NFL winter meetings began with a special session meant to discuss the problem of the Colts. Watner asked the other owners for help to build his team, meaning he wanted veteran players from them. They said no because the Korean War was causing problems with every team's personnel; the draft was taking all fit young men who weren't married and didn't have children. At the time of the meeting, none of the owners were really sure how many players that they'd be losing to the war. Watner responded by saying the Baltimore franchise would have to suspend operations because it didn't have enough veteran players to compete in '51. The owners replied negatively; either play or disband. Watner was disappointed, to say the least. He revealed that he personally lost $106,000 on the Colts in 1950. Could he have the $50,000 that he'd paid Marshall returned? Yes, said Bell and Marshall. Could he sell the contracts of his players and thus recoup some of his losses? Yes, the league would pay him $50,000 for his roster. As added incentive for Watner to go peacefully, Bell and the owners promised that, if and when the NFL decided to expand again in the next three years, Baltimore—and Watner—would get the first chance at the new franchise. Watner was a sound businessman who knew a deal when he saw one. He accepted, and the Baltimore Colts were out of the NFL—for the time being.

With the Colts gone, folks in the Green Bay area were breathing a lot easier. The NFL now had 12 teams, six in each conference. Nice numbers. The Packers survived another scare. *Whew!* Now it was time to get back to the business of building a winner.

Meanwhile, back in Chicago at the winter meetings, the owners argued over conference alignment.

Rumor had it that Halas wanted the Bears to play in the American Conference because he didn't want to travel to the West Coast and he wanted to play the Cardinals twice in Chicago and make two trips to New York where the Bears drew extremely well. This was strange considering how he was paid $48,000 for the first trip into LA, then $35,000 to play in San Francisco, then $65,000 for the playoff game against the Rams in December. Also, playing an extra game in New York hardly made up for playing the Packers in Chicago where the two rivals had performed in front of a record crowd in 1950.

In the end, the owners couldn't agree on anything except to turn the decision-making over to Bell who didn't want to make up the conference alignment but accepted the challenge anyway.

In rapid succession, the owners made the tackle eligible play illegal, ruled that in case of inclement weather a new ball would be introduced at the beginning of each quarter, modified the rule pertaining to a punted ball being downed by the punting team, and rejected a plan to number uniforms according to position.

In late January, the league announced that nine teams had turned a profit for 1950. Actually, it was 10 clubs. The Lions showed a deficit because the owner bought out the contract of head coach Bo McMillin at the end of the season creating a bookkeeping deficit. The other losers were the Colts, of course, the New York Yanks, and Curly Lambeau's Chicago Cardinals. Funny thing about that last item—or so it was whispered in Green Bay.

§§§

5

1951: A Second Rebuilding Year

Gene Ronzani's year started off poorly with the resignation of Ray Nolting, his backfield coach. Nolting quit to go into business in his home town of Cincinnati. He'd been very popular as a speaker with fans in the area. Ronzani remarked: "Ray's resignation was such a complete surprise that we haven't had time to look around yet" for a successor to Nolting.

Before he could think about hiring a new backfield coach, Ronzani and his remaining staff had to consider the NFL College Draft—and the Korean War. The coaches picked players who weren't likely to get drafted by the Army.

To make the Draft interesting, National Football League Commissioner Bert Bell added the names of players who had been under contract to the Baltimore Colts in 1950 to the list of college "eligibles." The Draft started with the bonus selection drawing. The Packers were eligible, but the Giants won the luck of the draw. New York took Kyle Rote (Tobin Rote's cousin), fullback from SMU, as the top choice for 1951. The Bears had the second choice due to a trade with Baltimore the year before, and Halas took Bob Williams, the quarterback from Notre Dame. Next was the coin flip for the teams that had finished with identical records, such as the Packers, Redskins, and 49ers who were all 3-9 in 1950 and were in line for the third pick overall. Washington won the toss and took Leon Heath, a fullback from Oklahoma. The 49ers won the next toss and took Y.A. Tittle off the Baltimore roster. Finally, the Packers got to choose.

Heading Ronzani's wish list was Bob Gain, a tackle from Kentucky. Gain never played a down for the Packers. Second on the list was Al "Rip" Collins, a halfback who had played for the Colts in 1950. Next was Fred Cone, a powerhouse fullback from Clemson. The fourth and eighth choices went to the Browns as compensation for acquiring Tom O'Malley and Bill Boedeker from Cleveland the previous summer. Of the remaining choices, few of them ever donned a Green Bay uniform. Among those who did were Dick Afflis, guard, Nevada; Ray Pelfry, end, Eastern Kentucky; and Art Felker, end, Marquette.

The annual stockholders meeting of the Green Bay Packers, Inc., held on January 22 revealed what everybody suspected: The Packers made a modest profit in 1950. The corporation earned $12,990 for the year, and this was without using any of the money raised from the sale of stock. This was good news all around. The Packers would be solvent again in 1951.

The officers of the corporation were re-elected and so were the 10 directors whose terms were up as of January 1. The officers were Emil Fischer, president; Lee Joannes, chairman of the board; Gene Ronzani, vice-president; and Frank Jonet, secretary-treasurer. The board members were William Servotte, Russell Bogda, Frank Jonet, Walter Scherf, H.J. Bero, Dominic Olejniczak, C.J. Renard, August A. Reimer, Ed Schuster, and Henry Washburn. The executive committee was also re-elected consisting of the three officers and chairman of the board plus Servotte, Bogda, Bero, Fred Leicht, Verne Lewellen, Fred Trowbridge, Max Murphy, and John Torinus.

Sadly, Frank J. Jonet, the friendly receiver appointed by the court when the Packers were in bankruptcy during the '30s and who had served the corporation and the community with honor and dignity for two decades, passed away during the summer. His position on the executive committee was given to Green Bay's Mayor Dominic Olejniczak, a director and a Packer Backer since boyhood. Jonet's office of secretary-treasurer would be filled at the regularly scheduled meeting of stockholders the following January with the election of William Servotte to the post.

With league and corporation business out of the way, Ronzani went about the task of signing players for the coming season. This was not

an easy job because, besides the usual interference of attracting players to Green Bay, the Korean War was getting in the way. Before the Draft, Ronzani lost linebacker Clayton Tonnemaker, halfback Larry Coutre, and guard Len Szafaryn. The first man called to active duty after the College Draft was halfback Wally Dreyer.

Another problem plaguing Ronzani and every other NFL coach was the Canadian Football League. The loop to the north had a rule that limited each team from hiring more than seven foreign—meaning American—players, and it seemed that every Canadian club was intent on getting its quota of U.S. citizens. Every week came an announcement that one player or another had signed to play in Canada in '51. The first Packer to go north was end Al Baldwin who joined the Ottawa Roughriders for the season. Another big loss to the Canadian league was Ronzani's first choice in the Draft, Bob Gain. the tackle from Kentucky. After the College All-Star game in Chicago, Gain signed to play with Ottawa.

The first veteran to sign his contract for '51 was perennial holdout Tony Canadeo. Following the "Grey Ghost into the fold were Don Stansauk, tackle; Ray "Dippy" DiPierro, guard; Carl Schuette, center; Bob Mann, end; Buddy Burris, guard; Leon Manley, guard; Ab Wimberly, end; Jack Cloud, fullback; Dick Wildung, tackle; Breezy Reid, halfback; Billy Grimes, halfback; Rebel Steiner, end; Tobin Rote, quarterback; Joe Spencer, tackle; Carleton Elliott, end; Jug Girard, halfback; Bob Summerhays, halfback; Ed Neal, guard; Dan Orlich, end; and Ed Ecker, tackle. A big surprise for Ronzani was the return of Jay Rhodemyre to professional football in '51.

Halfback Wally Dreyer received his discharge from the Army and joined the team two weeks into the training season.

Other newcomers to the team were Bob Thomason, a quarterback picked up from the Rams in a conditional deal that would give Los Angeles the Packers first and second draft choices in '52 if Green Bay kept Thomason beyond December 31, 1951; Ham Nichols, guard, Rice; Walt Michaels, a guard-linebacker from Washington & Lee who came to the Packers in a trade with the Browns for Dan Orlich who was returned to Green Bay in a subsequent trade; John Martinkovic, an end from Xavier who came to the Packers in a trade with the Redskins for Ted Cook; and Howie Ruetz, a tackle from Loras College picked up on waivers from the Rams. Three players were obtained in a blockbuster trade. The Packers received halfback Dom Moselle, halfback Ace Loomis, linebacker Charley Schroll as well the return of Dan Orlich in exchange for a '52 Draft choice and the negotiating rights to Bob Gain, the All-America tackle from Kentucky who decided to play in Canada instead of Wisconsin. The final three players to be added to the Green Bay roster for '51 were halfback Harper Davis, guard Dave Stephenson, and end Dick Moje. Davis came from the Bears on waivers, while Moje and Stephenson were purchased from the Rams.

The signing of Ray "Scooter" McLean as the backfield coach made headlines in the sports section of the *Green Bay Press-Gazette* in May. McLean gained Little All-America recognition at little St. Anselm College in Manchester, New Hampshire. George Halas drafted him, and he played eight years for the Bears. When his playing career came to an end, he became the head football and baseball coach at Lewis College in Lockport, Illinois. His football squads fashioned a 21-5 mark under his tutelage, including two conference titles.

Also joining Ronzani's staff was Chuck Drulis, the former Bear guard who had played for the Packers in 1950. Drulis would be an assistant line coach to Tarz Taylor.

The biggest news of the spring was the announcement that Ronzani had made a deal to take the team to Grand Rapids, Minnesota, to train prior to the exhibition season. He felt the site would give him an opportunity to "keep the squad together better" and as a result all concerned could "concentrate more on practice." This would only be the second time that the Packers trained away from the immediate Green Bay area, the other time being 1935 when Lambeau took the team to Rhinelander for preseason drills. Ronzani told a group of Kiwanians that the move to Minnesota would garner $20,000 for the corporation, consisting of a savings of about $2,000 for rooms for the players, payments of about $5,000 for each of a pair of intrasquad games, and a gate take of $10,000 or more for an exhibition game in Minneapolis. Even so, this was Ronzani's first really large mistake as the head man of the Packers.

After trimming the roster to 45 players, the Packers played their first exhibition game of the pre-season in Green Bay against Lambeau's Cardinals. Art Daley provided the usual hype in the *Press-Gazette*, but afternoon showers kept the crowd down to 16,168 die-hard fans. The Pack pulled the game out of the bag in the fourth quarter with a long TD pass from Tobin Rote to rookie Ray Pelfry and a field goal by Ted Fritsch to win by the identical score of the previous year's contest with the Cards, 17-14. Lambeau gave the Packers a grudging compliment by saying they were the better team—that night.

The next pre-season game was against the Eagles in Milwaukee. A crowd of 19,282 partisans showed up to watch the Packers beat themselves, 14-10, with penalties that called back two TDs. The Packers outplayed the Eagles in every facet of the game except where it counted-the scoreboard.

The 49ers provided the opposition for the Pack in their next non-league tilt, playing on a muddy field in Minneapolis. The defense did a fairly good job with San Francisco's potent attack, holding the Californians to 20 points; but the offense failed to show up as the Packers were unable to score at all. Once again, Ronzani went back to the old drawing board.

Buffalo was the site of the next pre-season encounter for the Pack, and the Steelers humbled the Packers, 35-7, in front of a crowd of 13,458 fans. Fumble-itis contributed greatly to this defeat as the Pittsburghers scooped up a pair of bouncing balls and returned them for third quarter scores. The only bright spot for Green Bay was the performance of Bob Mann who snared five passes for 65 yards.

In their final lineup before the home opener against the Bears, the Packers defeated the Redskins, 14-7, at Alexandria, Virginia. Green Bay scored first and last, while holding Washington to a solo TD in between. Both sixes came at the end of long drives.

The regular season opened late because Commissioner Bert Bell had planned to play the NFL title game on New Year's Day at the Rose Bowl in Pasadena, California. Earlier in the year when Bell was making up the schedule for the '51 campaign, the annual Rose Bowl game in Pasadena between the champions of the Big Ten and the Pacific Coast Conference was in jeopardy. Rose Bowl officials began negotiations with Bell to install the NFL title game as a replacement. The idea of playing a championship game at a neutral site was novel, although not unheard of. (The National Collegiate Athletic Association's basketball tournament was played at a neutral site each year.) Bell felt playing in Pasadena on New Year's Day would bring national attention to the NFL, and that meant more money for the owners in the forms of ticket sales and television rights. The plan fell through, however, when the Big Ten and PCC renewed their contracts with the Rose Bowl officials during the summer, and by that time, it was too late for Bell to change the NFL schedule for '51.

As they had done six times in the past, all in the '40s, the Packers opened championship play against the Bears in Green Bay. Art Daley wrote that starting the regular season with the Bears in Green Bay was a long tradition in the NFL, but the truth was the Bears had only provided the opposition for the home opener on two other occasions: 1944 and 1948. Of those eight donnybrooks, Chicago had won four, the Packers three, and one had ended in a deadlock.

In 1950, the two teams had split their season series, and Ronzani was looking to get a leg up on his old taskmaster, George Halas. In '51, Ronzani held secret practices throughout the week before the Bears arrived in town, and on Sunday, he unveiled a new, innovative offense that featured a single running back behind the quarterback with the other two backs spread wide outside the ends but behind the line of scrimmage. The wide-open attack didn't gel in the early going, and the Bears built up a 17-0 lead in the first half Green Bay got the sawdust out of the gear box late in the second quarter and mounted their first scoring drive to go into the locker room trailing, 17-6. The second half was a typical Bears-Packers game as both teams exchanged TDs. insults, and punches. The final score showed the Bears as the winner, 31-20, but statistically it was a draw. Ronzani's quarterbacks threw the ball 38 times and completed 22 for 238 yards. No Green Bay offense had done that since Don Hutson had retired. The 24,666 fans who left City Stadium that day went home disappointed in the final score, but nobody complained about not being entertained all afternoon.

George Halas made a famous statement after the game that has been used over and over by dozens of other magnates of the pro game in the ensuing years. He said:

> "This defeat doesn't mean a thing as far as Green Bay is concerned because it's going to be a mad scramble. There's no question but what the team that wins the championship will lose four games. It can't help but lose that many because all of the teams are so close. *Any team can beat any other on a given Sunday."* [Author's italics.]

Although Halas has been credited with originating much of the NFL's incredible history, he wasn't the first to utter this phrase, but he probably popularized it. Elmer Layden, the one-time NFL commissioner, spoke those words initially, and Curly Lambeau gave them credibility by repeating them often enough during the early days of World War II when the NFL moguls were trying to decide whether they should continue operations through the war.

Although the loss to the Bears was disappointing, as every loss to the Bears always was, the Packers picked themselves up off the floor and prepared for their match with the Pittsburgh Steelers in Milwaukee the following week. Pittsburgh, coached by John Michelosen, was one of the last teams to employ the single wing offense, primarily a running attack. Michelosen added a few twists to his game plan by making each back a potential passer-receiver-runner. This put some real excitement and more points into Steeler games, but it didn't add many more victories. Their first regular game ended in a tie with the defense minded Giants, and their second contest was a loss against the Packers.

A ferocious wind from the north was blowing on game day. Winning the toss, the Packers chose to have the wind at their backs in the first and fourth quarters. They scored 28 points in those stanzas. The Steelers scored all of their points, 33, when they had the wind at their backs. The difference in the game was the seven points the Packers scored at the start of the second period. Unfortunately, only 8,324 stalwart fans witnessed Green Bay's new offense as it piled up 393 yards and began to look like a real powerhouse destined for greatness.

Next into Green Bay were the unbeaten Philadelphia Eagles. Ronzani termed the game as crucial to any title hopes that the Packers might have. A crowd of 18,489 fans turned out, figuring the Pack might not win but that they'd at least be entertaining. Much to their delight, the Packers were more than entertaining as they blasted the Eagles, 37-24, scoring 30 second half points.

The win put the Packers (2-1) atop the National Conference standings— with four other clubs: Rams, Lions, Bears, and 49ers. The Yanks (0-3) rested on the bottom. Over in the American Conference, the Giants (2-0-1) took the early lead with the Eagles and Browns (both 2-1) close behind.

Riding on elation, the Packers faced the Rams the following week in Milwaukee. A good crowd of 21,339 fans turned out to watch the two teams fight to a scoreless first-half tie on a buttery field made muddy by an all-night and all-morning rainfall. The Packers had a good drive in the third quarter that fizzled on the one. The failure to score proved to be a real letdown for Green Bay and a real encouragement for the Rams as they stormed back to score 28 unanswered points in the final 18 minutes.

The loss dropped the Packers (2-2) into a fourth place tie with the 49ers behind the Bears (3-1), Rams (3-1), and Lions (2-1-1). In the American Conference, New York (3-0-1) remained on top with Cleveland (3-1) and Philadelphia (2-2).

In week five, the Packers traveled to New York for a match with the Yanks (0-3-1). For once, they were favored to win. A cold, cloudy day held down the crowd to 7,351 fans. Those who stayed away missed a whale of a game. The Yanks broke on top with two first quarter TDs before the Packers could complete a drive to the end zone. New York added another six before halftime, and the score stood 21-6 at intermission. After a zero third stanza, the Packers finally came to life and rode Bob Thomason's arm to three fourth period touchdowns but only two Fred Cone PATs. Trailing 26-21, the Yanks mounted a scoring drive and took back the lead with 1:12 remaining in the game. Taking the ensuing kickoff back to the 47, the Packers marched up the field to reach the New York nine with 11 seconds remaining. Cone, the probable goat for a loss because he'd missed two PAT tries that would have spelled victory, lined up for a 16-yard field goal try. He kicked it true and through, giving the Packers a 29-27 win that made the trip back to Green Bay very enjoyable for the whole team.

The well-earned victory moved the Packers (3-2) into a second-place tie with the Rams and 49ers, one game behind the Bears (4-1). The Lions (2-2-1), narrow losers to the Bears and the Packers' next opponent, were a close fifth. In the American Conference, the Browns (4-1) nipped the Giants (3-1-1) to move into first place, while the Eagles (2-3) dropped into a tie with the Redskins.

A record cold snap hit Wisconsin during the first week of November as the thermometer dipped to a low of seven degrees. At game time on Sunday, the temperature stood at 17, and a stiff wind out of the west swept across the field; cold, but not so cold that the Packers and Lions couldn't play football at City Stadium. Loyal fans, 18,800 strong, turned out to watch an odd game. Fred Cone and Doak Walker exchanged field goals in the first half to put the score at 3-3 going into the third period. On their first possession of the second half, the Packers started moving toward an apparent TD when the play of the game occurred. Tony Canadeo hauled in a Tobin Rote pass and ran down to the Detroit 20 with it where he was tackled, and a whistle was blown, ending the play—for the Packers, but not for the Lions. Detroit's Jack Christiansen took the ball from Canadeo, ran back up the field to be tackled on the 28. One official picked up the ball and took it back to the 20. Another official snatched up the ball again and returned it to the 28 and signaled a Detroit first down. Confusion reigned, but the

Lions kept the ball. Too stunned by the sudden turn of play, the Packers failed to stop the Lions on their next two possessions, and Detroit built a 17-3 lead early in the fourth period. The Packers recovered their composure and scored a six, but the Lions replied in kind. A last-minute TD by Green Bay only made the score close as the Lions went home to the Motor City winners, 24-17.

Now at the halfway mark in the season, Green Bay (3-3) slipped back to fourth with the 49ers. The Bears (5-1) continued to lead the hunt for a conference title, and the Rams (4-2) stayed close with Detroit (3-2-1) in third. On the American side, Cleveland (5-1) and New York (4-1-1) stayed ahead of the pack for another week.

The day before the Packers were set to play the Steelers in Pittsburgh, Ronzani said:

> "With all this talk about the fans booing players and riding the coaches and that protest against Frank Kilroy, the Steelers probably will play like a bunch of maniacs against us."

He was only right. Pittsburgh mauled the Packers, 28-7, but the score wasn't a good indicator of how the game was played. Green Bay managed to cross the 50-yard line only four times in the game, and the Pack's only TD came in the closing minutes after the outcome of the game was long decided.

With four losses now, Green Bay's title hopes were quickly vanishing. The Bears and Rams (both 5-2) stood atop the National Conference standings, and the Lions (4-2-1) were only a half-game behind. The 49ers (4-3) stood between the leaders and the Packers. In the American, the Browns (6-1) and the Giants (5-1-1) were head and shoulders above the rest of the conference.

The only bit of glory left for the Packers was the game with the Bears in Chicago. A win in the Windy City would go a long way toward salvaging the season. In order to achieve this goal, Ronzani unveiled yet another twist in his offense. With quarterback Bob Thomason sidelined for the game, Ronzani put Tobin Rote into a one-back formation where the big QB stood four yards behind the center while the halfbacks and fullback were spread out as flankers. Rote had the choice of running himself or passing. He ran 14 times and gained 150 yards. He passed 33 times but only completed 10. Therein was the difference in the game. Unable to move the ball through the air, the Packers came out on the short end of this one, 24-13, and their season was over-for the most part, anyway. For the first time in their history, the Packers played on national television on Thanksgiving Day. It didn't help Green Bay's decimated lineup win the game, but it did help professional football take a giant step toward financial stability. The Packers jumped ahead, 21-10, early in the second quarter, but the Lions' Bobby Layne brought his team back with three TD tosses to take a 31-21 lead into the locker room. Two punt returns for touchdowns by Jack Christiansen capped a 21-point third period for the Lions, and when the dust settled that afternoon, Detroit had another win over the Packers, 52-35. The very entertaining game drew an estimated audience of 24 million viewers.

The loss left the Packers (3-6) with little hope of a .500 season because of their impending trip to the West Coast to face the vaunted Rams (6-3) and the 49ers (4-4-1). Fortunately, they wouldn't have to face the conference leading Lions (6-2-1) or the Bears (6-3) again in '51. But they did have one more home game, and that was against the revitalized Yanks (0-7-2).

Only in Green Bay would a professional football fan be treated to an old-fashioned, college style homecoming. The Packers staged another one on December 2 when the Yanks came to town. Jug Earpe, the former Packer All-Pro and current publicity director for the Packers, conducted the ceremonies that welcomed back such notable Packers as Don Hutson, Clarke Hinkle, Lou Brock, Cal Hubbard, Arnie Herber, Johnny Blood, and 34 other former Packer players. Each of them was given a blanket commemorating their induction into the Helms Foundation Hall of Fame.

In the game, the Packers lost a close one that could have and should have gone their way. Only 14,297 loyal fans turned out on a mild day to watch the Pack blow a 21-10 lead in the fourth quarter to go down to defeat, 31-28. Once again, Ronzani employed his one-back offense when Tobin Rote was in the game, and the big QB from Rice responded with 92 yards rushing on three attempts and 95 yards passing on seven completions. Bob Thomason, a real T-formation QB, tossed 30 passes and completed 14 for 160 yards, but he had three aerials picked off. Those interceptions and the two thrown by Rote plus two fumbles lost proved to be very costly to the Packers.

The season-ending trip to the West Coast wasn't exactly a disaster for the Packers, but it did result in two more losses, extending their losing streak to seven games. They played the 49ers down to the wire before losing, 31-19, and they equaled the Rams for a half before succumbing, 42-14.

The 1951 campaign could be summed up in two words: hope and injuries. Green Bay had found hope for the future, but the present was wracked with injuries that cost them more than one game. Once again, the theme in Wisconsin was: We'll be better next year.

§§§

6
New Spark

The one big highlight of the 1951 season was Tony Canadeo becoming only the second man in National Football League history to push his career yards rushing total over the 4,000 mark* He accomplished this feat in the last game of the campaign against the Rams.

During his career, the "Grey Ghost" from Gonzaga gained, through the 1951 season, 8,211 all-purpose yards. He had been the primary source of offense for the Packers throughout the '40s. Canadeo had reached the pinnacle of popularity among Packer fans. When he announced his retirement at the end of the '52 season, it was like a death in the family.

The Packers were faced with the huge task of finding somebody in the 1952 NFL College Draft who could eventually fill the 31-year-old Canadeo's shoes. The man charged with finding that replacement was Jack Vainisi, the front office talent evaluator. Vainisi kept tabs on hundreds of college players for head coach Gene Ronzani and his staff of assistants who had the final say on who would be picked in the upcoming Draft.

---

* The other 4,000-yard man to that time was Steve Van Buren who was actually over 5,000 yards after the 1951 season.

Topping Ronzani's list of wants and needs was another quarterback to replace Bob Thomason who had to be released because of the terms by which he'd been acquired before the '51 season. If the Packers were to keep Thomason beyond December 31, 1951, they would have to surrender their first and second round draft choices to the Rams. In order to preserve those choices, and thus the future, Ronzani wisely let Thomason go free, returning him to the Rams who subsequently traded him to Philadelphia. Returning Thomason was a tough order for Ronzani because Thomason was one of the better passers in the NFL in '51, completing 125 of 221 for 1306 yards and 11 TDs. His completion percentage was among the best in the circuit, being topped only by all-time great Otto Graham of the Browns.

Ronzani filled his first priority by choosing and signing Vito "Babe" Parilli, QB, Kentucky, in the first round. His second choice was somebody to catch passes from Parilli and Rote. He picked Billy Howton, end, Rice. The Packers third glaring gap was in the defensive secondary. Ronzani needed a man who could stop the other team's passing attack. He put that responsibility on the shoulders of Bobby Dillon, defensive back, Texas. More help in the line? How about Dave Hanner, tackle, Arkansas, in the fifth round? Other draftees who signed and eventually played for the Packers were Tom Johnson, tackle, Michigan; Bill Reichardt, fullback, Iowa; Deral Teteak, guard, Wisconsin; Bobby Jack Floyd, fullback, TCU; and Chuck Boerio, linebacker, Illinois. All things considered; it was a good draft. Ronzani, with Vainisi's major input, was beginning to put together a respectable crew.

A native of Rochester, Pennsylvania, a stone's throw from Beaver Falls, Parilli was the first of a long line of great collegiate quarterbacks to be recruited by the immortal Paul "Bear" Bryant from the western Pennsylvania region. Parilli had some very remarkable college stats. He threw for 54 touchdowns, completed 354 of 634 passes, and gained 4,732 yards through the air. His college records on finishing school included:

Most Touchdown Passes in a Season, 23
Most Touchdown Passes in a Career, 50 (not including bowl games);
Most Yards Passing in a Career, 4,351 (not including bowl games);

Most Passes Complete in a Career, 331 (not including bowl games).

In his senior year at Rice, Howton caught 33 passes for 747 yards and seven TDs. His 22.6 yards per catch was the highest average in the nation.

A few days after signing Parilli the Packers announced the playing schedule for the '52 season, and it was a shocker because three regular season games were slated to be played in Milwaukee. Chairman of the Board Lee Joannes stated:

> "This move was taken solely with the best interests of the future of the Packers in mind. We are not moving the Packers to Milwaukee. The Packers can survive only as a Green Bay team, but we are asking all of Wisconsin and particularly Milwaukee to help us support the Packers so that Green Bay will always be in the National Football league."

Joannes gave several reasons for the move to three games in Milwaukee:

1. The Packers lost $18,000 in '51.
2. This was the first step toward building support for the Packers in Milwaukee.
3. Season ticket sales in Green Bay dropped off in '51, but they increased in Milwaukee.
4. Only half of the season ticket holders for games in Green Bay actually came from Green Bay and De Pere.
5. Milwaukee had a new stadium.

Once again, the Packers were faced with a financial crisis, and as they had done so often in the past, the executive committee rose to the occasion. Playing three games in Milwaukee at this time proved to be the right solution. The fly in the ointment was a construction strike in May that delayed the completion of Milwaukee County Stadium. This forced the trio of games to be moved to Marquette University's stadium.

In late April, Ronzani made a trade with the Cleveland Browns, sending Walt Michaels to Cleveland for three tackles: Forrest "Chubby" Grigg (not to be confused with Forrest Gregg of later Packer fame), Elmer "Zeke" Costa, and Dick Logan. Only Logan made the Packer squad in '52.

A few weeks later the head coach traded offensive back Al Collins to the Philadelphia Eagles for defensive back Dan Sandifer. Collins and Sandifer were teammates at LSU before joining the pro ranks.

Another trade had Ace Loomis going to Cleveland for Tony Adamle and Don "Dopey" Phelps. Some deal! Adamle chose to go to medical school, and Phelps walked out of training camp. Can you imagine a guy giving up a chance to play pro football for $8,000 a year to become a doctor and make $50,000 a year? Who wants a guy like that? And how about picking up a player with the nickname of "Dopey"? Makes one wonder who was smart here and who was really dopey.

But the Green Bay brain trust wasn't the only one making unusual trades in the NFL in '52. The Dallas Texans (nee New York Yanks) completed one of the all-time big trades in professional sports history. They sent all-pro linebacker Les Richter to the Rams for 11—count 'em—11 players, none of which ever amounted to much more than a blocking and tackling dummy.

As July rolled around, Ronzani and his coaching staff of Ray McLean (backfield), Dick Plasman (ends and defense), Tarz Taylor (line), Chuck Drulis (assistant line), and newly signed Bob Perina (assistant/game-talent scout) had 34 players under contract, but only five of these had pro experience, three with the Packers. Not to worry, though. Many of the veterans weren't being counted on anyway. By the time training camp opened July 28, Ronzani had 57 players under contract.

Two days before the team was to leave for training camp at Grand Rapids, Minnesota, Ronzani purchased the contract of Clarence Self from the Lions, then he traded popular Jug Girard to Detroit for veteran defensive end Ed Berrang, rookie tackle Steve Dowden who had been coached at Baylor by Hall of Famer Mike Michalske, and the famous player to be named later. On the opening day of camp, the coach purchased the contract of 10-year veteran guard Ray Bray from the Bears.

On the home front, Packer officials reported that sales of season tickets in the Milwaukee area had already surpassed the count for '51. The sales impetus was due to the hard work of corporation directors from the region, spearheaded by that former Packer great Charles "Buckets" Goldenberg.

While the team practiced in the cool Minnesota weather, a sextet of Green Bay rookies were in Delafield, Wisconsin, preparing for the College All-Star Game. Bobby Dillon, Billy Howton, Babe Parilli, Tom Johnson, Chuck Boerio, and Bill Reichardt were among the 61 college stars working out under Coach Bobby Dodd for their meeting with the Rams in Chicago on August 15.

With Ronzani in the stands paying particular attention to the play of his six draftees, the College All-Stars gave the Rams all they could handle before bowing, 10-7. Parilli on offense and Dillon on defense stood out as the game's stars, and Ronzani couldn't wait to get them into the green and gold uniforms of the Packers.

The Packers started their exhibition season the next night in Milwaukee, squaring off against the Giants at Marquette University's stadium. A good crowd, estimated at 22,000, turned out to see Green Bay go down by a 7-0 count. Tobin Rote carried the load at quarterback. Five Green Bay turnovers spelled the difference in the game.

Ronzani's squad still had 23 rookies on it the following week when the Browns visited City Stadium. Always a powerhouse under Paul Brown, Cleveland listed only nine rookies on their roster. The lack of experience showed but not the lack of talent as the Packers gave the Browns a good fight, although losing, 21-14, before 22,215 fans, the largest crowd to see a pre-season game in Green Bay to date.

The Packers traveled to Latrobe, Pennsylvania, for a game against the Steelers on a high school field. A sellout crowd estimated at 10,000 came out to see Pittsburgh slip by Green Bay, 7-6, in a game that was a celebration of the alleged first professional football game in the history of the sport. Supposedly, a contest between Latrobe [Pennsylvania] YMCA and a team from Greensburg, Pa., was the first pro game. Actually, the first pro game was played by elevens from Latrobe and Jeannette, Pa.

The Green Bay roster was down to 45 for the next exhibition game, a clash with the Cardinals at Comiskey Park in Chicago. Six were newcomers from other pro teams, 20 were holdovers from the '51 squad, and 19 were rookies. The Redbirds were primarily a veteran club under new head coach Joe Kuharich. The Cards showed their experience, drubbing the young Packers, 38-7.

What happened to Curly Lambeau? Wasn't he coaching the Cardinals in '51? He was. He threw a fit and got himself fired near the end of the season. Typical Lambeau logic. A man whose ego had out-grown his reputation.

Washington owner George Marshall possessed a temperament very much like Lambeau's, and they were old friends. When Washington coach Dick Todd resigned in the middle of the practice season, it was only natural that Marshall should hire Lambeau to coach his Redskins.

Lambeau thanked the boss with a loss in his first game as head coach, and he continued to show his gratitude for being removed from the list of the unemployed by bowing to the Packers, 13-7. This was the third straight game that Lambeau lost to his former team.

The Packers played a rematch against the Steelers in Minneapolis for their pre-season finale, and they showed some real signs of being a good football team for '52 as they dumped Pittsburgh, 23-10. A 79-yard TD bomb from Babe Parilli to Billy Howton gave Packer fans a hint of what the future held for them. Howton wasn't exactly Don Hutson, and Parilli wasn't Arnie Herber or Cecil Isbell, but both were exciting football players at a time when the Packers needed all the excitement they could get.

Cutdown time had finally arrived in Green Bay. The mythical "Turk" made his rounds of rookies and veterans alike, and when the sword wielding villain departed, the roster consisted of 33 players eager to begin the '52 campaign. The veterans for '52 were ends Bob Mann, John Martinkovic, Abner Wimberly, Ed Berrang, and Carleton Elliott; tackles Dick Afflis and Howard Ruetz; guards Dave Stephenson and

Ray Bray; center Jay Rhodemyre; and backs Tobin Rote, Bob Forte, Tony Canadeo, Ray Pelfrey, Fred Cone, Dan Sandifer, Billy Grimes, Dom Moselle, Breezy Reid, and...The rookies were tackles Steve Dowden, Tom Johnson, and Dave Hanner; guards Deral Teteak, Chuck Boerio, Steve Ruzich, and Dick Logan; center George Schmidt; end Billy Howton: and backs Babe Parilli, Bob Floyd, Bill Reichardt, and Bobby Dillon.

Ronzani owned a 1-3 record against his old team going into the '52 regular season. His first Packer team dumped the Bears in their first contest of 1950, but Green Bay had dropped three straight since then. After finishing strong in the pre-season, Packer fans had reasonable hopes of beginning the year with a win, especially since the game would be played in front of a sellout crowd in Green Bay. The Bears had other ideas. A fourth quarter letdown by the Pack allowed the Chicagoans to pull out a 24-14 win. The game did have a silver lining: no injuries to key personnel.

Ronzani picked up five players during the week on waivers: guard Washington Serini, rookie center Hal Faverty, end Jim Keane, all from the Bears; tackle Bob Dees from the Rams; and back Ace Loomis, drafted by the Browns and traded to the Packers in '51, then traded back to the Browns in '52 only to be cut before the first game of the season. To make room for this quintet, the coach released Pelfrey, Boerio, and Berrang with Johnson and Teteak going on the injured list.

Lambeau, now 0-3 against his old team but only in pre-season games, inspired the Redskins to a 23-7 upset of the Cardinals in a Monday night game at Comiskey Park in Chicago. Filled with this victory, he brought his team to Milwaukee the following Sunday to face the revitalized Packers.

Confident that he could outcoach Lambeau on any given day, Ronzani put his best foot forward against Washington in front of a disappointing crowd of only 9,657. Milwaukeeans as most of the Cream City's sports fans stayed home or went to local watering holes to watch the World Series on television. Parilli led a potent attack against the Redskins, completing seven of 12 passes for 248 yards and a pair of TDs, including a 90-yarder to Billy Howton in the first quarter.

Fred Cone hulled his way for 76 yards on only eight carries, and Tony Canadeo added 40 yards to his all-time total. Cone, Canadeo, Reid, and Rote also had touchdowns, and Cone booted all five extra points as Green Bay outscored Washington, 35-20.

Lambeau was now 0-4 against his old team.

Art Daley was calling the Packers' next game, another Milwaukee date against the defending NFL champion Rams, "THE BIG ONE." Green Bay had lost seven straight games to LA, and Ronzani hoped to reverse that trend. To date, the Rams were winless, scoring only 21 points while giving up 54; not exactly the mark of champs. Even so, Los Angeles was a veteran team with several All-Pros, and the Packers were young and inexperienced.

Daley reported the game best:

> The Packers buried themselves with the most dreadful collapse you'll ever see or hear, and the Rams won with one of the greatest—if not the greatest—rallies in the history of football.
>
> For three full quarters, the Packers were absolutely magnificent. They smashed to four touchdowns and held the offense-crazy Rams to two field goals for a 28 to 6 lead-yes, 28 to 6.
>
> The Packers and 21,693 fans in Marquette University Stadium started to reach for the chips...Then it happened—like a nightmare...The Rams scored 24-points...in the last 11 minutes and 10 seconds—the Packers scored none. Result: LA 30, GB 28.

As bitter as this defeat was, the season had only just begun, and a 1-2 start was not the end of the world. Or so Ronzani told his charges on Monday.

During the following week, tackle Howie Ruetz had an emergency appendectomy and had to be placed on the injured list. To replace him, Ronzani signed Bill Robinson, a halfback who played at Lincoln College in Pittsburgh before playing for the Steelers in '51 and early '52. Robinson joining the Packers was significant because he was the second player on the squad who had ancestors that came from

Africa. The other fellow was Bob Mann. Slowly, Green Bay was burying the past by recognizing that African-American athletes deserved their place on the playing field.

The Yanks, whether they played in Boston or New York, never amounted to much of a threat to cop an NFL title, and they never drew very well in the Big Apple. Thus, the franchise was shifted to Dallas for the '52 season. This was the NFL's first incursion into the old Confederacy, and it might have been its last if certain shameful laws below the Mason-Dixon Line hadn't been changed in succeeding years.

When the Packers traveled to Dallas for their fourth game of the '52 campaign, Robinson and Mann were forced to stay in a motel for "Negroes Only" because Texas still had racial segregation statutes. A Packer stockholder, Myron Kuhlman, who had moved to Texas from Wausau to work for a paper company there, drove Mann and Robinson to and from practice and the game. Art Daley excused the state of Texas for segregating the Packer players by stating:

> The Texans, incidentally, have two Negro stars, Buddy Young and George Taliaferro, who must live apart from their teammates.

This is not to say that Daley was a racist: far from it. His remark in print was merely a sign of the times. Not the best of times for all Americans, especially those of African and Hispanic ancestries.

Besides archaic racial segregation laws, Texas "Blue Laws" still forbade the playing of football on Sunday. Thus, the Packers and Texans met on Saturday night in the Cotton Bowl. After trailing Dallas at halftime, 14-7, Green Bay rallied in the third and fourth quarters to come away winners, 24-14. Tobin Rote had another big game, passing for 117 yards and rushing for 65 more, and Billy Howton hauled in three passes, two for TDs.

The win put the Packers (2-2) in second place behind San Francisco (4-0). Detroit and Chicago were tied with Green Bay, while the Rams (1-3) and Dallas (0-4) brought up the rear of the National Conference. Over in the American Conference, the Cardinals, Giants. and Browns (all 3-1) sat atop the standings with Washington and Philadelphia right behind them (both 2-2). The Steelers (0-4) *were the pits.* [Author's pun intentional]

"If the Packer-Ram game in Milwaukee recently was the BIG ONE," wrote Daley, "then the Packer-Detroit battle in City stadium next Sunday is the GREAT BIG ONE." Daley exaggerated because he was trying to drum up business for the Packers. The Lions seldom drew big crowds in Green Bay, and a little extra emphasis on the importance of the game just might put another thousand fans in the stadium. The stratagem helped as the two teams played to a sellout.

The Lions didn't have a single running back in the top NFL's 10: Bobby Layne, their quarterback, was 16th among passers: but Cloyce Box was 10th in pass receptions because he was the only guy on the team who could catch. In spite of this lack of offense, Detroit was a .500 team. Why? Defense. They held on to their leads against the powerful Rams for a pair of wins. Their two losses were against the division leading 49ers. Daley ran a headline:

Lions To Explode Against Pack? They're Overdue!

He was only right again. The Lions mauled the Packers, 52-17. strictly because the Pack committed nine turnovers to Detroit's two. The Packers gained 423 yards to Detroit's 384, but the Lions put the numbers where they counted the most: on the scoreboard.

The loss dropped the Packers (2-3) three games behind undefeated San Francisco (5-0). The Rams and Bears had identical records with Green Bay, putting the three of them a game behind Detroit (3-2). Dallas was hopelessly buried in last place without a win. The Browns (4-1) moved ahead of the herd in the American Conference. Knotted a game behind Cleveland were the Cardinals, Giants, and Eagles (all 3-2). The Redskins (2-3) were fifth, and the Steelers (1-4) got into the win column but stayed in last place.

With Parilli and Rote one-two in the passing stats for the entire league, the Packers met the Eagles in Milwaukee the next Sunday. Philadelphia owned two wins over the hapless Steelers and an upset victory over the Giants. Leading the Eagles was former Green Bay quarterback Bob Thomason. A meager crowd of 10,147 turned out to watch the Packers snuff the Eagles, 12-10, as Deral Teteak blocked a fourth-quarter punt and Big John Martinkovic scooped up the ball and ran it into end zone for the winning score.

The win kept the Pack (3-3) in the race because the Bears (3-3) dumped the 49ers (5-1). Detroit (4-2) also won, and so did Los Angeles (3-3). The only loser in the National Conference that Sunday was (big surprise!) the Dallas Texans (0-6). Over in the American Conference, Cleveland (4-2) lost to the Lions, but the Giants (4-2) bumped off the slipping Cardinals (3-3) who remained tied with the Eagles. The Steelers (2-4) made it two straight by nipping the Redskins (2-4).

Ronzani picked up another defensive back for the next game, the return match with the hated Bears. Marv Johnson played for the San Jose Packers in a semi-pro league in California before being signed for the '51 season by the Rams who put him on waivers in '52. Johnson replaced Clarence Self who broke a finger in the Philadelphia game.

Wrote Daley:

> Chicago's Wrigley field, known to millions of radio fans as the "world's most beautiful ball park," has been nothing but a big, black, ugly dungeon for the Packers.

Or so it had been since 1941, the last time the Pack beat the Bears in Chicago. Not so in '52. Ronzani inspired the Packers with a game plan that mounted a superior offensive attack and buried the Monsters of the Midway, 41-28. In a real team effort, Canadeo gained 61 yards on 11 carries; Cone, 46 yards on nine carries; Grimes, 45 yards on five carries; and Reid 30 yards on seven carries. Rote completed nine of 13 passes for 120 yards and a TD, while Parilli completed seven of 12 for 81 yards and two TDs. Howton caught six passes for 62 yards and a touchdown.

Two weeks earlier when the Packers were 2-3 their hopes of a conference title seemed remote at best. Once again, the old adage that "Time changes all things" was proven true. Green Bay (4-3) was still in a third-place tie with the Rams, but the two teams trailed the Lions and 49ers by only one game now. The Bears (3-4) slipped to fifth, and Dallas remained winless. Cleveland and New York (both 5-2) won that week to stay tied for first in the American Conference a game ahead of Philadelphia (4-3), winners over Lambeau's fading Redskins (2-5). The

Cardinals (3-4) lost their third straight, and Pittsburgh (2-5) failed to climb out of the cellar.

During the following week, the Packers hired Jumbo Joe" Stydahar as a special administrative assistant to Ronzani. The signing was necessitated by the illness of Jack Vainisi, the club's top talent hunter. Stydahar's duties would include evaluating collegiate talent for the coming Draft.

The schedule-makers usually had each team play every other team in their conference twice during a season. That meant 10 games. Then each team would play two teams in the other conference once to make a total of 12 games for the campaign. In '52, the schedule-makers did it a little differently for the Packers. Instead of playing the 49ers twice and two American Conference teams once each, Green Bay was set to play San Francisco once and three AC squads. Why? Who knows? This was the NFL in 1952.

Therefore, the Packers traveled to New York to take on the mighty Giants at the Polo Grounds. The Gothamites stood atop their division with the Browns when the day started. When the sun dropped below the Manhattan skyline that evening, Cleveland owned first place in the American Conference all by itself as the Packers put up a stone wall defense to stuff the Giants, 17-3.

The win was Green Bay's third straight, and it left the Packers (5-3) tied with LA, only a game out of first behind San Francisco and Detroit. The Bears (3-5) and Dallas (0-8) were no longer in the National Conference race, while the Browns (6-2) were beginning to take command in the American Conference over the Giants and Eagles (both 5-3) and the Cards (3-5), losers off our straight. Washington and Pittsburgh (2-6) were mathematically eliminated.

Ronzani warned his charges against getting fat heads over winning three straight because the winless Texans were coming to Green Bay and everybody knew how dangerous a team without a win can be. To add a little spice to the game and to help the draw, the Green Bay management chose the Dallas game to salute Tony Canadeo, the "Grey Ghost" from Gonzaga, who was planning to retire at the end of the season. This was a good idea because Dallas was on the verge of bankruptcy, a demise that its owners wished to avoid by playing the remainder of their schedule on the road. To make matters worse for the franchise, a new ownership group withdrew its offer to take over the team when Commissioner Bert Bell refused to let them off the hook for $200,000 in back stadium rent to the New York Yankees baseball team.

All of this prompted Ronzani to reiterate his warning about taking the Texans too lightly.

Art Daley wrote a piece about how tied up the NFL would be if the Bears, Packers, Rams, Giants, and Eagles won their respective games over the Lions, Texans, 49ers, Redskins, and Browns. If this were to happen, and the odds of it happening were high but not astronomical, then the Packers, Rams, 49ers, and Lions would be tied for first in the NC and the Browns, Eagles, and Giants would be atop the AC—all seven teams with identical 6-3 records. Well, guess what. It happened. For the first and only time in the history of the NFL, four teams were tied for first in a division in the ninth week of the season.

The Packers won their game by mauling Dallas, 42-14, behind several big TD pass plays: Rote to Canadeo for 21 yards; Parilli to Howton for 50 yards; Parilli to Mann for 18 yards; and Rote to Reid for 81 yards. Canadeo added a rushing six, and Loomis ran back an interception 45 yards for the final six-pointer. Surprisingly, the Packers committed seven turnovers and 10 penalties for 100 yards. Dallas was only slightly better in both categories, coughing up the ball only four times and committing 11 penalties for 95 yards. Field position helped Green Bay as well as the Packers booted five punts for an average of 42 yards while Dallas could only average 33 yards on their 13 kicks.

Entering the final quarter of the season, the Packers were masters of their own fate. Left on the schedule were a Thanksgiving Day grudge match with the Lions in Detroit and a trip to the West Coast to meet the Rams and 49ers. Three wins would give the Packers the conference title. Two wins would get them a tie for first as long as one was over the Lions and the other was over the winner of the Rams-49ers rematch. Two losses would probably mean no dessert for the Packers in December.

With revenge in their hearts, the Packers left for the Motor City on Wednesday. A national television audience of 30 million was expected, and a stadium crowd of 45,000 was a reasonable expectation as well. All those expectations failed to be met. Only 39,000 came to the park, the TV audience fell short by several million, and the Packers committed eight turnovers, including six lost fumbles, to get blown out by the Lions, 48-24. Enough said about this one.

The loss dropped the Packers (6-4) into a tie with San Francisco which lost to LA (7-3), leaders now of the NC with the Lions. The Bears (4-6) lost to Dallas (1-9) to put them out of the race for '52. In the AC, the Browns (7-3) crushed Lambeau's Redskins (2-8) to take over first place by themselves as the Giants (6-4) were steamrolled by the Steelers (4-6), 63-7, for the worst defeat in the history of the franchise, and the Cardinals (4-6) ended their five-game losing streak by besting Philadelphia (6-4), 28-22.

The Packers still had hope. All they had to do was beat the Rams in LA and the 49ers in San Francisco, while the Lions lost to the Bears or the Texans, and the Rams lost their finale to Pittsburgh. If that should happen, Green Bay would face the Browns for the NFL title. Of course, Hell might freeze over, too.

The only Green Bay regular to miss the game with the Rams was fullback Fred Cone who also did the placekicking. Thus, nobody could blame injuries for the 45-27 loss in front of 49,822 fans in the LA Coliseum. Trailing by a mere three points, 17-14, at the half, the Packers had two passes intercepted in rapid order in the third period, the first being returned for a TD and the second setting up another six point score that gave the Rams a commanding 31-14 lead. In all, the Rams intercepted five Green Bay aerials.

The game was marred from the start because the Packers showed up in their gold jerseys with green numerals. What's so unusual about that? The home team had the choice of uniforms for the game, and the Rams customarily wore their own gold jerseys with blue numbers when playing at home. Ronzani should have known this. The Green Bay equipment man should have known this. The Packers should have worn their other jerseys, the green ones with the yellow numbers. They might have had better luck. As it was, Hampton Pool, the LA coach, played the game under protest because he was steamed about the Packers wearing gold uniforms. Pool had a lot of nerve. When the Rams showed up in Milwaukee to play the Packers back in October, they only had their gold uniforms with them, and Pool asked Ronzani to switch his team to their green jerseys for the game. Gentleman that he was, Ronzani agreed, and the game was played without any problem. The Green Bay mentor made his mistake by expecting Pool to be an equal gentleman when the Packers traveled to LA.

The loss dropped the Packers (6-5) from the race in the National Conference. The Rams (8-3) stayed on top with the Lions who dumped the Bears (4-7) in Detroit, 45-21. San Francisco (6-5) was also eliminated, losing to Pittsburgh (5-6). Cleveland (8-3) clinched a tie for first in the AC by beating the Cardinals (4-7). The Eagles (7-4) stayed in the running by defeating Dallas (1-10), and Lambeau's Redskins (3-8) put the Giants (6-5) out of their misery for '52.

The only thing at stake in the season finale for the Packers was third place and pride. Ronzani wanted '52 to go out on a winning note and give him a good foundation to build on in '53. It wasn't to be. Reichardt missed four long field goal attempts of 48, 40, 45, and 42 yards, and a fifth possible attempt from the 32 was a fake that failed to gain a first down. If Reichardt had made four of those five tries…well, he didn't, and the Packers lost to San Francisco, 24-14.

The Rams and Lions finished the regular season tied for first and met in a playoff game in Detroit. The Lions won that one, then dumped the Browns in Cleveland for the NFL championship.

The Packers (6-6) finished in fourth place for their best season since '47 when they also came in fourth with a 6-5-1 mark. Statistically, they improved in several team categories.

Individually, Green Bay had some new stars in Billy Howton, Tobin Rote, Babe Parilli, and Bobby Dillon.

Howton caught 53 passes for 1,231 yards to break Don Hutson's record of 1,211 set in '42. He also had 13 TDs and averaged 23.2 yards a catch for a record that still stands as of this writing. Howton finished first in the league in yards, first in average per catch, second in TD catches, and sixth in total receptions.

Tobin Rote and Babe Parilli finished two-three in the passing race behind Norm Van Brocklin of the Rams, and Dillon was recognized as one of the better pass defenders in the league.

All things considered '52 was a good year. A little more defense and fewer fumbles and interceptions and the Packers could be a legitimate contender in '53.

§§§

7

Life After the Grey Ghost

Tony Canadeo was gone. The all-time greatest running back in the franchise's history to date had hung up his cleats for good. His slats included 4,197 yards on 1,025 carries and 31 touchdowns in an 11-year career. Although his numbers weren't all that great the last few years of his career, he still did some things-like block and give the team leadership-better than every other back on the squad. Would he be missed? Is the world round?

Ronzani needed a replacement for Canadeo; number one item on the shopping list for the '53 draft. The Packers had the seventh choice, sixth if the Bonus Pick didn't exist; but the Bonus Pick did exist, and the Packers didn't get it-again. San Francisco did.

Adding to Ronzani's roster problems for '53 were fullback Bill Reichardt and tackle Bob Dees, both of whom were entering the armed forces in January. If that wasn't enough of a headache, fullback/place kicker Fred Cone decided to call it quits to coach high school athletics back home in South Carolina. Cone changed his mind later in the year and returned to the Packers for his third season, but in January when the draft came around, as far as Ronzani was concerned, Cone was gone for good and had to be replaced.

On the good news side that winter, halfback Larry Coutre and center/linebacker Clayton Tonnemaker would be receiving their discharges from the Army in plenty of time for them to suit up for '53.

A week before the league meeting the Packers announced that Ronzani had been given a new three-year pact. This was considered to be a reward for bringing the Packers back to respectability. Satisfied that he was still in charge, Ronzani went to the NFL confab in Philadelphia in search of replacements for his retiring stars.

The 49ers opened the draft by taking Harry Babcock, an end from Georgia, as their bonus pick. In order thereafter, Baltimore took Heisman Trophy winner Billy Vessels, halfback, Oklahoma; Washington, Jack Scarbath, quarterback, Maryland; Cardinals, John Olszewksi, fullback, California; Pittsburgh, Ted Marchibroda, quarterback, Univ. of Detroit; Bears, William Anderson, halfback, Compton JC; and then it was Green Bay's turn. Ronzani made a good choice: Al Carmichael, a speedy six-foot halfback from the University of Southern California. Carmichael was an excellent choice when you look at the players chosen ahead of him; not a whole lot of Hall-of-Famers there.

Ronzani's second pick was a major mistake. He took Gil Reich, a halfback who finished his collegiate career at Kansas because he'd been kicked out of West Point for his involvement in a cribbing scandal in '51. He never amounted to much in anything.

After those two picks, Ronzani took future Packers Bill Forester, linebacker, SMU; Gib Dawson, halfback, Texas; Roger Zatkoff, linebacker, Michigan; Jim Ringo, center, Syracuse; Joe Johnson, halfback, Boston College; Bill Lucky, tackle, Baylor; and Al Barry, guard, Southern California/. Forester played tackle on both offense and defense in college, but he was switched to linebacker in the pros. Dawson ran the 100-yard dash in 9.6 seconds; Barry was selected in the 20th round; Lucky and Johnson were juniors; Zatkoff and Ringo were picked in the fifth and seventh rounds, respectively, without much fanfare or press. This was not a bad draft, considering the Packers took eight men who made it in the pro circuit. Not every team could make such a boast.

On the league front, the Dallas franchise was dead and buried. On the horizon? Baltimore.

When it became apparent that the NFL was dead in Dallas, Commissioner Bert Bell let the folks in Baltimore know that they could have another team if they could sell 15,000 season tickets by the NFL annual meeting in January and if they could find a buyer for the Dallas players, meaning somebody who would pick up the $200,000 debt owed to the New York baseball Yankees for rent on Yankee Stadium. On January 7, 1953, the powers that be in Baltimore announced that they had sold the 15,000 season ducats, and they thought they had a new owner in the person of Carroll Rosenbloom, a 45-year-old clothing manufacturer. Rosenbloom headed up a group of five investors, and this satisfied Bell and the owners of the 11 other NFL franchises who voted to admit the new group to their club. The Baltimore Colts would be back for '53. The next question was: In which conference?

George Marshall wanted the Colts in the American Conference because of their proximity to Washington and the fact that Baltimore would play his Redskins twice each year, meaning a better crowd in his stands for the Colts than for the Cardinals from distant Chicago. If Marshall got his way, the Cardinals would be switched back to the National Conference where they would have to play the Bears and the Packers' twice each year, meaning they would have two games at home with good draws. This only made good sense, right? But whoever accused professional sports owners of having good sense? The Colts replaced the Texans in the National Conference, which became the Western Conference, and the Cards remained in the American, which became the Eastern Conference.

Bell announced that attendance had reached the two million mark again, but that only four teams had made a profit. Good, but not best or even better. More teams needed to make money on a consistent basis for the league to progress.

The NFL rules committee rejected such proposals as a sudden death period if a game ended in a tie, a seven-point touchdown and elimination of the extra point try, and a time penalty instead of banishment from the game for unnecessary roughness.

As previously mentioned, the owners voted to change the names of the two conferences from American and National to Eastern and

Western, respectively. More importantly, they voted to permit no more than a 10% cut in any player's salary from one year to the next. They would have been wiser if they had voted to permit no more than a 10% raise in any player's salary. A precedent like that, which would have been followed by the other professional sports, would have kept salaries down but not so low that an athlete couldn't make a very good living from his pay. Let's see: a player making $10,000 this year would make $11,000 next year, then $12,100 the year after that, and $13,310 in his fourth year. For the '50s, this would have been a good salary. If the owners had increased the minimum salary a grand or so every year or every other year, players would have kept ahead of inflation. But this didn't happen then, and it most likely will never happen, and the fans will continue to pay the freight for the NFL.

Finally the schedule was adopted for the '53 season. Each team would play their conference opponents twice each, home and away, and each team would play two teams from the other division, one home a one away. This would give each team a 12-game schedule. The Pack drew the Browns for their non-conference home game and the Steelers for their non-conference road game. The contest against the Browns would be their first ever regular season meeting, and it would christen brand new Milwaukee County Stadium as the Packers' home-away from-home.

At the annual meeting of the Green Bay Packers, Inc., Emil Fischer resigned as president of the corporation after six years at the helm, but he was elected to the post of chairman of the board of directors to replace Lee Joannes who was re-elected as a vice-president, as was Ronzani. Replacing Fischer as president was Russell W. Bogda who had been a board member for the past six years. All board members up for re-election were voted to another term, and the executive commit remained unchanged.

Bogda's election to the corporation presidency proved to be pivotal step in Packer history, but no one realized it until it was too late to do anything about it. No one questioned whether or not it was wise to give the reins of the corporation to a man who was essentially, a car salesman and the son of a car salesman. This is not to disparage car salesmen as people, but as a profession, they rank right up there with lawyers and door-to-door snake oil salesmen. Think about it. When sales are off, car dealers slash their prices and they dump employees. In psychological terms, they panic and point fingers of blame at others. It's the "Chicken Little mentality." You know, Chicken Little who uttered, "The sky is falling, the sky is falling!" Russ Bogda was as fine a man as any other man on this earth, but he suffered from this sort mentality, as time would tell.

The really good news from the meeting was the financial statement. The Packers made money again in '52: $12,000. This was the second profitable year since Ronzani came aboard as head coach, the other year being 1950. Furthermore, the corporation nest egg of $100,000 (insurance payoff for Rockwood Lodge) remained untouched. The executive committee had invested it in treasury notes, and Fischer pointed out, "And this past year we were able to add to that nest egg." Stability appeared to be returning to the Packers.

In other off-field news, the Green Bay Packers Alumni Association elected Al Rose, the big Texan who decided to make his home in Green Bay after his first season with the Packers, as the organization's third president, succeeding Charley Brock and founder Fee Klaus. Rose played for the Providence Steamrollers in 1931, then came to the Packers for the next six seasons. He remained in Green Bay and became the district manager for Universal CIT Credit Corporation. The Alumni Association had nothing to do with the team except to help them draw fans when they needed them most to keep Green Bay in the NFL.

A week before the NFL annual meeting in Philadelphia a story appeared in the *Milwaukee Journal* stating that Ronzani had replaced line coach John "Tarzan" Taylor with Jumbo Joe Stydahar. Taylor's three-year contract with the club ended on January 1, and Jack Vainisi regained his health and no longer needed an assistant for evaluating college talent. Ronzani wanted Stydahar for his line coach when he first took the Green Bay job, but the former Bear All-Pro lineman opted to become the head coach of the Rams, coaching LA to the NFL title in '51. The trouble was the *Journal* got it all wrong. Stydahar signed with the Chicago Cardinals to replace Joe Kuharich who had replaced Curly Lambeau at the helm of the Redbirds.

Taylor leaving the Packers was only the first sign of leaks in Ronzani's ship. On January 19, Dick Plasman let it be known that he wouldn't be returning to the Packers to coach the ends and defense. In a letter to Ronzani, he stated that his cemetery business in Miami was too pressing for him to rejoin the Packers for the '53 season. Plasman played college ball at Vanderbilt before being signed by the Bears in 1937. World War II interrupted his career in the NFL, and when it was over, he returned to Chicago but with the Cardinals as a player and assistant coach under Jimmy Conzelman. With Plasman and Taylor gone, Ronzani's staff was down to Chuck Drulis and Ray McLean.

Besides the departures of two coaches, Ronzani suffered the loss of defensive end Abner Wimberly who took up coaching at his alma mater, Louisiana State. Ronzani stated that "his loss would be a crippling blow" to the Packers. Wimberly played for the Packers for three years, and he was chosen as a Pro Bowl player in '52. His retirement left the Packers with only one regular defensive end, big John Martinkovic, and fill-in Carleton Elliott.

Scat-back Larry Coutre of Notre Dame was the second Korean War veteran to return to the Packers, signing a contract in February. In his only season with the Packers, Coutre gained 283 yards on just 41 carries for an average of 6.9 yards per carry, and he caught 17 passes for 206 yards; all this as a backup to Billy Grimes. Those were not bad numbers.

The Packers led the NFL in passing in '52, thanks to the strong arms of Tobin Rote and Babe Parilli who finished second and third, respectively, behind league-leader Norm Van Brocklin of the Rams. Both passers signed their contracts for the '53 season in early March, and Ronzani slept a little better for the rest of the winter and spring.

Soon after signing Rote and Parilli, Ronzani pulled off another publicity coup when he brought in six draftees and signed them all at once. To show these potential Packers that Green Bay was a big league city, the corporation held a luncheon at the Beaumont Hotel for them that included veterans Bob Forte, Parilli, Wash Serini, Hal Faverty,

Fred Cone, Deral Teteak, and the retired Tony Canadeo. The guest speaker was the radio voice of the Packers Russ Winnie who made a rather profound prediction with the announcement that the Boston Braves baseball team would be moving to Milwaukee that spring. He predicted that the presence of the Braves would be beneficial to the Packers:

> "The fans will have a completely new feeling that will carry over into the football season. We're going to back the Packers all the way."

Winnie was only right. The fans of Milwaukee caught "a Major League fever," and it proved contagious for the Packers.

The shift of the Braves to Milwaukee caused the Packers a minor scheduling problem. The Boston Braves were slated to play the Cincinnati Reds in Boston on September 27, which was okay as long as the Braves were in Beantown, but when they moved to Milwaukee, they discovered the Packers had already contracted Milwaukee County Stadium for that date. Question: What to do about this conflict in scheduling? Bert Bell, NFL commish, made up the schedule for the whole league. He was faced with moving the Packers-Browns game from Milwaukee to Green Bay, which wasn't all bad in itself, but the Packers had to play a game in Milwaukee. Since the Rams and 49ers were already set to play the Packers in the Cream City, this meant Bell would have to switch another game from Green Bay to Milwaukee. Which one? The first contest available was the Packers-Bears game. The Packers and Bears in Milwaukee? The fans threatened to riot. Bell forced the issue by telling the Milwaukee County officials that the Packers had first choice on the stadium for that date and that the Braves could change their schedule instead. Well, a contract is a contract; the Braves agreed to the switch and the Packers kept that date with the Cleveland Browns in Milwaukee.

Ronzani found a coaching replacement in early April. He signed former Notre Dame head coach Hugh Devore to help him shape up the Packers for '53. Devore played for Notre Dame in the early '30s, then went into coaching. He started out coaching the freshmen at Notre Dame, then moved to Fordham where he was an assistant under

Jim Crowley, one of the legendary "Four Horsemen of Notre Dame." Three seasons later he became the head coach at Providence and filled that post for three years, after which he moved to Boston to become an assistant coach at Holy Cross. A year later he returned to Notre Dame as an assistant to Frank Leahy in '43 and interim head coach Ed McKeever in '44. With Leahy still in the U.S. Navy in '45, Devore took the reins at Notre Dame and posted a record of 7-2-1. His experience with the Fighting Irish catapulted him into another head coaching position at little St. Bonaventure where his teams posted 25 wins against only 10 losses and a tie over four campaigns. New York University hired him to revive their football fortunes in 1950, but that institution's leaders gave him little support. His teams managed only four wins and two ties in 23 games over three years, and the program was scuttled, putting Devore out of a job until Ronzani rescued him from the unemployed.

When he wrote about Devore in the *Press-Gazette*, Art Daley reported that Devore was the 15th assistant coach in Packer history, that Lambeau had coached the team with the help of some players in previous years. Daley mentioned that Cub Buck, Jug Earpe, Mike Michalske, and Verne Lewellen had assisted Lambeau during their playing days. He designated Red Smith as the first official assistant coach for the Packers when Lambeau hired him to direct the linemen in 1936. He failed to mention any of the men who served as "coach" on the early Packer squads. But why should he? Daley was the unwitting progenitor of the myth that Lambeau founded the Packers in 1919.

In the front office league news, Bert Bell announced an agreement between the NFL, Westinghouse Electric Company, the American Broadcasting Company and the Du Mont Broadcasting Network that would bring 19 games to national television for the fall of '53.

Seven games would be on Saturday nights, 10 telecasts of Sunday games, and two Saturday afternoon games after the end of the college playing season in December. This required a change in the schedule for some teams. For the Packers, it meant changing three dates. They would play at Pittsburgh and Baltimore on Saturday nights and at Los Angeles on Saturday afternoon instead of Sunday afternoon. These games as well as their traditional game in Detroit on Thanksgiving Day would be televised nationally. The networks would pay the NFL $1.3 million for the rights to telecast the games, which worked out to a hundred grand per team with the leftover hundred thousand going into the league pot. This money would pay about 13 players on each team. For the Packers, it meant a major step toward financial stability and survival in the NFL.

Adding more television to the Packers, station WBAY in Green Bay planned to air its "Packer TC Touchdown Club" with Tony Canadeo as the host. The 30-minute program would feature about 15 minutes of film of the previous weekend's game, edited to show the high spots of the contest, plus an interview with one of the coaches summarizing the game and with one of the players who starred in the contest. The fan submitting the most interesting question about the week's game would be awarded an autographed football. The show would be produced by Robert Houle of Green Bay for the Packers, and the sponsor would be the Westinghouse Electric Supply Company of Milwaukee and its dealers in Northeastern Wisconsin and Upper Michigan.

In June, the Packers launched a season ticket drive in Milwaukee, hoping to fill more than a few thousand of the 37,000-plus seats of new Milwaukee County Stadium for their three games that fall. Buckets Goldenberg, the ticket master for the Packers, set a goal of 10,000 season tickets for Milwaukee, and he began the big push in the second week of June. By the third week, the count was up to 8,208, which wasn't bad but not up to expectations. Goldenberg predicted that total sales would eventually rise to 14,000. In support of Goldenberg and the drive, Fred Miller of the Miller Brewing Company said:

> "...All of us want to see the Packers stay in Green Bay. The Packers wouldn't be the Packers if they weren't in Green Bay. And the way to keep the Packers in Green Bay is for Milwaukee to support the Packers in Milwaukee..."

Miller knew the truth. Imagine a modern-day New York marketing director getting his hands on the Packers.

> "First off, we have to change the name. Green Bay is out. Wisconsin is in. The Wisconsin Packers. It's got broader appeal to a wider market. Yup, Wisconsin Packers. Just like the Minnesota Vikings or the Arizona Cardinals. Broader appeal to a wider market. Now we need a logo. Let's see, what's a Packer look like? Any ordinary guy? Can't use it. We need to change the nickname, too. Let's see, what's Wisconsin got that's ferocious? Badgers? Already been done. Wolverines? Wrong state. Cows? Bulls? Wrong sport. Fish? Muskies? No one outside of the upper Midwest ever heard of a muskie. Won't do. We need something really wicked like a wolf. Timber Wolves has already been taken? How about snakes? Got any nasty venomous snakes in Wisconsin? Timber Rattlers? Hm-m! Not bad, not bad. Wisconsin Timber Rattlers. Great! Now if we can only catch one and use it for a mascot. They hibernate during football season? No problem. We'll wake it up for games. We can't? Too cold? How cold? That cold, huh? Only meat packers in some place like Green Bay, Wisconsin, work in that kind of cold! (A pause. A light comes on.) Oh. I get it now. I think."

Makes the skin crawl to think of the Packers as anything other than the Green Bay Packers. Miller knew the truth.

Approximately 800 fans gathered in Green Bay's Legion Park Sunday morning, July 26, to give the Packers a sendoff on their trip to training camp at Grand Rapids, Minnesota. The program started with a few sky-rockets being sent aloft, then brief speeches were given by corporation president Russ Bogda, director Walter C. Scherf, Ronzani, team captain Bob Forte, Tobin Rote, Hugh Devore, and Tony Canadeo. The coaches and players departed Green Bay on two busses shortly after 9:00 a.m., and rode all day, making three scheduled stops along the way: lunch, supper, and to pick up halfback Dom Moselle who lived in Superior, Wisconsin. They arrived at the training facility around 9:00 p.m. The next morning Ronzani had his charges out of bed at 6:00

a.m., and he herded them to the clinic for their physicals before breakfast. After lunch, they were issued their equipment. Over 50 veterans and rookies began two-a-day drills the next morning.

The list of players in camp was long and promising, but it was missing several key veterans. Gone were Ab Wimberly, Billy Grimes, Tom Johnson, Ace Loomis, Steve Dowden, Bill Reichardt, Ray Bray, Bob Dees, Jay Rhodemyre, and, of course, Tony Canadeo. Also not ever showing up would be second round draft choice Gil Reich, the All-American halfback from Kansas, the man Ronzani thought might fill Canadeo's shoes.

Despite such serious losses to the roster, fans back in Green Bay remained optimistic about the coming season. Some even talked about '53 being another championship year. Tempering this enthusiasm was Art Daley who asked some very important questions in the pages of the *Press-Gazette*. He brought to the attention of his readers one simple fact: Could all the hotshot rookies and free agents that Ronzani had signed for the coming season replace those veteran players who had carried so much of the load in '52? Throwing more cold water on the parade, he pointed out that the Packers had the worst pass defense in the NFL in '52 and that it didn't appear to have gotten any better over the winter. But no one wanted to read stuff like that. Instead, they wanted to hear how deadly Rote and Parilli would be throwing to Billy Howton, Bob Mann, Jim Keane, and Carleton Elliott. Daley obliged them, of course, because it was job to do that and because he was under orders from his bosses, one of whom happened to be on the executive committee.

After the Packers played their first intrasquad game, Ronzani traded an undisclosed draft choice to the 49ers for Bennie Aldridge, a three-year pro out of Oklahoma A&M who played defensive back. That was the plus side. In the negative column, two rookies, Bob Kennedy, a middle guard drafted in the sixth round out of Wisconsin, and Jim Ringo, a center drafted in the seventh round out of Syracuse, walked out of camp. Ringo returned to the club by the next intrasquad game, but Kennedy stayed away for good that year, choosing to further his education by attending graduate school. On the same day, Ronzani picked up speedy defensive back Val Joe Walker and the Giants first round draft pick in '54 for the famous player to be named later who turned out to be the Packers 18th round draft choice in 1950, quarterback Arnie Galiffa of Army who was soon to be released from active duty. Walker and four Packer picks—Bill Forester, Vic Rimkus, Gib Dawson, and Roger Zatkoff—reported to camp after playing in the College All-Star Game against the Detroit Lions. Their arrival signaled the departure of eight other players: veterans Dom Moselle and Lindell Pearson and six rookies.

The exhibition season got off to a good start when the Packers smacked the Giants, 31-7, in Minneapolis. The Green Bay regulars handled the New York starters with ease, and the rookies who finished the game played pretty even. The fans back home began to expect great things from this team as none of them gave a second thought to the players reports that the Giants were grossly out of shape for the game.

Before the next pre-season contest, Chicago Cardinals coach Joe Stydahar praised the Packers as potential champs of the Western Division, citing their overall team speed as the big reason for his highly complementary assessment. Then his Cardinals met the Packers in Spokane, Washington, and held all that quickness in check. 13-7. None of the Packer players had anything to say about the conditioning of the Chicagoans, meaning they were simply outplayed.

Curly Lambeau had an 0-4 record against his old team coming into the 1953 season; this mark included exhibition games. Art Daley wrote that the law of averages were on Curly's side for the pre-season scrap between his Washington Redskins and the Packers in Green Bay, and Daley was right Lambeau's Skins dumped the Packers, 13-6, in a game that was all defense and little offense. Daley also pointed out that the Packers were now playing teams in good condition, unlike the New York Giants, which hinted that the Packers weren't as good as their fans expected them to be.

The Packers managed to score 23 points against the Steelers in warm-up No. 4, but the defense gave up 26 as Pittsburgh came away with the win. For the third game in a row, Green Bay failed to put any numbers on the scoreboard in the second half Ronzani had admitted two weeks earlier that his '53 team was weaker in some key spots than the '52 squad had been. How right he was!

Ever wonder what geniuses make up NFL pre-season and regular season schedules? Whoever made up the slates for the Packers in '53 sure wasn't too bright. He scheduled the Browns the week before the regular season opener, and of course, Cleveland was due into Milwaukee to play the Pack for that initial contest of '53. Brilliant, right? Just before the last tune up for the regular season, the Packers did receive a shot in the arm when Ace Loomis decided to return to the team. The defensive halfback had spent the summer playing baseball for the Wausau Muskies in the Wisconsin State League, and the horse-hide campaign came to an end in late August.

Not wishing to show each other much of their offense or defense, the Browns and Packers merely went through the motions of a football game in their pre-season meeting. The Packers showed a few good signs of coming around by scoring 13 points and only allowing the powerful Browns to put 21 points on the board. The ground game looked good as Breezy Reid and Howie Ferguson picked up a total of 114 yards between them, but the passing game was disappointing.

Art Daley made what today would be considered a major career threatening remark when he wrote in the *Press-Gazette*:

> With Bob Mann working only the last few plays, the Packer passing game looked off color—only 69 yards being gained in the air.

In 1953, a racial pun such as this was considered good humor. Can you imagine what would happen to a writer, such as Dale Hoffman of the *Milwaukee Journal-Sentinel* or Bob Verdi of the *Chicago Tribune*, if one of them wrote something like that today? The so-called "politically correct thought police" would crucify either of them just the same as they did to television sports analyst Howard Cosell who in the excitement of the moment said over national television, "Look at that little monkey go!" in reference to an African-American running back for the Washington Redskins. Daley meant no racial slur back in 1953 any more than he would today, and Hoffman and Verdi, two of the better sports columnists in America today, would never write anything with racial overtones—or undertones. But words can be twisted and misunderstood and in time totally distorted as their meanings change with age and regional use, and in the future, someone could read one of their old columns and decide that they were racists because they used a certain word that in the centuries to come gained a new meaning. Lest someone else read Daley's words from 1953 and unfairly draw the conclusion that he was a racist, let the record be set straight in these pages: Art Daley was no racist then or now, and anyone reading all-and-all should be emphasized here—anyone reading all of his work would know that, just the same as anyone who saw and heard Howard Cosell as often as this writer did over the years would know that he was no racist and should not have his entire career and character judged by one innocent remark that lacked the intent of a racial slur.

With the exhibition season out of the way, Ronzani pared the roster to the league limit and then some. Remaining on the team for the opening of the 1953 season were: quarterbacks Babe Parilli and Tobin Rote; halfbacks Al Carmichael, Gib Dawson, J.R. Boone, Larry Coutre, Floyd Reid, Ace Loomis, Don Barton, Bobby Dillon, Bennie Aldridge, Marv Johnson, and Val Joe Walker; fullbacks Fred Cone and Howie Ferguson; centers Dave Stephenson and Jim Ringo; guards Steve Ruzich, Len Szafaryn, and Dick Logan; tackles Dave Hanner, Dick Wildung, Dick Afflis, Howie Ruetz, and Bill Forester; ends Bob Mann, Bill Howton, Carleton Elliott, John Martinkovic, and George Hays; and linebackers Bob Forte, Clayton Tonnemaker, Deral Teteak, and Roger Zatkoff. During the week, Ronzani traded draft choices to Cleveland and Washington, respectively, for tackle Gus Cifelli out of Notre Dame and running back Johnny Papit out of Virginia, and added them to the opening day roster.

Art Daley made predictions for the outcomes of the six NFL games on the opening weekend. He picked the Browns to beat the Packers by 10 points, which was a courageous choice in Packerland. He also figured Washington would beat the Cardinals, Detroit would down Pittsburgh, the Bears might nip Baltimore, Los Angeles would take New York, and San Francisco would defeat Philadelphia. His picks were pretty accurate as he chose five winners in the six games. Only the Bears let him down, and he didn't mind getting that one wrong.

Daley did mind getting the Packers-Browns game right, though. Green Bay went into the game without ace receiver Billy Howton who was injured in the pre-season game against the Browns when a Cleveland player piled on him after he was tackled. This was not to mention that the Packers had several new faces on the team and that some of the veterans, such as Ace Loomis and Dick Wildung, had not had the benefit of a complete training camp. These factors and the talent, experience, and organization of Paul Brown's squads were the key reasons that Cleveland smashed the Pack in Milwaukee on opening day, 27-0. Not only did the Packers fail to score, but they also failed to gain a hundred yards through the air. Rote and Parilli were both very ineffectual against a superb Cleveland defense.

Ronzani picked up more new players during the week. Byron Bailey, a halfback from the Lions; Bill "Buddy" Brown, a guard from the Redskins; and Clive Rush, an end and punter from the Cardinals. More roster confusion for the Packers.

But first, the hated Bears!

Under Ronzani, the Packers had yet to win an opening game, and at the same time, Green Bay had yet to lose the second game of a season. The Packers had lost to the Lions in 1950's opener, then the Bears in both '51 and '52, and the Browns, of course, in '53; only to turn around the next week and beat the Redskins in '50 and '52 and the Steelers in '51. Daley was hoping that history would continue to repeat itself when he picked the Packers to beat the Bears. He also picked the Eagles over the Redskins, the Lions over the Colts, the Giants over the Steelers, the Browns over the Cards, and the Rams over the 49ers.

The Bears committed eight turnovers in their opener at Baltimore, which denied them several scoring opportunities and allowed the Colts to put just enough points on the board to beat them, 13-9. Papa Bear Halas wasn't about to let that happen again. He brought a predominantly veteran club to Green Bay led by future Pro Football Hall of Famers George Connor and George Blanda and he intended to give the younger, faster Packers and his protege Ronzani a lesson in football.

A sellout crowd of 24,835 packed City Stadium to watch the Pack take on the Bears for their 68th regular season meeting. The navy blue and orange Bears scored first on a Blanda field goal in the opening frame, but the Packers bounced back with a touchdown on a 19-yard pass from Rote to Bob Mann. The PAT was muffed, and the Packers led the Bears, 6-3, after one. Gib Dawson ran back a punt for 60 yards and TD in the second stanza, and Fred Cone booted the point-after to put the Packers up by 10, 13-3. The Bears mounted an 89-yard scoring drive to close out the first half, and the scoreboard read: Packers 13, Bears 10. Neither team could threaten in the third quarter, but the Packers mounted a good drive that took them to a first down on the Bears two in the fourth. Still leading by three, a touchdown at this point might have put the game out of reach for the Bears, but it didn't happen. The Packers fumbled for the fourth time in the game, and the Bears marched back up the field to score the go-ahead TD with a little less than four minutes left in the game. A final attempt by the Packers to pull out a win was thwarted when Byron Bailey fumbled on the Bears' 49 and Ed Sprinkle recovered it for the Monsters of the Midway. The Bears ate up the remaining time and took a 17-13 victory back to Chicago.

Halas, always magnanimous in victory, praised the Packers for playing a fine game, while his Bears played poorly. Let's see. The Packers had five turnovers, and the Bears lost the ball four times. Plus one to the Bears. The Packers were 11 of 25 passing; the Bears 12 of 27; plus .004 better completion percentage to the Bears. Packers gained 281 yards; the Bears only 232; Packers plus 49 yards. Packers had 13 first downs; Bears 16; Bears plus three. Both had five punts, but the Packers averaged 36 yards per kick, while Bears averaged 43; advantage Bears by seven yards per kick. Packers scored 13 points; Bears 17. Looks to this writer that the Bears outplayed the Packers on the field as well as on the scoreboard. Gracious George Halas:

"We played one of our poorest games today. Perhaps the
Packers made us look that way, but nevertheless, we did play
one of our poorest games this season."

Truth? Both teams smelled to high heaven, only the Packers broke
one too many rotten eggs and once again had goose eggs on the
scoreboard for the second half for the sixth consecutive game,
including the four—pre-season affairs when they failed to score after
intermission.

Art Daley's predictions were terrible for the week. The Redskins and
Eagles tied; Pittsburgh dumped the Giants; the 49ers nipped the Rams; and
the Bears slipped by the Packers. Only the Browns and Lions came through
for him to make his record 7-5 for the season. He did predict the correct
score for the Bears; however, he said the Packers would score 20
points. Too bad he was only half-right on that game.

For Week Three, Daley picked the Rams over the Packers, Browns
over Eagles, Bears over Colts, Steelers over Cards, Giants over
Redskins, and Lions over 49ers. He must be applauded for picking
with his head instead of his heart.

Next up for the Packers was Los Angeles in Milwaukee. A year
earlier the Packers blew a big lead, 28-6, in the fourth quarter to lose,
30-28, in the final minute. Ronzani was determined not to let that
happen again in '53.

With the exception of the retired Bob Waterfield, the Rams were
pretty much the same club that they had been in '52 when they won
both games from the Packers. The one big addition to LA was the
return from the Army of end Bob Boyd, the speediest man on the team
who played behind Elroy "Crazy Legs" Hirsch. Norm Van Brocklin
was now the number one quarterback with Tank Younger and Dan
Towler splitting time at fullback and future Hall of Famer Tom Fears
complimenting Hirsch at end. On paper, the Rams looked
unstoppable. On the field, they almost were.

Ronzani surprised the Rams with new defenses and a new offense
for the game. He inserted a double wing-T attack that put both Rote
and Parilli in the backfield. The result was the Rams running game was
stunted and held to a mere 92 yards, but their passing game piled up

334 yards. On the plus side for the Packers, the new formation accounted for 327 yards and 20 points on the board, 10 in each half. Once again, the Packers lost the turnover battle, recovering two LA fumbles but throwing four interceptions. Furthermore, Packer passers were thrown for losses of 49 yards compared to only 14 for the Rams. Final score: LA 38, Packers 20.

Daley predicted four right and only two wrong this week, giving him a season record of 11-7. The Browns remained undefeated and in first in the Eastern Conference, and Lambeau's Redskins (2-0-1) were surprising so far. The Steelers (2-1) were now in third place, while the remainder of the division had yet to win a game between them. Detroit continued to ride the crest in the Western Conference, remaining undefeated, while San Francisco, LA, and the very surprising Colts with two wins over the Bears stood tied for second (all 2-1). The Packers brought up the rear of the West, one game behind the struggling Bears.

Smarting over getting the Colts wrong twice against the Bears, Art Daley picked the Packers to beat Baltimore in Week Four. He picked upsets by Lambeau's Redskins over the Browns and by the Rams over the Lions. In other games, he picked the 49ers over the Bears, the Steelers over the Eagles, and the Giants over the Cardinals.

Picking the Packers over the Colts was no big deal. The Bears had played really bad football in both games against Baltimore, meaning the Colts were luckier than they were good. The fans knew that, and Carl Mraz had his hands full trying to sell all the tickets to the game in Green Bay. To help the ticket master, the *Press-Gazette* bought 675 ducats for their carriers and newsstand dealers. The game still wasn't a sellout. Too bad, because the Packers finally put on a decent showing.

The Packers rolled up an astounding 303 yards on the ground and completely dominated the Colts, 37-14. After a scoreless first quarter, Green Bay scored a pair of sixes in the second frame to take a 13-0 lead into the locker room. Parilli tallied the first TD on a one-yard plunge, then Cone barged 11 yards for the second only two minutes later. In the third stanza, Reid scooted seven yards around the end for the third tally ending 67-yard drive. Carmichael dashed 41 yards for the next score put the Packers up, 27-0. The Colts finally got on the board before the period ended, but Cone booted a 19-yard field goal to stretch the lead to 23 points, 30-7. Val Joe Walker picked off a pass and ran it back 54 yards for the final TD, and Baltimore scored a meaningless touchdown near the end of the game. The Packers committed only two turnovers, but the Colts threw five interceptions and lost two fumbles, proving once again you can't score without the ball.

Daley's picks were no better this week than the week before. Lambeau let him down, as did the Steelers. His record was still good at 15-9 for four weeks.

The only remaining undefeated team in the NFL after four weeks was Cleveland. The Browns were trailed by the Redskins (2-1-1). Philadelphia (1-2-1), New York (1-3), and the Cards (0-4) who had yet to come close to winning a game. In the Western Conference Lions, Rams, and 49ers (all 3-l) were mounting a three-way race with Baltimore (2-2) in fourth and the Bears and Packers (both 1-3) bringing up the rear.

Five, Daley picked the Packers to beat the Steelers in Pittsburgh, Rams to beat the Bears in Chicago, San Francisco over New York

over Cleveland, Philadelphia over the Cardinals and Washington.

The local fans gave the Packers a parade before the team left for the nationally televised Saturday night game in Pittsburgh. The players were impressed with the support, but it didn't help them much on the field. The Steelers put on a defensive show to hold the Packers scoreless well into the third quarter, while the Pittsburgh offense put 24 points on the board, gaining yard after yard on the ground. Steeler fullback Fran Vogel piled up 163 yards on just 19 carries. The Packers scored a touchdown late in the third quarter after recovering a fumble on the Pitt one-yard line. Johnny Papit did the honors on that one, then Fred Cone scored a token TD in the last period to make the final score 31-14.

There once was a time when losing to Pittsburgh was a major disgrace for the Packers, but in 1953, the football fortunes of the NFL's collar teams were reversed. The Steelers (3-2) stood second in the Eastern Conference behind Cleveland (5-0), while the Packers and Bears held up the Western Conference. Detroit and Los Angeles (both 4-1) won to remain on the top in the West, while Baltimore(3-2) moved up to tie the 49ers for third place. Lambeau's Redskins (2-2-1) suffered defeat at the hands of the Colts to drop into a tie with the Eagles for third in the East, and the Giants (1-4) and Cards (0-5) continued to hold down fifth and sixth place, respectively. Daley was now 18-12 for the year.

During the week before the second Baltimore game, Ronzani released Papit and Howie Ruetz as Len Szafaryn and J.R. Boone came off the injured list. These roster changes put Art Daley in a sour mood as he picked the Colts to dump the Packers in Saturday night's nationally televised contest from Baltimore. He also picked the 49ers to beat the Bears again, LA to tame the Lions, the Giants to gain their second win over the Cardinals, Pittsburgh to nip Philadelphia, and the Browns to crush Lambeau's Redskins.

The good news of the week was how the Packers overcame a 14-7 deficit in the first half to trim the Colts, 35-24, but the bad news was the report of a rash of injuries. Tackle Gus Cifelli broke a hand; Marv Johnson separated his shoulder; Al Carmichael had his chest banged up; and Bobby Dillon had to be carried from the field. Cone, Reid, and Boone each scored a single TD, and Billy Howton, back from the injury list, hauled in two TD passes, one each from Rote and Parilli. Reid rushed for 120 yards on only nine carries, and the passers suffered only one interception. The team was so charged up after the victory that they carried Ronzani off the field on their shoulders. The coach was so caught up with the emotion of the moment that he had difficulty speaking to the press without showing tears.

On the prediction front, Art Daley missed on two games: the Packers (2-4) who climbed out of last place and the Eagles (3-2-1) now in second place in the East. LA (5-1) wrested control of first in the West from the Lions (4-2) who were joined in second by the 49ers (4-2). The Colts (3-3) held down fourth, while the Bears (1-5) rested comfortably in the basement. In the Eastern Conference, the Browns (6-0) continued to hold the top spot, while the Cardinals (0-6) remained winless on the bottom of the pile below the Eagles, Steelers (3-3), Redskins (2-3-1), and Giants (2-4). Daley's record improved to a respectable 22-14.

When he made his predictions for Week Seven, Daley picked the Pack to dump the Bears by a field goal, 27-24; Detroit over Baltimore, 42-28; Washington over the Cardinals, 22-20; Philadelphia over New York, 31-24; Cleveland over Pittsburgh, 17-15; and San Francisco over Los Angeles, 28-24. Except for one game, Daley had a great week.

The one exception, of course, was the Packers-Bears "sister kissin" act. As Daley put it:

"The Packers were lucky to sneak off with a tie."

Over 40,000 fans packed Wrigley Field to watch the two long-time rivals finish in a dead heat, 21-all. The Packers scored 14 points in the first six minutes, then had to come back in the fourth quarter to score on a very late 80-yard drive to pull out the tie. Fred Cone missed on two field goal attempts in the first half from 31 and 34 yards out, and he missed another on the final play of the game from 45 yards away. But Cone was not the reason the Packers failed to win the game. The usually magnanimous Halas summed it up in his post-game remarks:

"I didn't think the Packers were in the game in the second half until that last drive."

Daley's 5-1 week raised his record for the year to 27-15. San Francisco beating the Rams and the Lions winning again put the three teams in a tie for first in Western Conference, while Baltimore (3-4), Green Bay (2-4-1), and Chicago (1-5-1) stayed in the same slots. The only change in the Eastern Conference standings had the Redskins (3-3-1) switching places with the Steelers (3-4). The Browns (7-0) remained ahead of the Eagles (4-2-1) by two and a half games, while the Giants (2-5) and Cardinals (0-7) started planning for '54.

In Week Eight, Daley went for the upsets. He picked the Packers to nip Detroit, the Bears over Washington, the Giants over the Steelers, and San Francisco over the Browns. In his only two sensible choices, he took LA over the Cards and Philadelphia over Baltimore. He admitted he was picking with his heart instead of his head, especially in the case of the Packers and Lions because this would be "Homecoming Week" for the Packers. The guest of honor for the game was former Packer Fred Vant Hull who had been stricken with polio a few years earlier and had struggled to stay alive and overcome the often fatal and very painful disease.

As for the game itself, Ronzani just couldn't catch a break. Maybe it was all that negative karma coming from the brass who infected a large portion of Packerdom with their downer vibes for the Italian from the U.P. Anyway, the Packers outplayed the Lions and still lost, 14-7.

The Packers charged into Detroit territory 10 times and five times they had clear cut chances to score; only to lose the ball twice on interceptions, twice on missed field goals, and once on a fumble. But turnovers weren't the problem; the Lions gave up the ball just as often as Green Bay did. The key was field position. The Lions punted for an average of 44 yards, while the Packers could only average 37 yards. Also, Detroit ran back kickoffs farther than the Packers did. That's why they call it football.

Maybe Daley learned to pick with his head after this week in the NFL. The only two games he got right were the Bears (2-5-1) over Lambeau's Redskins (3-4-1) and Philadelphia (5-2-1) over slumping Baltimore (3-5). San Francisco (5-3) failed to put an end to Cleveland's (8-0) winning string, although the game was close, 23-21. Pittsburgh (4-4) moved into third place, while the Giants (2-6) were mathematically eliminated from the Eastern Conference race. The Cardinals (0-7-1) didn't win, but they didn't lose either as they pulled the Rams (5-2-1) out of a first-place tie with the Lions (6-2) whose victory put the Packers (2-5-1) back into a tie for last in the Western Conference. Daley's record for the season fell to 29-19.

In Week Nine, Daley proved that he hadn't learned not to pick with his heart. He predicted the Packers to upset the 49ers by a point in Milwaukee. Furthermore, he picked the Bears over the Lions and the Giants over the Redskins when common sense said Detroit and Washington should win. With more sensibility, he chose Philadelphia over the Cardinals, Cleveland over Pittsburgh, and LA over the Colts.

Little rain had fallen for several weeks in Wisconsin, and the extreme dryness forced the postponement of deer hunting season. Too bad it didn't stay that way, or so Ronzani wished. A steady snowfall of large flakes and an overnight drop in the temperature made playing conditions in Milwaukee rather slick and hazardous for the Packers. As they had so many times before in the 1953 season, the Packers committed several more turnovers than their opponent; in this case, six to San Francisco's one. The result was a 37-7 shellacking by the 49ers. Ronzani felt the eggs breaking under his feet.

Daley didn't do much better with his picks than the Packers (2-6-1) did with the 49ers (6-3) that Sunday, barely breaking even. He lost all three of his upsets. The Lions (7-2) held on to the top spot in the West by dumping the Bears (2-6-1), and Lambeau's Redskins (4-4-1) beat the Giants (2-7). Cleveland (9-0) moved within a win or a Philadelphia (6-2-1) loss of taking first in the East, while LA (6-2-1) stayed on Detroit's heels by eliminating the Colts from the race. This put Daley's record at 32-22.

Faced by a short week, Ronzani called his team together earlier than usual to prepare for Green Bay's next opponent: the Lions on Thanksgiving Day in Detroit. Besides this burden, the coach had to contend with the local rumor mill grinding out predictions of his demise at the helm of the Packers. All this pressure showed when his team took the field at Briggs Stadium. The Packers won the first half, 15-7, and they were on the verge of scoring early in the third period when a fumble killed a drive on the Detroit three. From that point on, it was all Lions as they stormed back to win, 34-15.

The next morning Gene Ronzani resigned, but that's not the whole story or the truth.

The executive committee turned the team over to Devore and McLean for the final two games on the West Coast, but they couldn't do any better than their ex-boss. The Packers finished a miserable 2-9-1 and in last place in the Western Conference.

As for Daley's picks, the editor didn't make a public prediction of the Packer game, but taking all things into consideration, he more than likely would have taken the Lions. He did pick the Rams over the

Bears, the 49ers over the Colts, the Browns over the Cards, the Eagles over the Giants, and the Steelers over the Redskins. He had a bad week as the Bears (3-6-1) upset LA (6-3-1), Lambeau's Redskins (5-4-1) dumped the Steelers (4-6), and the improving Giants (3-7) beat the Eagles (6-3-1) to give the Eastern Conference title to Cleveland's Browns (10-0) who crushed the Cards (0-9-1). The 49ers (7-3) did defeat the Colts (3-7) to remain one game behind the Lions (8-2).

Daley made no more picks for the '53 season after Ronzani left the team. He finished 35-25. Not too hot for a sportswriter with his finger on the pulse of the NFL. The Lions (10-2) won the Western Conference title again as the 49ers (9-3) and Rams (8-3-1) won the remainder of their games, while the Bears (3-8-1) managed to stay ahead of the Colts (3-9) and the Packers. The Browns (11-1) lost their chance at an undefeated season when the runner-up Eagles (7-4-1) beat them in their final game. Lambeau brought the Redskins (6-5-1) in third half a notch ahead of the Steelers (6-6), while the Giants (3-9) finished one of the worst campaigns in their history. And the Chicago Cardinals (1-10-1) finally won a game, beating the Bears on the last Sunday of the season, 24-17. Detroit eked out a victory over the Browns in the championship game, 17-16, to win their second straight NFL title, and 1953 came to a close.

For the Packers and their fans, it had been a greatly disappointing year. Unfortunately, it wouldn't be the last for some time to come.

8

The Lynching
of Gene Ronzani

The morning after the Lions came roaring from behind to crush his team, 37-15, on Thanksgiving Day, 1953, in Detroit, Gene Ronzani "resigned" as head coach of the Green Bay Packers. It was either "resign" or be fired, but that was only the surface story. The truth is pretty bad, a real black eye for the Packers, for the corporation. for the city of Green Bay, and for the state of Wisconsin.

The fall of Gene Ronzani started the day after Russell W. Bogda was elected to the presidency of the corporation. It was a well-known fact within the inner circle of the organization that Bogda had been opposed to Ronzani being hired in the first place. This fact was revealed by the late John Torinus, Sr., who once told this author the sad tale of Gene Ronzani's experience in Green Bay and whose words were supported and embellished by the late Jim K. Ford. By Ford's account:

> "Gene Ronzani got a raw deal from Russ Bogda and the executive committee."

Torinus corroborated Ford's remark by admitting to feeling a certain amount of guilt over tacitly supporting Bogda in his handling of Ronzani. He wrote in his book on the Packers:

"I always felt badly about Ronzani's unsuccessful career with the Packers because he was a fine gentleman and continued to be one of the Packers' great supporters in the years after he had given up coaching."

On the other hand, Ronzani could have overcome Bogda's prejudice against him if other circumstances had gone his way and he had produced a winning team in '53.

Ronzani's problems began with the retirement of Tony Canadeo at the end of the '52 season. Although Canadeo's best games were behind him before the '52 campaign, his experience and leadership gave the Packers a kind of coach on the field, and he was a major reason for Green Bay's six wins. Finding a replacement for the "Grey Ghost" was a major concern for the coach; therefore, Ronzani drafted a trio of half-backs, hoping one of them would turn out to be the superstar who could replace Canadeo. Topping the list of draftees was Al Carmichael, a first-class college back with a lot of heart and speed but not much else. In the second round, Ronzani took Gil Reich of Kansas, a fellow with more ego than common sense, having been expelled from West Point in a cheating scandal before attending KU, but he turned down the Packers offer. Ronzani 's fourth-round pick was Gib Dawson, a real speedster from Texas who lacked the shiftiness and stamina to be a solid pro player. None of these three could carry Canadeo's supporter, let alone, take his place on the field and in the hearts of his teammates.

Tarz Taylor leaving the coaching staff was the next problem for Ronzani. Taylor went looking for greener pastures when his contract ran out on New Year's Day. Why? Not because he had a problem with Ronzani or the other members of the coaching staff. He did have a problem with the executive committee, Packer stockholders, and Packer fans telling him how to coach. Then Dick Plasman chose to make serious money in the cemetery business instead of having fun coaching professional football. The cemetery business was just an excuse to get out of Green Bay. Plasman had the same concerns that Taylor had.

This left Ronzani with two big holes to fill, which he only patched by hiring one new assistant: Hugh Devore, a former college head coach. This was a mistake because once a man becomes a head coach it's hard for him to work as anything less after that. Devore proved this theory to be true.

Besides losing coaches and a future Hall of Fame player, Ronzani lost other players. Good players. Veteran players who understood what it takes to win a game in the NFL. Gone were Ab Wimberly, Billy Grimes, Tom Johnson, Steve Dowden, Bill Reichardt, Ray Bray, Bob Dees, and Jay Rhodemyre. These eight plus Canadeo made up over 25% of the Green Bay roster in '52. When commenting on Wimberly's retirement, Ronzani stated that "his loss would be a crippling blow" to the Packers. He was only right. The departures of these veterans made the '53 season a rebuilding year, and if anybody of importance had pointed that out, the fans would have understood. Excuse me. Ronzani did point it out, and Art Daley mentioned it in the *Press-Gazette*. But nobody wanted to listen to Ronzani or believe Daley—In this instance, anyway. Bogda and others said Ronzani was only making excuses before the season even began.

Despite such serious losses to the roster, fans back in Green Bay remained overly optimistic about the coming season. Some even talked about '53 being another title year. Daley tried to temper their enthusiasm by asking some very important questions in the pages of the *Press-Gazette*. He brought to the attention of his readers one simple fact: Could all the hotshot rookies and free agents that Ronzani had signed replace those veteran players who carried so much of the load in '52? Throwing more cold water on the parade, he pointed out that the Packers had the worst pass defense in the NFL in '52 and that it didn't appear to have gotten any better over the winter. But no one wanted to read stuff like that. Instead, they wanted to hear how deadly Rote and Parilli would be throwing to Billy Howton, Bob Mann, Jim Keane, and Carleton Elliott. Daley obliged them, of course, because it was his job to do that.

Fueling the fans' false hopes of a winning season was an opening exhibition blowout of the poorly conditioned New York Giants in Minneapolis. Ronzani had cautioned the public before the game that his team had some serious holes in it, but Daley downplayed this warning until after the second pre-season encounter when the Cardinals, a really poor team that was being totally rebuilt by Jumbo Joe Stydahar, slipped by the Packers, 13-7. After losing two more games to Washington and Pittsburgh, respectively, Ronzani stated again that his team was weaker in some places than it had been in '52. No one listened because they didn't want to hear that kind of defeatist talk. They wanted to hear the Curly Lambeau line:

"The boys are working real hard, and they'll give a good account of themselves on Sunday."

That wasn't Ronzani's style; he didn't know how to blow smoke in the faces of the fans like Lambeau had done for so many years. He gave Green Bay the truth, but the fans didn't want the truth. They wanted a championship, and no one more than Gene Ronzani wanted to give them one. They couldn't see that, however.

The pre-season ended on a really sour note. Billy Howton was blind-sided by a Cleveland tackler while another had a hold on him. The result was several cracked ribs, and Howton missed the first four games of the regular season. His absence left a huge hole in a passing offense that already had problems.

Two days after the opening game against Cleveland the executive committee called a meeting at the YMCA that involved the board of directors, players, and coaching staff. Packer President Russell W. Bogda told the coaches and players in the presence of the committee:

"This meeting today is called to carry to you the feeling that the executive committee has confidence in its coaching staff and in its players—all rumors to the contrary notwithstanding. We wish to make it clear here and now that insofar as the coaching staff is concerned, there will be no changes, and the confidence of the board in the ability of the present coaching staff to bring to the front the capacity of the ball club is unimpaired. The executive committee, along with the coaching staff, feels that we have the nucleus of a good ball club, with personnel capable, if it gives its best, of competing with any club in the National league."

Now what was that all about? Rumors? What rumors? The rumors that Bogda was prejudiced against Ronzani right from the start because Ronzani was Italian and from the Upper Peninsula of Michigan? Or maybe it was the roster changes that the players kept hearing about.

Daley explained in his *Sports Cocktails* column that Ronzani's last minute roster changes had unsettled a number of players during the week before the opening game. Word had it that five new players were coming into camp to replace five players already there, and this started several Packers worrying about their jobs instead of concentrating on the upcoming game. As one player told Daley the week before:

> "These boys should be thinking about who I'm supposed to take out on this play, etc.; instead they don't even know if they'll play against the Browns."

In defense of Ronzani, Daley wrote that the coach refused to stand pat if he thought he could get a better man for any position. Thus, he traded for Gus Cifelli and Johnny Papit before the first game, and he gave tryouts to three players released by other NFL teams. After the Cleveland game, he added two more men to the roster, causing even more confusion among the players, or so it was rumored.

This was the first public crack in the dam for Ronzani, and it wouldn't be the last.

After the first game with Los Angeles, the off-field plot thickened when the Packer Alumni Association made a statement in the press. The article read:

Packer Alumni Not
Behind Hinkle Move

The Packer Alumni Association, through President Al Rose, today stated its position on a telegram sent by former Packer fullback Clarke Hinkle to Packer President Russ Bogda last Friday.

Hinkle, here for an address of the Quarterback club meeting, applied for the Packer head coaching job in a wire to Bogda. The Packer prexy had "no comment" on the telegram.

Rose pointed out today that "we did not sponsor anything like that, nor did we suggest it. Hinkle apparently did it on his own."

Hinkle addressed the QB club Thursday night and indirectly defended Packer coach Gene Ronzani in his talk, making no mention of any job-seeking intentions he might have.

How about them apples? Hinkle sent Bogda a telegram expressing interest in the head coaching job, and Bogda, when asked about it said, "No comment." Mighty suspicious. Bogda had been caught with his pants down when Hinkle opened the men's room door at the wrong time. Hinkle would pay for this *faux pas* down the road.

Ronzani's ship sprung another leak the week of the second game against the Colts when line coach Chuck Drulis didn't board the plane to Baltimore with the team. Ronzani announced that Drulis was ill, but Daley reported a hint that this was not the case:

"It is understood that Drulis situation and the entire matter of Packer coaching may come up for discussion at the regular meeting of the Packer executive committee."

At the routine team meeting before the game, Ronzani told players he still had confidence in them and felt they could take the Colts a second time. After that, team captain Bob Forte called a second meeting of players only, where everyone was allowed to speak his piece. The consensus was a vote of confidence in Ronzani and his staff. After the team returned to Green Bay from Baltimore, the executive committee asked a group of player representatives to attend their weekly meeting. Out of that gathering came two official announcements. This one from the Packer brass:

A committee representing Packer players met with the executive committee at the Northland Hotel and expressed their confidence in the present coaching staff.

And this one from the player group of Forte, Rote, Wildung, Tonnemaker, and Cifelli:

> We have nothing farther to add to the official report of the meeting other than we're planning to go down to Chicago and give the Bears a good, hard game.

Why was there so much smoke here and everybody was saying there was no fire?

Whatever. Chuck Drulis was back on the practice field with the team as the Packers prepared for the Bears in Chicago.

Oddly, in his column *Sports Cocktails*, Daley made no more mention of Ronzani or the rumors that Bogda wanted him out of Green Bay. Once again, the *Press-Gazette* bosses appeared to be muzzling their reporters.

Then came the fiasco in Detroit followed by Ronzani's "resignation."

The executive committee turned the team over to Ronzani's assistants for the final two games on the West Coast, but Devore and McLean couldn't do any better than their ex-boss. The Packers finished a miserable 2-9-1 and in last place in the Western Conference.

The fans were told to blame Ronzani for this lousy year, and they did. The truth wasn't as easy as that, and it was a harder pill to swallow.

In the simple words of one-time Packer quarterback Paul Christman when he addressed the Men's Quarterback Club the week before the first game with Detroit—"your team is out of balance—a star here, then a mediocre player, then a star, etc. *You need 18 to 22 good pros or stars, to get into that championship bracket.* "
[Author's italics.]

In reflecting on the Cardinals when he played for their title team in the late '40s, he added, "They drafted for years building up their team and gradually we got 22 or so stars, most of whom were not sensations as freshmen." He then advised Packer fans and management to be patient with Ronzani because—he is a good fundamentalist."

That was the truth that the executive committee didn't want the fans to hear. Instead, Bogda pointed the finger at Ronzani's back and told everybody it was the coach's fault for the team's poor showing. The late John Torinus, Sr., a member of the executive committee for more than 30 years told this writer that "Russ Bogda had it in for

Ronzani right from the start." The late Jim Ford said that—Ronzani got a raw deal from Russ Bogda and the executive committee. Russ Bogda didn't like him because he was Italian, because he was from the U.P., and because he'd played for the Bears." These were also the reasons many Packer fans didn't like Ronzani right from the start of his tenure at the Packers' helm. Some people in Wisconsin made ethnic jokes about UP'ers (pronounced YOU-pers), disdaining them for living in the U.P., and for working at menial occupations in the mining and logging industries. Some of the older ones continued to harbor ethnic prejudice against Mediterranean peoples. At the bottom of the list were Packer fans who resented Ronzani for having played and coached for the Chicago Bears.

Daley reported on Ronzani's "resignation":

> Russ Bogda...announced that the executive committee has accepted the resignation, effective immediately.

Translation: Bogda asked for Ronzani's "resignation" and got it under threat of being fired or so the executive committee wanted everyone to believe. Daley went on:

> Ronzani had been under fire by the fans for most of the current season which is approaching the worst in the team's history.

Translation: Bogda and the executive committee didn't want to take the blame for Ronzani leaving the organization. Sounds like Pontius Pilate washing his hands.

In the *Milwaukee Journal*, the unnamed correspondent wrote:

> "Gene Ronzani '*resigned*' Friday morning..." [Author's italics.]

The reporter placed the quotation marks around resigned, then explained the two little facts that Daley left out of his story. Ronzani's contract contained an escape clause that allowed the executive committee to fire him at any time if they paid him $7,500 and gave him 60-days' notice. With his signing date of February 1, Ronzani had to be dismissed before December 1, 1953, or the Packers would have to pay his salary of $12,500 for 1954 as well. Bogda exercised that clause to remove Ronzani and saved the money. After all, it wasn't his idea to give Ronzani a new contract after the '52 season.

Ronzani maintained a sportsmanlike composure in the first interview after he "resigned." He said things like:

> "The Packers will always be a credit to Green Bay and the National league where ever they play. I know they'll always give 100 per cent and I hope it's good enough to win; so far it hasn't been."

About the current team, he added:

> "It was the best squad I've ever coached; the spirit never was higher than during this season in view of all the adverse publicity about the team and the staff. At no time during the season did the Packers become disorganized and lose control of a game. [Author's italics.] With additional help the Packers will become a contending team and will stay that way."

Behind closed doors, Ronzani was incredulous. "I can't believe it, I can't," the *Milwaukee Journal* reported he told a subcommittee of the executive committee consisting of Fred Leicht, Fred Trowbridge, and Verne Lewellen. He walked out on them, refusing to accept their demand that he resign. Finally, Green Bay's Mayor Dominic Olejniczak a man who was just beginning to figure so prominently in Packer history, was able to meet with Ronzani and calm him down long enough to discuss the matter. It was after this meeting that Ronzani accepted the executive committee's decision that he should "resign" with dignity.

A few days later it was announced in Green Bay that Chuck Drulis left

the team *because his father was ill back in Pennsylvania.* [Author's italics.] Okay, that was as good as an excuse as any for a smart man to jump a leaky ship before it left port. Drulis was only getting a head start at looking for a new job. Or so the executive committee wanted the Green Bay public to think. But the truth was reported in the *Milwaukee Journal.* He was fired just like Ronzani was. Like Ronzani and McLean,

Drulis was an ex-Bear, an unforgivable offense, and like Ronzani but unlike McLean, he was a tough competitor who coached his way and wouldn't take any interference from outsiders. It cost him his job.

Bogda addressed the remaining coaches and the players prior to their first workout after Ronzani left the team:

> "We've had our troubles this season but remember that all of Green Bay will be backing you all the way in your last two games. We're expecting you to do your absolute best and every Packer fan is expecting the same. You can be sure that every Packer backer will be behind you in these last two games. We hope to see you all back again next year."

Sounds like the corporate baloney that's handed out just before the pink slips show up in the pay envelopes.

Now that Ronzani was officially out of the picture he became fair game for the cryptic typewriter of Art Daley just the same as Curly Lambeau had been after he was chased out of town. The *Press-Gazette* sports editor wasted little time, turning his wrath on Ronzani in his column of December 2, 1953, quoted here in its entirety with certain key words underlined by this author:

> The Packer organization——in the process of accepting the resignation of Gene Ronzani as head coach——was careful to <u>protect the future</u> of the onetime Chicago Bear star…At no time did the group <u>publicly announce that Ronzani was being</u> fired for the simple reason that such a maneuver would make it difficult for Ronzani to find a job with some other club in the National league——or even Canada…<u>the horrible details that generally attach themselves to such a situation were withheld</u>——to make it easier for Ronzani in his future coaching life…We thought Gene was allowed to resign with complete ease; no <u>public airing of "uncomfortables" that actually set in after Ronzani grabbed Parilli, Howton, and Dillon in the 1952 draft</u>…In short, everything was forgotten——for Ronzani's protection in the future…
>
> What did Ronzani do in return for this "official protective silence"?…He holed up in his office from Friday afternoon

(the announcement was made at 12:30 last Friday afternoon) until around 10 o'clock Tuesday morning...Granting a little time to clean out his desk, etc., Ronzani should have been cleared out by sometime Saturday...His presence mined all chances of the co-coaches to prepare for the San Francisco game and accustom themselves to the change...The heat was fierce in the Packer office these past few days...It was no secret that Co-Coaches Hugh Devore and Ray McLean were anxious to get on the train Tuesday and start preparation for the Forty Niners...

But what happens?...Ronzani gets on the train, too...He wasn't permitted in the Packer car but his mere presence made it "uncomfortable" for the two coaches—not to mention the 30-odd players...At first it appeared that Ronzani was only going to Chicago...The Associated Press office in Chicago, upon the request of this department. was asked to check when the team arrived at 3:25 yesterday afternoon...The AP man got this quote from Ronzani: "I'm not a member of the party, naturally, but I'm interested in some of the players and if I can give them any tips I'll be glad to."...We received a wire from Packer publicist Jug Earp [sic] as the train stopped in Clinton, Iowa, about 7 o'clock last night...The Jugger said: "Gene on same train with squad. Going to San Francisco. So far so good. Going for rest."...We can think of a lot better place than San Francisco to go for a rest at this time of the year...But the fact remains that Ronzani apparently insists on creating as much turmoil as he can by just being present like a ghost of the immediate past - ready to haunt and confuse the minds of the players...We'd like to know what Ronzani has in mind...His statement to the AP about "tips to the players" was to put it mildly, stupid... Maybe the San Francisco press can unearth some of Ronzani's intentions...The statements coming back should be interesting...Under it all is Ronzani 's complete lack of willingness to give the Packers a fair shake in return for <u>the gentleness with which they let him off the hook</u>...

We (the Press-Gazette) received that proverbial last straw last Friday afternoon...We encountered Ronzani in the Packer office about two hours after the announcement and, in the presence of Devore, McLean and Chuck Drulis and the office girl, told Ronzani this: "Sorry, Gene, that this had to happen"...We had the feeling that anyone would toward a man who had just lost his job...But here's what he said: "Well, the stories in the Press-Gazette didn't help.

These things, not to mention a million "discourtesies" (and that's a mild word) along the line, could have been left unsaid. But as long as Ronzani continues to plague the "bigger-than-any-man" Packers, it will become increasingly more difficult for him to find a head coaching job in the National league..."These things" get around. you know!"

Daley was right: "These things" get around. Now his column has come back to haunt him and the Green Bay Packers. Inc.

Let's take it from the top.

The opening statement in Daley's column cries out for a few questions: How was the Packer organization careful to protect Ronzani's future? And why did it need protecting?

Next his remark excusing the front office for not publicly announcing that Ronzani was being fired implies without any hesitation that he was forced to resign, a standard corporate method of making the employee look bad instead of the corporation—or someone in it-being the bad guy. *The horrible details that generally attach themselves to such a situation were withheld—to make it easier for Ronzani in his future coaching life.* This was true: the "horrible details...were withheld, but not to protect Ronzani. No! They were withheld to protect Russ Bogda and the executive committee, a group that failed to understand the workings of a football team—or any other professional franchise sport for that matter.

Baseball manager Leo Duroucher said it best when he was hired to manage the Chicago Cubs for the 1966 season. Keep in mind that the Cubs had been run by a committee of "rotating head coaches" since

1961. Duroucher said in reply to a question by a reporter who asked him if he was being hired as the new head coach: "Make no mistake about it. I am the manager of the Chicago Cubs." In other words, he was stating that he was in charge and that was that.

Curly Lambeau had tried to make this clear to the executive committee while he was the head coach and the man who hired and fired players, and the executive committee was willing to go along with Curly as long as he won and the stands were filled with fans. Curly ruined a good thing by abusing his authority, wasting corporation money, misusing corporation funds, and by conspiring to abscond with the franchise.

Let's continue with Daley's column.

Gene was allowed to resign with complete ease; no public airing of "uncomfortables" that actually set in after Ronzani grabbed Parilli, Howton, and Dillon, and others in the 1952 draft. The first statement here again implies that Ronzani was given the choice of resigning quietly or being fired for a list of grievances against him that would blackball him from coaching again. What were these grievances, these so-called "uncomfortables" that actually set in after Ronzani grabbed Parilli, Howton and Dillon and others in the 1952 draft? If these "uncomfortables" had existed since the 1952 draft, why did then Packer president Emil Fischer and the executive committee reward Ronzani with a new three-year contract after the '52 season? Also, Daley's words make Ronzani sound like some kind of pervert with the use of the word "grabbed" in reference to the named players.

Daley seemed to be overly concerned about Ronzani's presence on the same train to San Francisco on which the Packers were traveling. Why? At the time of Ronzani's "resignation" being announced, Daley reported that Ronzani would be allowed to address the players one last time. If he did speak to them, his words were not reported in the *Press-Gazette*, which implies that he was not allowed to speak to them after all because he might state his side of the story and this would not bode well for Bogda and the executive committee.

Next part of the column to be scrutinized: *Under it all is Ronzani's complete lack of willingness to give the Packers a fair shake in return for the gentleness with which they let him off the hook.* The Packers let him off the hook? For what?

Next part: "*Sorry Gene, that this had to happen*"…*We had the feeling that anyone would toward a man who had just lost his job.* Only people who are fired or who are forced to "resign" lose their jobs. People who "resign" on their own volition don't lose their jobs because they quit.

And finally: *These things, not to mention a million "discourtesies" (and that's a mild word) along the line, could have been left unsaid.* Not once before this column appeared in print had Daley ever mentioned or even hinted that Gene Ronzani was anything less than a decent person, a gentleman in every sense of the term. Could it be that Daley was trying to cover his own tracks as an unwitting party to the conspiracy to remove Ronzani from the head coaching post of the Green Bay Packers? Or was he merely bitter that Ronzani had possessed the courage to slap him verbally in front of other people? Daley won't say, but as Torinus put it in his book: "…he [Ronzani] was a fine gentleman and continued to be one of the Packers great supporters in the years after he had given up coaching." If Ronzani had committed *a million "discourtesies" (and that's a mild word) along the line,* why would Torinus consider him to have been a fine gentleman and why would Ronzani continue to support the Packers in years to come? Just another man's point of view? Or was Daley under orders to make Ronzani look bad in order to cover Bogda's tracks in forcing Ronzani out of Green Bay? Most likely, the latter.

Bruce Lee, not the martial arts expert but a reporter for the *San Francisco Chronicle,* in a story from San Francisco three days later, wrote: "Ronzani was deposed Friday night after the Packers had lost to Detroit…" Deposed? In the same story, Lee quoted Ronzani: "*And if this messy business of firing me helps the Packers any, I'm all for it. If it really helps, I'd rather have that than an undefeated season.*" There it was! The truth! Ronzani was fired. Saying he "resigned" was only a coverup. If he did resign, it was definitely under duress, an illegal act in this day and age.

Why was Ronzani dumped? The answer lay in an article where Art Daley listed the qualifications that the executive committee desired in Ronzani's replacement:

> ...he must have a knowledge of modern football and ability to coach it...He must be a leader of men...He must have executive ability as it applies to head coaching...He must have ability to organize his own staff and work harmoniously with all members of his staff... He must have a sense of public relations. And he must have a good personal reputation and a happy home life.

How did Ronzani measure up to this list of necessary qualifications to be the head coach of the Green Bay Packers?

From the top, he knew modern football and he proved that he could coach it.

He was a leader of men, which was proven when his players carried him off the field after they came from behind to beat the Colts in Baltimore.

He organized a good staff that was moving the Packers in the right direction, but the executive committee, other stockholders, and Packer fans in general broke up that team. He had no trouble working with his staff until Hugh Devore came on board. Devore rocked the coaching ship by second-guessing his former assistant at the weekly meetings of the coaches with the executive committee.

He failed in the public relations department because Ronzani was rather reticent. A good man at heart he wasn't an insurance salesman like Curly Lambeau had been.

He failed in the last two items—personal reputation and happy home life—because he was Italian, came from the U.P., and because he was single, which made him suspect in a day when being homosexual was a secret that, if ever let out, led to being totally ostracized from society. Remember the line Daley used in his column? *no public airing of "uncomfortables" that actually set in after Ronzani grabbed* Parilli, Howton, and Dillon *in the 1952 draft.* Was this an insinuation that Ronzani was homosexual, planted in the minds of the Green Bay public in order to make his dismissal acceptable to them without question? If it was, it smacked of the propaganda tactics that the Nazis used in Germany and the Communists used in the old Soviet Union. At the very least, it was character assassination by innuendo, an old newspaper gambit that often ruined whole careers. In this case, it helped to finish Ronzani's career as a head coach.

More than likely, Daley was referring to the fact that Ronzani had listened to certain members of the executive committee and a few so-called more knowledgeable Packer fans when the '51 Draft was being conducted and he made his choices according to their recommendations, but in the '52 Draft, he told them all to butt out and let him do his job. A look back at those two Drafts shows that Ronzani knew football talent better than the freelance advisors of the executive committee and the so-called more knowledgeable Packer fans. Of the top 15 choices in '51, only one man made it in the NFL, and that was Fred Cone who made the Packers more because he was a decent placekicker than because of his talent as a fullback. In '52, when Ronzani made his own picks, of the top 15, eight men made the team—Parilli, Howton, Dillon, Hanner, Johnson, Reichardt, Teteak, and Floyd. Four of these men went on to have remarkable pro careers. No one likes to be shown up, and that was why those local "experts" resented Ronzani.

Ronzani told Ollie Kuechle of the *Milwaukee Journal:*

> "They [the Packers] have something they shouldn't lose, but the situation has grown so serious that unless the 'powers that be' take the bull by the horns, the same thing will happen to the next coach, and maybe the ball team. If I was the cause of our failure, they can now prove it. I'm glad to be out of it."

No one knew at the time how prophetic Ronzani was being, but that's another story for later in these pages.

Concerning heavy fan pressure, he said:

> "Situations in the past have forced the Packers to go to the public for aid and now everybody in town feels he has a voice in the club. And probably rightly, too."

This was his reference to those so-called local "experts" butting into his job of drafting college talent and running the team.

Team captain Bob Forte told the following story to Chuck Johnson, reporter for the *Milwaukee Journal*. The story appeared in Johnson's 1960 book on the Packers:

> Ronzani knew a lot about football. He had some troubles, many of his own making, but I think he could have done the job if they had left him alone.
>
> Every Tuesday in Green Bay after practice the whole team would have lunch with the executive committee at the YMCA. The committee members would question the coaches carefully. When lunch was over, each of the thirteen men on the committee would corner two or three or four of the players and try to find out what was wrong with the coaches, the other players and the team.
>
> After one defeat in 1953 my wife met me at the airport in Green Bay when the team got back and we drove to Milwaukee for the weekend. I got back to Green Bay Monday night and at seven o'clock the next morning I got a call from a member of the executive committee.
>
> 'Bob, I want to see you this morning,' he said. I said, 'I can't, I've got practice.'
>
> 'He asked what time practice was. I told him eight-thirty.'
>
> 'Well,' he said, I've got to see you before practice. It's urgent. I'll pick you up at quarter to eight.'
>
> He came by and I got in and he drove to a dead end street and parked the car. He turned to me and said, 'Now, Bob, tell me what's wrong with the team.'
>
> I told him I was just a player and wasn't in any position to know everything that went on. He asked me about some of the players and assistant coaches, the team spirit and strategy. I didn't give him any satisfaction. Finally, I told him I had to get to practice, that I'd be late, so he quit questioning me and drove me to the field.
>
> The next morning another member of the executive committee called me and wanted to see me. I said I wouldn't be able to see him. I didn't see any sense in it and then they quit bothering me.

Johnson also wrote:

> The four-year stay of Gene Ronzani was controversial and strife-torn from start to finish. He was hired only six days after Lambeau quit, so some thought the whole thing had been arranged in advance.
>
> A faction of the executive committee and many of the fans never accepted Ronzani. Their loyalty still belonged to Lambeau. What's more, they couldn't forget Ronzani had been a Chicago Bear, both as a player and assistant coach.

A faction of the executive committee... *"A faction of the executive committee"* Now who could that have been?

The executive committee for 1949-50, the guys who hired Ronzani, consisted of Emil Fischer, Frank Jonet, Russ Bogda, Bill Servotte, Fred Leicht, Howard Bero, Gerald Clifford, John Torinus, Lee Joannes, Milan Boex, and H.G. Wintgens. The executive committee for 1953-54. the guys who fired Ronzani, consisted of Fischer, Bogda, Servotte. Leicht, Bero, Torinus, Joannes, Verne Lewellen, Fred Trowbridge, Max Murphy, and Dominic Olejniczak.

So, who was there when Ronzani was hired and was still there when he was fired'? Fischer, Bogda, Servotte, Leicht, Bero, Torinus, and Joannes.

So who was opposed to Ronzani being hired in the first place? Couldn't have been Joannes because he proposed hiring Ronzani. Couldn't have been Torinus because he put Ronzani's name in the hat in the first place. Couldn't have been Fischer because he pushed for a new contract for Ronzani after the '52 season. Couldn't have been Bero because he and Olejniczak threatened to resign over the handling of Ronzani's dismissal. So that leaves Bogda, Servotte, and Leicht. Bogda and Servotte became members of the executive committee in the same year, 1947, while Leicht was an original member of the committee when it was established back in the '30s. Since he usually went along with old chums Joannes and Fischer nearly all the time. Leicht can be ruled out as part of the "faction of the executive committee...that never accepted Ronzani." That leaves Bogda and Servotte. Throw in Trowbridge and Murphy, both of whom were ax-wielders as time would tell, and you have four members of the executive committee who were solidly opposed to Ronzani. Add Lewellen to that mix because he stood to gain from Ronzani's firing, and add Torinus, too. That makes six opposed to Ronzani, three for, and two on the fence. Three for Olejniczak, Bero, and Joannes. On the fence? Fischer and Leicht.

The big question here: Why would Torinus be opposed to Ronzani after being the impetus for his hiring?

This writer had the privilege of being a very close friend to John Torinus, Sr., over the last four years of that man's remarkable life. How close were we? After John's funeral in October 1985, his son Tom said to me: "Thanks for being there for Dad these past few years. I think you were closer to him than any of us [his children] in his last years." Tom also told me: "I don't recall Dad ever saying 'I love you' to any of us, but we knew he loved us by how he treated us. He showed us his love in a lot of little ways." I can vouch for that because John, a newspaperman all his adult life, ironically was not a man of words when it came to expressing his feelings. The warmest thing he ever said to me was spoken in our last conversation, a phone call just days before his passing. I had just expressed my feelings to him about how much he meant to me as a friend, and he replied: "I've enjoyed the relationship, too, Larry." When I repeated this to Tom after the funeral, he put his hand on my shoulder and said: "That's more than he ever said to any of us."

As much as I cared for John, I accepted him as being human and all that goes with that label. He had his faults as well as a wonderful soul. One of his faults, if it can be called that, was his ability to blow with the prevailing wind. When the Honorable Lee Dreyfus was governor of Wisconsin, John and I took him a copy of John's book, *The Packer Legend: An Inside Look*. They were good friends. John had supported Dreyfus in his campaign for governor. When the Honorable Anthony Earl was governor of Wisconsin, John and I took him a copy of his book. They were good friends. John had supported Earl in his campaign for governor. Dreyfus was a Republican, and Earl was a Democrat who had been a frontrunner in the polls throughout the election. Fortunately, for John, they didn't run against each other.

Other memories of John's tendency to waffle come to mind, but they are unnecessary to this work. Suffice it to say that I have first-hand knowledge of this trait in John Torinus.

In 1953, John Torinus blew with the prevailing wind, and Gene Ronzani got the axe. John Torinus was the deciding vote. He told me so when he explained why he wrote in his book:

> I always felt badly about Ronzani's unsuccessful career with the Packers because he was a fine gentleman and continued to be one of the Packers' great supporters in the years after he had given up coaching. His family continued to reside in Iron Mountain while he was coaching in Green Bay, and he made frequent trips to the Upper Peninsula to go trout fishing, which he loved. He would always bring back a supply of Italian sausage for members of the Executive Committee, a favor which I badly missed after his leaving.

That was John's way of apologizing to Gene Ronzani for putting him in harm's way in the first place, then throwing him a rock when he needed a Mae West.

Jim Ford said that "Ronzani got a raw deal from Russ Bogda and the executive committee." Sadly, Gene Ronzani wouldn't be the last man to suffer humiliation at their hands.

§§§

9

The Search for
a New Scapegoat

Searching for a new coach was not an exact science, and the executive committee of the Green Bay Packers proved this to be a true axiom.

Said John Torinus to the *Milwaukee Journal* shortly after Gene Ronzani was fired:

> "We're not going to rush into anything this time. We've got ample time before the league meeting late in January. We want our new coach there, of course, but that's still two months off."

The first name in the hat, thrown there by the Green Bay press, was that of Ivy Williamson, the highly successful head coach of the University of Wisconsin Badgers. Williamson's '51 team had won the Big Ten title and had gone to the Rose Bowl.

The Milwaukee newspapers added Tom "Red" Hearden to the list as a formal applicant for the job. Rearden had played for the Packers back in the '20s, stayed around after his playing days, coached on the high school level, then became a very successful head coach of St. Norbert College in nearby De Pere.

The next name to appear in print as a prospective new head coach for the Packers was that of George Trafton. Bob Moir of the *Winnipeg (Canada) Free Press* called Art Daley at the *Press-Gazette* and told him that Trafton, the head coach of the Winnipeg Blue Bombers in the Canadian Football League, was headed to Green Bay to take the Packer post. Moir also told Daley that Trafton was on his way out the door as Winnipeg head coach no matter what and that former Packer assistant coach Bob Snyder was soon to be dismissed from the Calgary Stampeders' top post.

The same day, December 2, the executive committee made the official announcement that they were seeking a new head coach:

> "All applications will be treated in the strictest confidence and will be screened for final action by the executive committee. Applications should be addressed to President Russell W. Bogda."

Daley listed the qualifications that the executive committee wanted in their new head coach:

> ...he must have a knowledge of modern football and ability to coach it...He must be a leader of men...He must have executive ability as it applies to head coaching...He must have ability to organize his own staff and work harmoniously with all members of his staff...He must have a sense of public relations...And he must have a good personal reputation and a happy home life."

In the same article, Daley reported that the names of the applicants would not be made public, and he implied that henceforth rumors of potential coaches would no longer be printed the *Press-Gazette*. Without saying it, he had his orders from the top.

In his *Sports Cocktails* column of December 10, Daley wrote about Paul Brown, head mentor of the Cleveland Browns, and other head coaches in the NFL who had come out of the college ranks. He wrote:

"This seems to be the trend these days." Couple this remark with an earlier story about Ivy Williamson coming to Green Bay to address the Quarterback Club, and you can see what people were thinking back then. Simply this: the fans wanted a successful head coach from a college, preferably a Wisconsin college.

Daley let it be known that Hugh Devore would be interviewed by the executive committee when he returned from the West Coast trip for the final two games of the season, and a subcommittee did talk to him before he left Green Bay for the holidays.

Officially, the public knew that former Packer player Clarke Hinkle wanted the job and so did Red Hearden. Now Hugh Devore. Through press agent Rigs Rigsby, a Hollywood type drum-beater for the *West Coast News Service,* former Packer assistant coaches George Trafton and Bob Snyder had let it be known that they would accept the Packer coaching job. Daley wanted Ivy Williamson to take the post, but Williamson had expressed no interest in the position and had not been officially contacted by the Packers. Daley even wrote a kind piece about Curly Lambeau wanting to see the Packers succeed on the field: the tone suggested that the Packers would take Curly back.

Joining the official applicant ranks just before Christmas was Clark Van Galder, the head coach for Fresno State in California. Van Galder hailed from Wisconsin. His coaching career included stops at South Milwaukee and Racine Washington Park High Schools and LaCrosse State Teachers College where his 1950 team had gone undefeated and had won the Cigar Bowl in Tampa, Florida. His only connection with the Packers was having coached Packer Ace Loomis, a member of that unbeaten 1950 squad.

Complicating the search for a new coach were the New York Giants and Baltimore Colts, both of which had fired their mentors Steve Owen and Keith Molesworth, respectively. Owen had been at the helm of the Giants since 1931 and the volatile Molesworth had not done well with the Colts and the organization's management. New York being one of the richer teams in the NFL put the Giants in the driver's seat in hiring the best available man, and Baltimore had weather going for it over Green Bay as well as being a big city compared to

Packerville. The members of the executive committee were well aware of these factors as they sought a new man to lead the Packers to glory again.

Another factor in the search for a solid coach was the college ranks.

Five top schools were also looking for new men to run their teams. Pennsylvania, Idaho, Kansas, Iowa State, and Minnesota were all trying to find replacements at the same time as the pro teams. With greater stability on the college level most coaches were apt to accept positions at a university before joining the pros. The executive committee was also aware of this fact.

The day after Ronzani was fired John Torinus told the *Milwaukee Journal*:

> "We might get a fulltime business manager, but a general manager—I don't think so. Our executive committee has served well and in many ways."

Thus, Russ Bogda and the executive committee really surprised the whole world three days before Christmas when they announced that former Packer halfback Verne C. Lewellen, a lawyer by profession, had been named as general manager of the Packers. The selection of Lewellen for this position heralded a general reorganization of the administration of the Packers. Lewellen was given complete charge of the corporation's business affairs. Lewellen's qualifications for the job included four years as Brown County, Wisconsin, district attorney; 12 years with the Standard Oil Company as personnel supervisor; and four years on the Packer executive committee. He was the first man to hold the position of general manager alone. Lambeau had been both coach and general manager, and the late Frank J. Jonet, Sr., had been the business manager for the organization in the latter years of his life.

In order to take the post of general manager, Lewellen had to resign from the board of directors and the executive committee. Replacing him on the board was Harrison "Mickey" McCormick who owned a car dealership in Menominee, Michigan. Also elected to the board were Charles "Buckets" Goldenberg who replaced Charles E.

Kohlhepp of Milwaukee and W. Heraly MacDonald of Green Bay who replaced Ronzani. Goldenberg was a former Packer player who now was in the restaurant business in Milwaukee. MacDonald was a division manager for Wisconsin Public Service. This put the board of directors back up to its full complement of 36.

As the new year of 1954 began, the Packers were still without a new coach. Several names were being bandied about. Among the new ones were Biggie Munn, the head coach at Michigan State, who was leaving the field to take the athletic director's post at MSU; and Jim Tatum, the head coach at Maryland, whose team had gone undefeated during the regular season only to lose to Bud Wilkinson's Oklahoma Sooners in the Orange Bowl. Closer to home, the fans were talking about Ivy Williamson, Tom Hearden, and Lisle Blackbourn, the head coach at Marquette in Milwaukee. Devore had his backers who were saying: "We know what we got, let's give him a try instead of bringing in somebody new..." Others supported Ray McLean. But detractors of McLean and Devore said: "Let's start fresh. Get a whole new bunch."

In sideline news, Lewellen and talent evaluator Jack Vainisi flew off to Cincinnati to confer with NCAA officials about the available players for the upcoming draft. The two Packer representatives would be looking at miles of game film and reading over reports by coaches. Or so the Packers and the *Press-Gazette* wanted everyone to believe.

John Biolo, the former Packer guard and presently head football coach at Green Bay West High School, was elected the new president of the Packer Alumni Association. He succeeded Al Rose. Other members taking office were Bernard "Boob" Darling as vice-president, J.A. "Gus" Rosenow as secretary-treasurer, and Al Petcka as sergeant-at-arms. This organization had a profound influence on the executive committee.

Back to the circus surrounding the search for a new head coach, the truth about Lewellen's trip to Cincinnati came out on January 7 with the announcement that a new head coach had been hired. Lewellen went there to sign Hugh Devore to the post, but Devore passed on the Packer job to return to the college ranks as he accepted the top spot at Dayton University. Devore had seen firsthand what had happened to Ronzani, and now that he had been away from the pressure cooker in Green Bay for a few weeks he realized that he wanted nothing to do with Russ Bogda and the Packer executive committee. Therefore, Lewellen turned to the executive committee's second choice for the job: Lisle Blackbourn, the 54-year-old coach at Marquette University in Milwaukee.

Known as Liz, Blackbourn was born in Beetown, Wisconsin, near Lancaster where he went to high school. He played collegiate football at Lawrence College in Appleton, Wisconsin, then went into coaching. He became the head football coach and athletic director at Washington High School in Milwaukee in 1925, and over the next 22 years, his teams amassed a record of 140 wins, just 30 losses, and six ties. His squads won 10 championships and tied for another. He retired from Washington High in 1946 and became a scout and instructor for the Wisconsin Badgers, and in 1948, he joined Harry Stuhldreher's Badger coaching staff as the backfield mentor. After he was passed over as head coach at Wisconsin for Ivy Williamson, he moved to Marquette as line coach under Frank Murray. When Murray resigned a year later, Blackbourn was named the head coach at the Milwaukee university. His record in four seasons was a mediocre 18 wins against 17 losses and four ties.

Several Packer officials made public statements after Blackbourn was hired.

Attorney Victor McCormick of Green Bay, long active in Marquette affairs, called the selection of Blackbourn "an outstanding appointment."

Verne Lewellen said:

> "Liz will grow on our community and he's the type of man that will bring the Packers out of their present predicament. He's a really hard worker, a good organizer, a disciplinarian, and a top public relations man."

Jug Earpe said:

> " I used to bang heads against him in some scrimmages in Milwaukee years ago, and I've known him ever since. He's just

" the man we need up here."

Blackbourn was hardly prepared for the job of head coach in the professional ranks. He had absolutely no experience on that level, and his collegiate performance was nothing to write home about. Furthermore, he was a second choice. Of course, none of this bothered Bogda, the executive committee, and Packer fans. Blackbourn would have plenty of coaching help—from them.

§§§

10

Another Rebuilding Year

Lisle Blackbourn's first task as the new head coach of the Packers was to assemble a coaching staff. He had plenty of volunteers in the organization and in the community, but he wisely sought real football men to aid him.

The first man Blackbourn hired for his staff was Thomas "Red" Hearden who was then attending graduate school at the University of Wisconsin in Madison and was coaching the freshman team there. Hearden played college football at Notre Dame under Knute Rockne, then played for the Packers in 1927 and 1928 and the Bears in 1929. He coached high school ball at Racine St. Catherine's where his record was 34-8-6 and at East High in Green Bay where his teams posted a mark of 51-3-2 over seven seasons. After a stint in the Navy during World War II, he returned to Wisconsin to coach St. Norbert College in De Pere, Wisconsin, where he put up a 41-13 record over seven years. Hearden would coach the backfield.

Art Daley wrote in the *Press-Gazette:*

> Addition of Hearden adds to the college theme being introduced to the Packers who, especially in the earlier years, were known as the "pro team with the college spirit."

In that one sentence, Daley said it all. He explained Russ Bogda's game plan. Can't you just hear him giving a Rockne-esque type of speech to the board of directors?

"We gotta get back to the old days, the old ways, the ways that worked, that brought home championships. We need that college spirit again."

Granted, the college spirit was a good thing—in its time and place. But this was the '50s, the first years of the television era, the extension of mass communication begun by radio in '20s. Super highways four lanes wide and with limited access were being built all across America, and airline travel was having a dramatic increase. No longer were businesses dependent strictly on their hometown markets; they could now reach out and touch new customers hundreds of miles away.

Professional sports were discovering the same thing. Their fan bases extended for hundreds of miles from the cities where the franchise was located. Chicago Cubs fans were found in Iowa, Indiana, Minnesota, Michigan, Wisconsin; just about everywhere WGN radio could reach in daytime. St. Louis Cardinals fans heard games in Iowa, Missouri, Arkansas, Tennessee, Kentucky, and Illinois. The Cincinnati Reds drew spectators from the coal fields of Kentucky and West Virginia as well as the farmlands of Indiana and Ohio. The Packers already had people driving into Green Bay for games from as far away as Madison and Eau Claire, and football fans in Minnesota sometimes made the trek across Wisconsin to sit in the bleachers at City Stadium on a cool autumn afternoon.

Unfortunately, Bogda and the executive committee had yet to realize that the Packers were now the team for the entire state of Wisconsin and Upper Michigan as well as those transplanted Wisconsinites living in Illinois and elsewhere in America. They had yet to recognize exactly what it was that the Packers symbolized in the minds of working America, and not seeing the obvious, they failed to capitalize on it. Instead, they chose to turn back the clock in an attempt to capture that old spirit of the small town football team that could beat the big baddies from the big cities of Chicago and New York. Their good intentions were totally misguided as they suffered from that small town myopia, which has always been the major cause of stagnation and eventually the erosion and death of the very thing that such well-meaning people seek to protect with their obsolete attitude. In other words, they behave like a dog chasing its own tail: they run around in circles getting absolutely nowhere while time and the rest of the world passes them by.

Only a few men in Green Bay realized this at the time, but they were in the very small minority. They would remain silent until their time would come to take command. In the meantime, they would sit back and watch Bogda and his majority on the executive committee slowly tighten their own nooses around their necks.

The Packer community threw a welcoming party for Liz Blackbourn, charging $2.25 a plate for a chance to hear him speak to the dinner crowd in the Crystal Ball Room of the Northland Hotel. Blackbourn made a speech, and everyone applauded him as if he had already won the NFL title. Actually, the Packer officials, former Packer players, current Packer players, and fans would have put their hands together for just about anybody at this point because they were all tired of the cold war that had been raging between Ronzani and Bogda for nearly a year and a new man meant a fresh start on the future. Blackbourn didn't know it, but he had just won *the lottery*, not that one where the winner gets a zillion bucks in cash but the one in the classic short story of the same name.[*]

Going into the league meeting in Philadelphia in late January, Blackbourn had yet to hire a line coach. He still had Jack Vainisi as the team's talent scout, and he kept Ray "Scooter" McLean on his staff as an assistant coach and college scout. This trio checked into the annual NFL confab with a pile of reports on hundreds of collegiate players, and they intended to find themselves a few good men, preferably linemen of quality, to play in the NFL.

[*] For those readers who never read *The Lottery by Shirley Jackson,* maybe you know the story in Tom Tryon's novel *The Dark Secret of Harvest Home.* In the former, the winner gets stoned to death, and in the latter, the winner gets his throat cut with a sickle. The outcome is the same in both, but before the winner is sacrificed, he gets one last good time, sort of a condemned man's last meal but a lot more.

The Packers owned the third pick in the NFL College Draft. The top spot, the Bonus Pick, was won by the Cleveland Browns—as if they needed another great player-who took Stanford's outstanding quarterback Bob Garrett. The Cardinals, with the worst record in the league in '53, owned the next choice, and they took Arkansas quarterback Lamar McHan, who would eventually wind up with the Packers; but that's in the future. For now, the Packers chose Notre Dame tackle Art Hunter with their first pick in the first round. With their second pick in the first round, a choice obtained in the trade with the New York Giants for the rights to 1950 18th-round draftee Arnie Galiffa, the Packers took Veryl Switzer, a speedy halfback out of Kansas State. In succession, the Colts took Francis "Cotton" Davidson, QB, Baylor; the Bears Stan Wallace, B. Illinois; the Steelers Johnny Lattner, HB, Notre Dame; the Redskins Steve Meilinger, HB-E, Kentucky; the Eagles Neil Worden, FB, Notre Dame; the Rams Ed Beatty, C. Mississippi; the 49ers Bernie Faloney, QB, Maryland; the Browns John Baumer, G, Illinois; and the Lions Richard Chafman, T, Rice.

The Packer brain trust continued picking for 29 more rounds, and when they had finished, they had taken 19 linemen and 10 backs. Of these, only Hunter, Switzer, George Timberlake (G, USC), Max McGee (HB. Tulane), Gene Knutson (E, Michigan), and Emery Barnes (E. Oregon) would ever play in a regular season game with the Packers, and the only one who would make any real impact on Green Bay's football fortunes was McGee. This was not a good Draft for the Packers, and from the looks of the first-round choices of the other teams, it was no great shakes for the whole league.

Blackbourn's last bit of business in Philadelphia was the hiring of a line coach. He signed former Notre Dame and Cleveland Browns tackle Lou Rymkus to the job. Rymkus hailed from Chicago where he went to Tilden Tech High School before graduating to Notre Dame where he played for Frank Leahy for three years before being drafted and signed by the Redskins in '43. After one year in Washington, he enlisted in the Navy for the next two years, and upon his release, he signed with the Browns in the new AAC. When his playing career ended, he became an assistant coach at Indiana under Bernie Crimmins, then assisted Bob Snyder at Calgary in the Canadian League in '53.

Although he wanted an ends coach to work with his line coach, Blackbourn decided to renew the contract of Ray "Scooter" McLean instead. Throughout the entire Ronzani ordeal, McLean had been cooperative with the executive committee, so much so that some thought he sold Ronzani down the river, as the expression went in those days. This could explain why nice guy Scooter was still working when Ronzani and Chuck Drulis were out of their jobs. Food for thought.

In front office news, the corporation reported a profit of $29,267 for 1953. Apparently, Ronzani was good for business, if nothing else, or so most fans and stockholders said openly now. Actually, the profit was due entirely to the new television contract that Bert Bell had struck the networks for televising league games. The Packers received $12,000 from their Thanksgiving Day date with Detroit and $20,000 from the league deal.

The stockholders elected one new director, Richard Falk of Milwaukee who replaced Joe Krueger, and they re-elected 11 others whose terms were up. These men were Erv Bushman of Sturgeon Bay, Don Hutson of Racine, H.J. Bero, Russell W. Bogda, L.J. Levitas,, Dominic Olejniczak, August Reimer, C.J. Renard, Walter Scherf, Edward Schuster, and William J. Servotte all of Green Bay.

The board of directors then elected Olejniczak as one vice-president to replace Ronzani, and they re-elected Lee Joannes as the other vice-president, Bogda as president, Servotte as secretary-treasurer, and Emil Fischer as chairman of the board. Max Murphy, John Torinus, Fred Leicht, and Fred Trowbridge were re-elected to the executive committee with the corporation's officers.

A letter from the Sullivan-Wallen American Legion Post in Green Bay recommended that some consideration be given to construction of a new stadium and suggested that rental fees from each game be placed in a trust fund and used to build onto the stadium in later years as the need would arise. This was the first official thought given to building a new playing facility, but more about this subject in a later chapter. Suffice it to say that the corporation was starting to make some sensible moves.

Another thing that made sense was the cutting of ticket prices for the '54 season, or so the Packers had their public believe. The truth was the federal government cut the tax on admission tickets from 20% to 10%, but the Packers actually increased their share on most of their tickets. In 1953, the best seats were sold for $5.00 each. Of that $5.00, five-sixths or $4.17 went to the Packers, and 83 cents went to the federal treasury. The same ticket would cost the public $4.75 in 1954. Of this $4.75, nine-tenths or $4.28 would stay with the Packers, and 57 cents would wind up with the government. The Packers received an 11-cent raise courtesy of the United States government. On the next level of tickets—$3.80 in '53 and $3.50 in '54—the Packers' share went down two cents, but on the cheap seats—$2.50 in '53 and $2.40 in 54—the Packers gained eight cents more per ticket sold. The extra revenue—about $10,000—would come in handy for the Packers in the future.

Finally, publicity director Francis L. "Jug" Earpe resigned from the organization in May to go into the beer distributing business as generalmanager of Packerland Distributors, Inc. Lewellen hired Bonnie Ryan to replace the very popular Earpe.

From this point, Blackbourn went about rebuilding the 1954 Packers in his own image of what a professional football team should be. He started with signing draft picks Art Hunter, Gene Knutson, and Veryl Switzer in February; 1952 pick Joe Johnson in March; Max McGee in April; 1953 pick Al Barry from USC and free agent Gene White from Georgia in June. He also signed George Timberlake, the guard from USC, but he broke his arm in pre-season practice and missed the entire season.

Along with the rookies, he signed veterans Fred Cone, Jim Ringo, Bobby Dillon, Tobin Rote, and Clayton Tonnemaker in May; Dave "Hog" Hanner, Deral Teteak, Dick Afflis, Carleton "Stretch" Elliott, Howie Ferguson, Bill Brown, and Billy Howton in June; Al

Carmichael, Dave Stephenson, Roger Zatkoff, John Martinkovic, Bill Forester, Steve Ruzich, Val Joe Walker, Len Szafaryn, and Breezy Reid.

Besides signing their own players, Blackbourn traded for another. He picked up Francis "Jerry" Helluin, a defensive lineman who went to Tulane, from the Browns for the Packers' fourth-round pick in the 1955 draft, and he signed Clarence Self, the defensive back from Wisconsin who had played for the Cardinals and Steelers before joining the Packers in '52 but was cut during the exhibition season in '53. Also, defensive back Lou Mihajlovich out of Indiana who had been cut by the Bears in '52 was discharged from the Navy in time to join the Packers for the '54 season.

Not every veteran returned to the fold. Veteran J.R. Boone retired in April. Clive Rush signed on as assistant to Hugh Devore at Dayton. Ace Loomis, Benny Aldridge, Bob Forte, and Dick Wildung decided it was time to move on with their lives. Gib Dawson reported to camp, but an injury put an end to his career with the Packers.

The military took its toll on the Green Bay roster as well. Quarterback Babe Parilli went into the Air Force. Veterans—guard Dick Logan and halfback Don Barton; rookie, end Emery Barnes, Green Bay's 18th draft choice in '54; rookie middle guard Bob Kennedy, the Packers sixth-round pick in '53; and rookie center Bob Fleck, the Pack's second-round choice in '54 from Syracuse; all entered the Army.

And the Canadian Football League also caused problems for the Packers. Halfback J.D. Roberts, Green Bay's 17th-round pick from Oklahoma, and veteran halfback Byron Bailey went north of the border to play.

Blackbourn and his staff did take 60 players to the Packers new training camp at Stevens Point (Wisconsin) State Teachers College in late July. The new coach demanded discipline from his team. and he set down several rules for them to obey.

1. No smoking is permitted at any official meeting of the squad. This includes squad meetings. in locker or dressing rooms and at official dinners. Squad members will refrain from smoking in the

immediate vicinity of dressing room or locker rooms before and after games and practices.

2. Drinking of "hard liquor" is prohibited anytime during the course of the season.

3. Curfew for all players is 10:30 p.m. unless told otherwise by the Head Coach.

4. No phone calls unless emergency may be received after 10:30 p.m.

5. All members will be attired in Suit Coats when traveling with the team and when relaxing in Hotel Lobbies.

6. Profanity will not be allowed on or off the field.

7. Each player must turn in a game report on the second day following any football game scheduled by the club.

8. Poker playing and dice games will not be tolerated. One tenth of a cent a point is the maximum limit in any card game. Gambling resorts or book-making establishments are strictly "Off Limits" for all football personnel.

9. A small sum will be withheld from the last paycheck of each player until all miscellaneous expenses incurred by the individual are cleared by the Club Treasurer.

10. The Head Coach determines which places are detrimental to the player and organization and can be placed "Off Limits" to all personnel.

11. During training season the Club is responsible only for room and board of each player. Personal expenses will be paid by the individual.

12. The time designated for all practices and meetings means to be ready to start at that given time. No one is excused without the permission of the Head Coach. Any players late for practice, meetings, and train trips are subject to disciplinarian action.

13. All news items concerning the ball club and its members are to be kept in strict confidence and any announcements will be made by the Head Coach.

14. Any player receiving medical care, either during or after the season, must have it sanctioned by the Head Coach. The Club will not be

responsible for any medical bills received without them being granted previous permission.

15. Any loss of equipment through carelessness will be divided among the squad and taken from the squad's salary.

16. Each player is required to have two good pairs of shoes, a pair for game and another for practice, which will be checked periodically by the club equipment man.

17. All players must have on file at the club office their home address and phone number as well as their Green Bay address and telephone number. This can be turned in to the Coach's secretary.

18. All squad members must report to the trainer the day following a game. The trainer will decide whether you need a "jog" and shower or treatment for injuries.

19. All players must participate in public relations and goodwill work of the club. A player may keep any financial remuneration received.

20. No wives are allowed at training camp nor are they allowed to travel on trips with the team.

Well, well, well. God needed only Ten Commandments. At the very least, the players knew where they stood with the coach. To those who had done military service, only the uniform and drill sergeant had changed. To those who hadn't experienced such rigid discipline before, Packer training camp might as well be compared to Alcatraz and Blackbourn was the warden.

Although they were in the Army, Babe Parilli and rookie Bob Fleck were traded to the Cleveland Browns just before the beginning of the exhibition season. In return for the rights to Fleck and Parilli, the Packers received four players: quarterback Bob Garrett of Stanford, Bonus Pick in the '54 draft; tackle John Bauer of Illinois, the Browns first round draft choice in '54; defensive back Jack Miller of SMU, the Browns No. 7 pick in '54; and tackle Chester Gierula of Maryland. Bauer was later traded to the Giants, and Gierula never reported to the Packers. Garrett and Miller made the team.

Blackbourn finally made his debut in a professional game, albeit an exhibition encounter against the Chicago Cardinals in Minneapolis. It was hardly a success as the Packers bowed to the league's worst team in '53,

27-10. The *Press-Gazette* quoted Blackbourn as saying: "They really sock out there." He probably said: "They really suck out there." But the newspaper that had built up Blackbourn as the second coming of Curly Lambeau certainly wouldn't print something like that. Truthfully, the Packers looked pathetic in the game, but no one wanted to admit that—not this early in the campaign. Besides, it was only a pre-season contest. The locals decided to give Blackbourn the benefit of the doubt; after all, it was Ronzani who had screwed up their Packers the year before or so they had convinced themselves to believe.

The Packers lost a close one to the Browns the following week in Green Bay, 14-13, but don't let the score fool you. Coach Paul Brown of Cleveland pulled his starters after the first two drives of the first quarter because his offense simply marched up the field on the Packers and scored easily both times, while his defense stymied the Packers in their first possession with equal ease. Playing against Cleveland's rookies and "wannabees," the Packers managed two second-half TDs and one extra point. Like most games where second and third units face each other, the play was sloppy, but the *Press-Gazette* didn't want their readers, i.e., Packer fans, to know this; they might not buy regular season tickets if they thought that their '54 Packers weren't any better than Ronzani's '53 version.

The Packers played a dispirited Pittsburgh team the next week in the Smoky City, and Green Bay looked good, stomping the Steelers, 36-14. The Steelers were so bad in this game that their coach, Joe Bach, quit in the locker room that night, but nobody in Green Bay cared. Packer fans were elated that their boys had finally won a game. Exhibition or whatever, it was a win, and that was all that mattered to them.

Blackbourn allegedly said that the Packers played well enough to win their next exhibition bout, a loss to the Eagles, 24-13; but eight turnovers—five passes intercepted and three lost fumbles—do not indicate good play. This was another case of the newspaper trying to hide the truth from the fans: the Packers of '54 were no better than the Packers of '53. Oh, yes. Philadelphia played mostly rookies and "wannabees" in this game because it was the Eagles third game in eight days and the Philly coach, youthful Jim Trimble, didn't want to risk injury to any of his first line players.

Using rookies and "wannabees" in the exhibition season in order to better evaluate them had yet to dawn upon the Green Bay press and Packer fans as a sensible plan. Evidence of this fact was given in a story by Art Daley. He wrote:

> Packer Coach Liz Blackbourn had brief looks at Quarterback Garrett and Tackle Bauer, mostly in the 36-14 victory over Pittsburgh. The closeness of the 24-13 loss to Philadelphia last Saturday kept Liz from giving the two ex-Browns a good shot.

Obviously, Daley and his readers had yet to understand the purpose of the pre-season was not to win games but to let the rookies and "wannabees" show the coaching staff what they could do and to allow the veterans to get into shape and hone their skills gradually without risking injury. Had Blackbourn understood this, he might not have cut some players who never received a fair shake from him and his staff.

The Packers stomped on another team in disarray the next week when they met the Redskins in Raleigh, North Carolina.

Curly Lambeau had been fired two weeks earlier by Washington's volatile owner George Preston Marshall after the Skins had been dumped by the 49ers, 30-7, at Sacramento. Marshall complained that Lambeau was too soft on the team, allowing them to get into shape gradually instead of pushing them with punishing drills and exercises. Lambeau told Marshall to mind his own business and let him do the coaching, and the owner told Curly to hit the road. Joining Lambeau were four of his players who walked out in protest of the coach's dismissal.

The Packers met this bunch and beat them soundly, 31-3, but not a word was written in the *Press-Gazette* about the Redskins being in a state of utter confusion. Daley did play down the win a little bit by not gloating and by not praising every minor aspect of the game. Blackbourn held his tongue as well.

In their final tune-up for the regular season, the Packers once again played down to their abilities, losing to a rebuilding New York team in Milwaukee, 38-27. The difference in the game was the result of Green Bay mistakes: poor passing (14 for 39) and poor blocking (blocked punt and several sacks by New York). Daley made the usual excuses in the newspaper, but Blackbourn either had nothing to say that was worth printing or he had nothing to say at all because his team had played badly—again.

With the regular season opener staring him in the face, Blackbourn was forced to do the hardest part of his job, which was pare down the roster to meet the league limit of 33 men in uniform. Of these, seven were draft choices of their own and the two more were Garrett and Miller, Cleveland draft choices obtained by trade. Of the 24 veterans on the '54 opening roster, Clarence Self and Jerry Helluin were the only players that did not play for the Packers in '53. Thus, Blackbourn began his first regular season at the Packer helm with a team that was only one-third his and a good two-thirds Gene Ronzani's. Now the question remained: How much of an impact would Blackbourn's newcomers make to the '54 effort?

When Joe Bach walked out on the Steelers, Pittsburgh's owner, Art Rooney, turned the head coaching job over to former Packer player and assistant coach Walt Kiesling. At the urging of his backfield coach, Kiesling had scrapped Bach's conservative attack for a more wide-open assault on enemy defenses.

Hearing about the changes in Pittsburgh's offense, Art Daley warned his readers that the Packers would be in for a real fight this time around, unlike the piece of cake that they had gorged on in Pittsburgh a few weeks earlier. He was only right.

The Steelers opened up their offense behind quarterback Jim Finks who completed 27 of 40 passes for 327 yards and a touchdown, and Pittsburgh's ground game added another 128 yards as the Steelers came from behind to beat the Packers, 21-20, in Green Bay. The Packers were held to 262 yards in total, but they could only amass 101 yards through the air. This lack of aerial production was due to the constant pressure put on Tobin Rote by the Pittsburgh defense. The backfield coach of the Steelers had tipped Kiesling that forcing Rote out of the pocket would make him throw on the run or throw early; either way would result in a poor pass. This strategy worked as Rote could only complete five of 18 passes with two intercepted. The game wasn't as close as the score indicated, and Blackbourn admitted in the post-game interview that the Steelers had outplayed the Packers. Much to the coach's credit, he refused to make excuses, although he could have because middle guard Bill Forester suffered an injury early in the contest and had to sit out the remainder of the game. With Forester healthy and in the game, the outcome might have been different, but it wasn't.

Oh, the backfield coach for the Steelers? A new guy in Pittsburgh. Name? Gene Ronzani.

After the Pittsburgh game, Blackbourn picked up another defensive back off the waiver wire. His name was Jim Psaltis who had played college ball for USC before turning pro.

Next up for Blackbourn was George Halas and the Chicago Bears. Halas had hired some extra beefy boys for the '54 season, and scouts Jack Vainisi and Wally Cruice reported the increased weight in the Chicago linemen. Blackbourn knew that to beat the Bears his charges would have to outsmart the Chicagoans because they sure as heck couldn't outmuscle them; therefore, he held practices behind closed doors as he prepared a special defense for the hefty Bears.

A record rain fell that Sunday when the Bears invaded City Stadium to face the Packers for 70th time. * Despite the sloppy weather, both teams gained more yards through the air than on the ground. Both teams also committed five turnovers, but the Packers made the one mistake that cost them the game. Tobin Rote swept around right end, pitched out to Howie Ferguson who missed it, and former Packer Paul Lipscomb fell on the loose pigskin at the Green Bay seven. Three plays later George Blanda passed to Billy Stone along the end line of the end zone. The Bears said touchdown.

The Packers said incomplete, out-of-bounds.

* The *Green Bay Press-Gazette* reported it was the 71st meeting, but the 1921 game was actually against the Chicago Staleys. The Chicago Bears did not come into existence until the NFL granted a franchise to George Halas on January 28. 1922. The Chicago Staleys franchise was owned by A.E. Staley and was returned to the league at the winter meeting of 1922. Also, the Staley franchise was granted the right play in Decatur. Illinois, not Chicago, although Halas did take the 1920 Staleys to play several games in Chicago.

The official with the best view said nothing. Another official signaled touchdown, and the Bears had the winning points on a controversial play, only one of many in the longest series in NFL history. Papa Bear slept well that night with a 10-3 win under his pillow.

Blackbourn's career as head coach of the Packers was not off to a rip-roaring start. Green Bay (0-2) sat at the bottom of the Western

Division looking up at everybody else. Detroit (1-0) stood on top. followed by the Rams and 49ers (both 1-0-1), then the Colts

and Bears (both 1-1). Over in the Eastern Conference, the two Pennsylvania teams. the Steelers and Eagles (both 2-0), were off to a good start, a game ahead of New York (1-1), one and a half ahead of the perennially tough Browns (0-1), and two over the ever meek

Cardinals and floundering Redskins (0-2). Detroit and Cleveland had their game postponed because the World Series was played in Cleveland that Sunday. Better for the Indians that their game had been postponed as New York's baseball Giants completed a four-game sweep of the powerful American League champs.

Blackbourn dropped defensive back Don Miller from the team and claimed an end on waivers from the Chicago Cardinals. Why the Cardinals released Gary Knafelc is still a mystery, but the Packers were glad they did. The former Colorado player stood six-four and weighed 215 pounds, and he had been Chicago's second choice in the '54 draft. In his last year in college, he caught 22 passes for 451 yards and eight TDs. This was his first of nine seasons playing for the Packers.

After two close games in Green Bay, the Packers changed their venue to Milwaukee where they met the 49ers for Week Three of the season. The San Francisco club had a powerful attack and a solid defense, which made the 49ers heavy favorites to demolish the rebuilding Packers. A backfield of Y.A Tittle, Hugh McElhenny, Joe "The Jet" Perry, and John Henry Johnson presented every opposing coach with headaches on defense, and a pair of tackles like Bob St. Clair and Leo Nomellini made life tough for running backs and quarterbacks across the line from them.

San Francisco put 10 points on the board in the first quarter, but the Packers stiffened in the second stanza to go into the locker room down only 10-0. Fired up by their first half performance, the Packers put up 17 points in third period on two Rote TD passes of five yards to Veryl Switzer and 10 yards to Max McGee and a Fred Cone field goal from 45 yards out. Stunned but not out, the 49ers roared back in the final 15 minutes with a pair of touchdowns to snatch a victory away from Green Bay, 23-17.

Although Green Bay (0-3) still remained on the bottom of the Western Division, the game with the 49ers (2-0-1) proved the Packers could compete with the best teams in the league. This was encouraging for the team and its fans.

Detroit (2-0) won again, downing the Rams (1-1-1), and the Bears (2-1) showed some life with a win over the Colts (1-2). In the East, the Eagles (3-0) ended the Steelers' (2-1) hopes for an undefeated season, while the Giants (2-1) beat the Redskins (0-3) and the Browns (1-1) pummeled the Cardinals (0-3).

The Packers entered their fourth game of the season as underdogs to the Rams in Milwaukee. The once super-powerful team from LA was beginning to show its age at several key positions, especially at receiver, where Elroy "Crazy Legs" Hirsch was nearing the end of his long career. The youthful Packers took advantage of the older Rams and came away with a stunning victory over LA, 35-17. Green Bay held the Rams scoreless in the first period, then gave up a solo TD in the second, while scoring a six of their own on a 15-yard TD pass from Rote to McGee. Rote put the Packers ahead in the third quarter on a 16-yard scoring strike to Veryl Switzer, and the Rams countered with a field goal to make score after three, 14-10. Rote climaxed an 80-yard drive with a one-yard dive into the end zone early in the final frame, and the Rams countered with seven on their next possession. The Packers added two more touchdowns on a 28-yard Rote-to-Howton pass play and a two-yard plunge by Reid. The key to the game, as with many NFL contests, was turnovers. Both teams intercepted one pass, but the Rams lost three fumbles to the Packers who kept a firm grip on the ball all afternoon. The Green Bay victory ended a nine-game winless streak over the last two years, and it also halted an 11-game losing string to the Rams that stretched back to 1948.

The Packers (1-3) moved into a tie with the Colts (1-3) for last place in the Western Division, while the Rams (1-2-1) remained in fourth behind the Lions (3-0), 49ers (3-0-1), and Bears (2-2). The Eagles (4-0) continued their bid to unseat the Browns (1-2) as champs of the Eastern Division, and Pittsburgh and New York (both 3-1) put distance between themselves and the hapless Cardinals and Redskins (both 0-4).

Feeding the fiery spirit that was suddenly rekindled in Packer fans, Art Daley wasted no time in pointing out how much better the Packers were than their co-cellar-dweller. The Colts had scored only 29 points in four games to the Pack's 75; Green Bay had surrendered only 71 points to Baltimore's 125. Surely, the Packers would maul the Colts and climb out of the basement when the two squads met in Baltimore the following Sunday. Furthermore, the Rams had demolished the Colts, 48-0. which gave life to some more foolishness in the sports pages. The Packers beat the Rams by 18 points. Add the 18 to the 48 LA stomped on Baltimore and maybe the Packers would win by 66 points. Sure they would. Just to hedge his bet, Daley also wrote that the Colts had a reputation for being a scrappy team. Good insurance on that wager. The Packers managed to squeak by the Colts, 7-6, on a TD by Reid and a PAT by Cone that held up through a scoreless fourth quarter.

The Packers (2-3) moved into a tie with the Bears for fourth place in the division, while the 49ers (4-0-1) climbed over the Lions (3-1) into first. The Rams (2-2-1) also moved up. Pittsburgh (4-1) turned the tables on the Eagles (4-1) in their second meeting of the season, and the Giants (4-1) joined them in first place. The Browns bided their time with a win over the Cardinals (0-5) who still had the Redskins (0-5) for company in the cellar.

Okay, the Packers had beaten one good team at home (actually, in Milwaukee) and one bad team on the road. Now they faced a good squad away from Wisconsin, meaning the Philadelphia Eagles in a nationally televised Saturday night contest. A short work week, road game, national TV. It all added up to disaster. For the Eagles. The Packers played their best game of the year as they embarrassed

Philadelphia right from the start, putting up a three after Switzer ran back the opening kickoff 88 yards to the Philly nine. Bobby Dillon then intercepted an Adrian Burk pass and returned it 59 yards for a TD that put Green Bay ahead, 10-0, in the first quarter. The Eagles came back with seven, but the Pack countered with one of their own on a pass play of 25 yards from Rote to McGee, and Green Bay led after two, 17-7. Another Rote-to-McGee scoring strike, this one 51 yards, put the Pack ahead by 16 points. Moments later, the same tandem connected on a 30-yarder to put the game out of reach, 30-7. One more six on a plunge by Rote in the fourth quarter finished the scoring for Green Bay, then Philly added a meaningless touchdown to make the final, 37-14.

Daley's headline in the *Press-Gazette* stated that the Packers (3-3) were now in the title picture, and in his story on the game, he mentioned that Green Bay's next game against the hated Bears (3-3) would have a real bearing (pun intended) on the season's final standings. Of course, the 49ers (4-1-l), Lions (4-1), Rams (2-3-l), and Colts (1-5) might have a few things to say about the outcome of the '54 campaign in the Western Division. The loss didn't hurt Philadelphia (4-2) all that much as the Giants (4-2) took it on the chin from the Browns (3-2) and the Steelers (4-2) were upset by the Cardinals (1-5) who thought they had escaped the cellar until they heard that the Washington Redskins (1-5) had nipped Baltimore.

An incredible crowd estimated at 10,000 fans turned out to greet the Packers when they landed at Austin Straubel Field the next day. With the Lumberjack band furnishing the pep music and some of the fans setting off fireworks, a stranger would have thought that the Packers had just won the NFL title and not just another regular season game. Those fans were really hungry for a winning season.

Game Seven of the campaign was the second Bear week. Like the Packers, the Monsters of the Midway were also improving from game to game, and this time they had the home field, a fact that never escaped Papa Bear Halas. A football field is a football field, right? Not when that 100 yards of grass was lined out inside windy Wrigley Field. Knowing the turf and the winds gave the Chicago receivers—a bevy of them by the names of Harlon Hill, Bill McColl, Jim Dooley, Billy Stone, and Gene Schroeder—and their passers—particularly crafty George Blanda—a distinct advantage over visiting teams. The home field factor and all the statistics favored the Bears to win this one, but as always when the Packers and Bears face off, the site and the numbers mean absolutely nothing.

Daley summed up the game in superb fashion when he wrote: "The Packers did just about everything but beat the Bears..." Green Bay overcame a 14-0 deficit, scoring 23 points on two touchdowns by McGee on Rote passes of four and 37 yards, a TD on a record-setting punt return of 93 yards by Veryl Switzer, and Fred Cone's two PATs and a field goal. Then the roof caved in. With less than eight minutes to play, the Bears punted to Switzer who dropped the ball on his own 14. Wayne Hansen of the Bears scooped up the ball and ran it into the end zone to close the gap to 23-21. Cone missed a field goal from 39 yards out on Green Bay's next possession, and the Bears marched up field to score on a Blanda TD pass to make the final score, 28-23. The Packers did make a last-minute charge at scoring a winning touchdown, but the clock ran out on them on the Bears' 16.

The loss dropped the Packers (3-4) to three losses behind the Lions (5-1), while the Bears (4-3) stayed in contention. The Rams (3-3-1) upset the 49ers (4-2-1) to keep LA's hopes alive, while the Colts (1-6) fell deeper into the cellar. In the East, the Giants (5-2) crushed the Steelers (4-3) to stay on top with the Eagles (5-2) who did likewise to the Cardinals (1-6) who remained in the basement with the Redskins, huge losers, 62-3, to the Browns (4-2).

The Packers could very easily have owned a record of six or even seven wins with only one or no losses. Each of their defeats had been by seven points or less, and in three of them, they held a lead in the fourth quarter only to lose on a bad break. At the same time, one of their wins had been by only one point, and that game, against their next foe, the Colts, could have gone the other way just as easily as those four losses.

Going into the contest with the Colts, a Saturday night affair in Milwaukee that would be shown on national TV, Tobin Rote had not been intercepted in 94 straight attempts. The last time he was robbed? Don Shula of the Colts in the first meeting in Baltimore. Rote extended the string to 104 in the Baltimore game until—you guessed it!—Shula snared another one. Never mind that. The Packers overcame a poor week of practice and a poor start of the game to trim the Colts, 24-13, scoring all 24 markers after the Colts had put up their unlucky 13.

Once again at .500, the Packers (4-4) remained in the race for the Western Division title. All they had to do to win the crown was climb over the Lions (6-1), 49ers, and Rams (both 4-3-1), and as Fate would have it, those teams were their opponents for the final four games of the season. If they should be the victor in all four, the Packers would still need some help from somebody else because beating the Lions twice would only leave Detroit with three losses; two other teams would also have to tame the Lions who were playing up to their name by this part of the season. In the Eastern Division, the Giants (6-2) were now on top all by themselves, but the Browns (5-2) were keeping pace. Philadelphia (5-3) and Pittsburgh (4-4) were fading fast, while Washington (2-6) and the Cardinals (1-7) were looking forward to 1955.

Ah, the schedule-makers! Who were these people? A pair of chimps at the Bronx Zoo? No, they were allegedly intelligent people in the commissioner's office who set the dates and places for NFL teams to play each other. They were supposed to know what they were doing, but that was easily questioned when they wrote Detroit at Green Bay, November 21, 1955, and Green Bay at Detroit, November 25, 1955, Thanksgiving Day four days later. It boggles the mind.

Anyway, the Packers prepared to play the best team in the NFL to date the following Sunday in Green Bay. Besides having only the one loss, the Lions were scoring an average of 33.9 points per game, while their stingy defense was only allowing 13.9 points per game. These guys were already NFL champs for 1953, and they had every intention of repeating.

The Packers had plans to cage the Lions, and they almost worked. A paid crowd of 20,767 witnessed another heartbreaker in Green Bay. The Packers scored first on a plunge by Reid that culminated an opening drive of 69-yards. Detroit came back to score twice before the Packers closed out the half with a Fred Cone field goal to trail, 14-10. The Lions put up seven more in the third period, and the Packers countered with a six of their own on another plunge, this one by Rote, after a monster drive of 92 yards. The Packers continued to fight back in the fourth quarter. The usually sure-handed Max McGee dropped a potential TD pass in the end zone with eight minutes left, then Cone missed a 41-yard field goal attempt. With three minutes left and the Packers driving again, Howie Ferguson fumbled the ball on the Detroit 35, and the Lions recovered it. The Packers never saw the ball again that day, losing another close one, 21-17.

The loss eliminated the Packers (4-5) from the division race, but the win put the Lions (7-1) only a victory away from another Western crown. All Detroit had to do was beat the Packers again on Thanksgiving Day, and they could plan on playing for the NFL title again.

The Packers suffered some injuries in the first meeting with the Lions. Rote, Val Joe Walker, and Veryl Switzer were all banged np and question marks for the turkey day affair. Walker was definitely out, and Switzer was really doubtful. Rote would play with the pain.

Art Daley reported on the game:

> If ever Detroit was going to break loose for its usual "45" yesterday was the day. The Packers played without Val Joe Walker, their ace defensive halfback; John Martinkovic was so sick with the stomach flu right up to game time that he could hardly walk; and the other defensive end, Stretch Elliott, went out with a leg injury in the second quarter.
>
> And to top it all off, Packer pass catchers dropped eight (8) throws from Quarterback Tobin Rote who was operating brilliantly on a leg and a half.
>
> Yet the Packers picked up 24 points, held leads of 7-0, 14-7 and 17-14 in the ding-dong battle, and captured all of the statistical honors—most notable of which was holding the Lions' vaunted running game to 85 yards while rushing for 133 themselves.

The Packers did everything except win the game. Unfortunately, they suffered the same result six times that season, losing those games by a total of 27 points. Only three of their wins were totally one-sided affairs. A split with the Bears, a split with the Lions, a win over the Steelers, and the Packers would have been 7-3 after 10 games and only one loss behind Detroit. But that ain't what happened, and the Packers were looking ahead to the Draft and the 1955 season the day after Thanksgiving.

Green Bay (4-8) lost its last two games on the West Coast, getting crushed by the 49ers, 35-0, and dropping another close one to the Rams, 35-27. The Packers finished in fifth place, a game ahead of the Colts (3-9) and well behind the division winning Detroit Lions (9-2-1). Bears (8-4), 49ers (7-4-1), and Rams (6-5-1). The Cleveland Browns (9-3) won the Eastern Division for the fifth consecutive year, while the Eagles (7-4-1) finished strong again with too little too late. The Giants (7-5) came in third. followed by Pittsburgh (5-7), Washington (3-9). and the Cardinals (2-10).

The Lions and Browns played their regular season game after the rest of the NFL had packed up and gone home for the off-season, then they played for the NFL title the next week for the third straight year. Detroit won the season finale, 14-10, and the Lions were looking to making it three title game wins in a row over the Browns to become the first team since the Packers of 1929-30-31 to capture the NFL crown three years running. No soap, Detroit. The Lions lost the championship big, big time, 56-10, and the title streak record remained in the sole possession of the Green Bay Packers for at least two more years.

§§§

11
Back to Even

The year 1954 ended on a very sad note for the Packer organization. Fred Miller, president of the Miller Brewing Company in Milwaukee, died from injuries sustained in an airplane crash. Miller and his son, Fred, Jr., were leaving Milwaukee for a hunting trip in Canada when their plane went down in a field not far from the airport. The son and two pilots were killed in the crash, while the father died five hours later in the hospital.

Miller had served on the board of directors for the Packers, and he had picked up the advertising contract for broadcasting Packer games on the radio, paying the corporation much needed cash that helped keep the franchise afloat during those difficult years when the NFL and AAC were at war. Although it was rumored often that Miller had designs on moving the team to Milwaukee, those close to Miller knew that he believed the Packers belonged in Green Bay and no other place, not even Milwaukee except on a part-time basis. His guiding hand would be sorely missed in the coming years.

Attendance for the 1954 season rose by almost 15,000 fans over 1953. Uh, that's misleading, which is what Art Daley and the *Press-Gazette* did to their readers in 1954. The facts? Attendance was up in Green Bay but only by 1,474 customers, and it was down in

Milwaukee—big-time!—by 9,522 fans. On the road, the Packers played before 22,955 more spectators than in 1953; most of the increase coming in Detroit where better weather '54 brought out more people than in '53.

What did this attendance business mean in the profit-and-loss statement? As the home team, the Packers got to keep 75% of the gate, and when they were the visitors, they were given 25% of the gate. Let's see. The Packers sold 8,048 fewer tickets in '54, and their opponents sold 22,955 more when the Packers were in town. One fourth of 22,955 is 5,591, while three-fourths of 8,048 is 6,036. That's almost a wash except that the Packers had the cheapest tickets in the NFL. In dollars and cents, the Packers once again made more money on the road than they did at home.

When the bottom line was announced in March, the Packers showed a profit of $69,594, the largest in the corporation's history. All of this was due entirely to $114,350 from radio and television rights revenue. Without the media money, the Packers would have shown a loss of about $28,000.

The stockholders reelected Fred Cobb, Emil Fischer, Les Kelly, Fred Leicht, Ed Liebmann, W. Heraly MacDonald, Herb Olson, A.C Witteborg, Charles "Buckets" Goldenberg, and Herb Mount to the board of directors, and they elected Bernard "Boob" Darling to complete the unexpired term of William J. Servotte who had resigned and Albert S. Puelicher to complete the late Fred Miller's term. The board elected the corporation's officers: Bogda, president; Lee Joannes and Dominic Olejniczak, vice-presidents; and John Torinus, secretary-treasurer. Next, they voted to expand the executive committee from 12 to 13 members. MacDonald, Bill Sullivan, and Kelly were elected to replace Servotte, Verne Lewellen, and Gene Ronzani, and Darling was elected to the new seat on the committee.

The new year of 1955 began with a few questions, and Uncle Sam had all the answers. This was an era when the military draft was a constant in American society. When a young man turned 18 years of age, he went down to his local draft board and registered for the possibility of serving his country in the Army, Navy, or Marine Corps, and with his 19th birthday, he became eligible to be called for peace-time duty. Attendance at an accredited college deferred him from being drafted until after graduation and being married with children could preserve his civilian life until a real war made his appearance in uniform absolutely necessary to the survival of his country.

When the sixth decade of the 20th Century began in 1951, the United States was heavily involved in the Korean War, and once all the reservists were called to active-duty, the government increased the number of draftees in order to fuel the needs of the war machine. Hundreds of thousands of young men across America were called to duty. Included in their number were hundreds of professional athletes. They were called up, served two years usually, then they were discharged. Some returned to their former careers, while others used their military experience to vault themselves into other professions.

Professional football was particularly subjected to the draft because a vast majority of its players were college graduates and the Army needed junior officers to command all those working-class draftees in the front lines. Because of the military's needs, NFL coaches were hard-pressed to fill their rosters each year with the NFL College Draft. Did they pick a player who might be called up that year and hope he would come out of the service in one piece and still want to play pro football? Or did they pick players with minor physical infirmities that kept them out of the service, such as Bobby Dillon who was blind in one eye or Val Joe Walker who was missing three fingers because of an oil field accident, and hope they could overcome those slight handicaps to play in the pro game? Often, it was a little of both.

The College Draft was a crap shoot without the military interference. Picking players was more like Muskie fishing with it. (Muskie fishing? Sometimes known as the fish of a thousand casts because Muskie fishers often have to go that long before they even get a bite.)

When the Green Bay brain trust prepared for the '55 College Draft, they kept in mind the possibility that they might lose a draftee or two to the armed forces and they might also lose a veteran or two the same way. They had to do their best to outguess the draft boards all across the country. Sometimes they did, and sometimes they didn't.

In the past, Packer alumni had informally aided the official team scouts and coaches in their search for new talent, but in 1955, the Packer Alumni Association openly declared that it was on a mission to survey the college ranks for potential pro players. Association president Bernard "Boob" Darling revealed that a questionnaire had been sent out to nearly 150 former Packer players asking them to evaluate collegiate talent in their area. Coach Blackbourn and his staff welcomed this assistance.

The first task at hand was the replacement of the team captain. Clayton Tonnemaker, middle linebacker in the Packers' 5-3-3 defensive scheme, called it quits in January. He took a job with Cargill, Inc., and his new position required him to enter a training program that would last at least six months and possibly a whole year. Besides the career opportunity, Tonnemaker cited the injuries to his knees as another reason for hanging up his cleats.

Just like Tonnemaker, who was a first-round draft choice in 1950, Art Hunter was a first-round pick in 1954, and also like Tonnemaker, he played one season in Green Bay before he received his draft notice. Hunter had been a starting tackle on offense in '54 and had acquitted himself well. He had been counted on to be one of the building blocks of a solid offensive line for years to come. Now he was off to spend two years in the Army.

Now Blackbourn had to replace two frontliners. Who would be next to go? he wondered as the Draft came closer and questions about the status of several other young players remained in doubt.

On the good news side, Tobin Rote signed a two-year pact with the Packers, putting an end to the rumors and fears that the former Rice Owl would jump to the Canadian League for '55. At the time of the signing, Rote ranked as the Packers' all-time greatest passer, having topped four of Cecil Isbell's marks and one of Arnie Herber's in the previous season. He now held the records for most passes completed career, 523; most passes completed one season, 180; most passes attempted one season, 382; most yards gained passing career, 7,355; and most yards gained passing in one game, 335. The most passes attempted in a season was also an NFL standard, breaking Otto

Graham's record of 364 in '52. Rote and Billy Howton, once he signed, assured Blackbourn of having one of the best passing combos in the NFL again in the fall.

Finally, Draft day came, and the Packers once again missed out on the Bonus Pick, which went to the Colts who chose quarterback George Shaw from Oregon. The Cardinals had the first pick in the regular phase of the draft, and they selected Max Boydston, an end from Oklahoma. The Redskins came next, taking Ralph Guglielmi, QB, Notre Dame. The Colts had the number three pick, and with it, they grabbed the man Packer fans wanted the most, Alan "The Horse" Ameche, the powerful fullback from Wisconsin. With the fourth pick in the regular draft, the Packers took Tom Bettis, a 6'2", 235-pound All-America guard from Purdue. In order after the Packers, Pittsburgh chose Frank Varrichione, T, Notre Dame; Los Angeles, Larry Morris, C, Georgia Tech; New York, Joe Heap, HB, Notre Dame; Philadelphia, and Dick Bielski, FB, Maryland; San Francisco, Dick Moegle, HB, Rice; Bears, Ron Drzewiecki, HB, Marquette; Detroit, Dave Middleton, HB, Auburn; and Cleveland, Kurt Burris, C, Oklahoma.

For the rest of the Draft, Blackbourn chose future Packers Jim Temp, E, Wisconsin, second round; Hank Bullough, G, Michigan State, fifth round; Norm Amundsen, G, Wisconsin, sixth round; Bob Clemens, FB, Georgia, seventh round; Charles 'Choo-Choo' Brackins, QB, Prairie View A&M, 16th round; Doyle Nix, DB, SMU, 18th round; Nate Borden, DE, Indiana, 25th round; and Jim Jennings, E, Missouri, 26th round. Temp and Amundsen would not play for the Packers until '57 while the rest made the squad in '55. Brackins was the first African-American quarterback in Green Bay history and the second in NFL history; the first being Willie Thrower (great name for a quarterback) who threw one pass in one game for the Bears in '53.

With the draft out of the way, Blackbourn and his staff had to go about the business of signing their team for 1955. Rote was already in the fold. That left Gene Knutson and Fred Cone who signed their contracts in February: Deral Teteak and Al Carmichael in March: Buddy Brown, Howie Ferguson, Clarence Self, Dave Hanner (whose contract included a weight clause that demanded he weigh no more than 245 pounds by the opening of training-camp in July or face being fined).

Steve Ruzich, and Roger Zatkoff in April: Billy Howton in May: Jim Ringo, Carleton Elliott, Bill Forester, and John Martinkovic in June: Val Joe Walker, Jerry Helluin, Gary Knafelc, Len Szafaryn, Breez Reid, Joe Johnson, Veryl Switzer, Jim Psaltis, and Bobby Dillon in July.

Newcomers to the team were fullback Jack Spinks who played for the Steelers in '52 and the Cardinals in '53 and sat out '54 after being cut by Chicago; Jim Capuzzi, a quarterback who only played his freshman year at Cincinnati University before enlisting in the Marines for three years; and Billy Bookout, a defensive back from Austin College. Although not exactly a newcomer, George Timberlake, Green Bay's eighth round draft choice in '54 who broke his wrist in training camp and couldn't play that season, returned to the Packers for the '55 season.

In addition to Art Hunter, veterans lost to duty in the armed forces were Bob Garrett, Al Barry, and Max McGee. Blackbourn added an old face to his coaching staff for training camp. He signed Ab Wimberly to coach the defensive ends for two weeks before Wimberly had to begin his regular coaching duties at LSU in August.

The Packers signed over 30 rookies and brought them to an early, one-week camp at Stevens Point. Most of these men were simply blocking and tackling dummies that the coaching staff was shaping up for the veterans to practice on when they reported a week later, but Blackbourn did hope to find a few replacements for the four players who had been drafted into the armed forces out of this bunch. Not finding many and needing offensive line help right now and not a year or two down the road when Art Hunter and Al Barry would be released from the service, Blackbourn traded the rights to Hunter to the Browns for tackle Bill Lucky and guard Joe Skibinski. Lucky, a 250-pounder from Baylor, was drafted by the Packers in '53 in the 19th round as a junior for '54 delivery, but he turned out not to be eligible which moved the NFL front office to forfeit the choice. The Browns drafted him in '54 as their fifth pick, but he didn't play because of family problems. Skibinski attended Purdue, then played for the Browns in '52 before being drafted into the Army.

In another trade before the pre-season games began, Blackbourn sent defensive end Carleton "Stretch" Elliott and a draft pick to the Rams for offensive tackle Torn Dahms, a four-year veteran out of San Diego State. The trade was necessitated when newly acquired Bill Lucky went down with an appendectomy a few days after he came over from Cleveland.

The Packers traveled to Spokane, Washington, to take on the New York Giants in their first exhibition game of the pre-season, and much to every fan in Packerdom's delight, Green Bay came away a winner, 31-24. After the game, Blackbourn cut veteran Jim Psaltis and six rookies, and he added punter Dick Deschaine from nearby Menominee, Michigan, who played for the Marinette-Menominee Hornets semi-pro team, and also played in the service.

In their second tune-up for the season, the Packers fell a touchdown short of defeating the Cleveland Browns, losing, 13-7, at Akron, Ohio. Number Three got away from the Packers in Green Bay when Pittsburgh kicked a late field goal to win, 16-14, and Blackbourn reduced the roster to 41 by releasing one free agent—Sisto Averno, a five-year pro guard—and three rookies. Their fourth exhibition game was played in Charleston, West Virginia, against the Eagles, a team on the decline in the NFL, and Philadelphia came away a winner, 24-10. Pre-season Game Five went to the Redskins, 33-31, at Winston-Salem, North Carolina. The final warm-up for '55 pitted the Packers against the rebuilding Cardinals in Milwaukee, and Green Bay put it all together to beat Chicago, 37-28.

Blackbourn trimmed the roster to one under the limit of 35 by releasing three-year veteran guard Steve Ruzich and placing Gene Knutson on the disabled list. Then he added end Pat O'Donahue who played on Wisconsin's Rose Bowl squad before being drafted by the 49ers in '52, playing one year in the NFL, then serving in the Army for two years before returning to the NFL in '55.

The Packers opened the 1955 regular season looking to break a few losing streaks. To begin with, they had a four-game skid at the end of the previous season that they wanted to halt. Next, they hadn't beaten the Lions, their first opponent of the campaign, since playing them in Milwaukee in 1949 when Curly Lambeau was still the head coach. That was a skein of 11 straight losses. They hadn't beaten the Bears since the second game against the Monsters of the Midway in '52, and they had never beaten the Browns in regular or exhibition season. They also had a seven-game losing streak to the 49ers and another seven-gamer to the Cardinals that stretched back to 1946. Worst of all, the Packers hadn't won on their own field in Green Bay in their last four tries. Ending half of these would be a real accomplishment, but first things first: the Lions in Green Bay.

The Lions had won the Western Division title three years in a row, and few people expected them to be dethroned in '55, especially since they returned a healthy nucleus of the same teams that won those crowns. The Packers had other thoughts on the subject.

A solid crowd of 22,217 paid customers turned out to watch the match at City Stadium, and none of them went home disappointed. The Lions benefited from a deflected pass and scored a touchdown in the first quarter to take a 7-0 lead, but the Packers countered with a pair of Fred Cone field goals in the second stanza. Detroit received a gift TD in the same period when Rote muffed a lateral and Gil Maine of the Lions recovered it in the end zone. Doak Walker booted a short field goal in the third frame to put Detroit ahead, 17-6, setting up a great Green Bay finish. The Packers mounted an 80-yard drive on the ensuing kickoff, and Breezy Reid capped it with a four-yard burst into the end zone to bring the Pack to within four. Another strong drive in the final quarter came to a halt when Billy Howton fumbled on the Detroit 15 with five minutes to play. Former Packer Jug Girard then punted out of bounds on the Packer five. This was followed by Howie Ferguson fumbling on the five, and Joe Schmidt of the Lions recovered it. The end didn't look good for Green Bay. After a five-yard penalty that put Detroit back on the 10, the Lions could only muster a single yard before Walker missed a chip shot from the 16. With only 1:45 showing on the clock, Green Bay took over on the 20. Then –

Rote passes to Switzer for 14-yards.

Rote scrambles for 28 yards to the Detroit 38, and Rote calls time with 1:15 left.

Rote throws short incomplete to Joe Johnson.

Rote passes to Johnson for a minus six yards and another timeout.

Rote passes to Switzer for 17 yards and a first down on the Detroit 27.

Rote passes to Howton for 9 yards and out of bounds on the 18 to stop the clock.

Rote drops back finds Gary Knafelc open down the middle, fires a huller. Knafelc snares the ball in the middle of three Detroit defenders, fights his way free of their collective grasp and bowls into the end zone for the winning touchdown with 20 seconds left.

Cone kicks the extra point, and the Packers have a victory. 20-17, to open the 1955 season.

In one stretch of the referee's arms, the Packers had ended their 11-game losing streak to the Lions, their four-game losing streak at City Stadium, and their four-game losing streak in regular season play. Joy and pandemonium reigned in Packerdom.

In a little human-interest sidebar, just after the winning touchdown was scored, a diminutive fan, supposedly about seven years old, pushed a 50-cent piece into Knafelc's hand then disappeared into the stands. Knafelc looked for the boy because he wanted to return the coin to him, but he had no luck finding the lad until Daley ran the story in the *Press-Gazette*. As it turned out, the boy was 14-year-old Mike Culligan who gave the coin to Knafelc. Culligan and two pals, John Kozicki and Jeff Funk, put up the reward for Knafelc scoring the winning touchdown. Knafelc kept the money; he earned it.

Next up: The Bears.

George Halas had once again assembled the makings of a championship club in 1955. Some of the more famous names on this squad were Ed Brown at quarterback, Harlon Hill and Bill McColl at ends, Bobby Watkins and Rick Casares at running backs, Bill George and Stan Jones in the offensive line, George Connor, Ed Sprinkle, Doug Atkins, Joe Fortunato, and Bill Bishop on the defense. This much talent mixed with the fire that Halas could put into a team and the rivalry with the Packers insured spectators a whale of a game.

The Packers had a little talent of their own, and they had the same fire in them because of the rivalry. A solid game plan by the coaching staff and the team's spirit carried them to a 24-3 win as they completely dominated Chicago from start to finish. The Packers scored on a second quarter TD pass from Rote to Howton, a field goal by Cone in the same frame, a plunge by Rote in the third period, and another TD pass from Rote, this time to Knafelc in the fourth stanza. A sell-out crowd of 24,662 went home with visions of another title in Green Bay, and the Bears just went home.

Blackbourn had to trim his roster to 33 players before the third game, so he let veteran Clarence Self and rookies Jim Jennings and Bob Clemens go on waivers. To replace Clemens, the coach picked up defensive halfback Al Romine, a numbers victim of the Bears out of Alabama State Teachers College.

Green Bay's quick start surprised a lot of people around the league, but the Packers weren't the only team causing a stir in the NFL so early in the campaign. The Colts had also beaten the Bears and the Lions to begin the season, and now they headed for a showdown with the Packers in Milwaukee in a nationally televised contest on Saturday night. Ever since becoming an NFL franchise the Colts had been building a winner. Their roster included such names as Alan "The Horse" Ameche, L.G. Dupre, Gino Marchetti, Art Donovan, Ray Berry, and Dick Szymanski, and they were coached by the great Weeb Ewbank, a protege of Paul Brown of the Cleveland Browns.

The meteorologists predicted perfect weather for the game, and for once, they got it right. A record crowd of 40,199 turned out to watch the two undefeated teams clash in Milwaukee County Stadium. The game started quickly with Rote hitting Howton on a 38-yard scoring strike just 41 seconds into the first quarter, and Baltimore struck right back. Just two minutes and 18 seconds later when Ameche crashed over from five yards out two plays after Rote lost a fumble on the Packer 12. The Colts added two more sixes in the period on two long passes of 82 and 40 yards to lead after one, 21-7, but that was all the offense they could muster for the night. Howie Ferguson scored a touchdown in the second quarter to make the halftime score, 21-14, and Fred Cone added a field goal in the third to close the gap to four, 21-17. A second fumble lost by Rote in the fourth stanza set up a field goal by Baltimore's Bert Rechichar, and Cone added another three of his own in the period. The Packers were marching for a winning touchdown when time expired, and the Colts went back to Baltimore sharing the top of the Western Division with the Rams.

For the fourth straight week, the Packers faced a highly talented opponent, this time the Los Angeles Rams in Milwaukee. LA had a new coach in Sid Gillman, and the lineup included Norm Van Brocklin, Billy Wade, Elroy Hirsch, Tom Fears, Tank Younger, Andy Robustelli, Bob Boyd, and Les Richter. A Green Bay victory coupled with a Baltimore loss would create a three-way tie for first in the West, and that was exactly what happened. Fred Cone, quietly known as "Pineapple" because that was the name of the town in Alabama where he was born, kicked a winning 25-yard field goal with 24 seconds remaining in the game to give the win to the Packers, 30-28. After a poor start that saw LA score on a fumble in the first two minutes of the game, the Packers came back to lead, 17-7, at halftime on touchdowns by Switzer and Knafelc on passes of eight and 16 yards from Rote and a field goal by Cone. Rote connected with Howton for 57 yards and a score early in the third period to increase the margin to 24-7, but the Rams came charging back, scoring two touchdowns to trail by only three early in the final stanza. Cone booted his second field goal to increase the spread to six, and the Packers seemed to have the game in hand until Jim Cason picked off a Rote pass and ran it 24 yards into the end zone to give the Rams the lead, 28-27, with only 3:40 left on the clock. Cason intercepted another Rote pass—the fifth interception of the day by the Rams—a little over a minute later, and the game seemed lost. But the Packer defense forced the Rams to punt, and Al Carmichael returned the ball 40 yards to the LA 30. Two plays later, both runs by Rote, Cone performed his heroics, and the Packers had their third win of the season.

After four weeks of play, the Packers, Colts, and Rams (all 3-1) sat atop the Western Division. The 49ers (2-2) were doing okay, and the Bears (1-3) finally got into the win column. The Lions (0-4) were having their problems, though. Walt Kiesling had his Steelers (3-1) in a tie with the perennial powerhouse of the Eastern Division, the Browns, while the usual Eastern doormats, Chicago and Washington (both 2-2) were showing signs of respectability. New York and Philadelphia (both 1-3) had gotten off to a terrible start, but the math said they could still win a crown and make it to the championship game.

After four games in Wisconsin, the time had come for the Packers to hit the road. First stop Cleveland.

The Browns were the Browns. Mighty and seemingly invincible. Otto Graham retired after the '54 season, then came out of retirement to lead Cleveland once again. Lou Groza was still kicking the PATs and field goals. Fred Morrison, Ray Renfro, and Ed Modzelewski were in the backfield with Graham. When the Packers came to town, they were a well-tuned football machine, and they mauled the boys from Green Bay, 41-10. The only Packer highlight was a 100-yard kickoff return by Al Carmichael.

The Packers (3-2) dropped to second place with the Colts a game behind LA (4-1). The Bears (2-3) beat the 49ers (2-3), while Detroit remained winless. In the East, Pittsburgh (4-1) kept pace with the Browns, while the surprising Redskins (3-2) held on to third. The Cardinals (2-2-1) managed a tie with the Eagles (1-3-1), while New York's Giants (1-4) brought up the rear.

Next port-of-call for the Packers was Baltimore for another Saturday night television game. The Packers were looking for revenge for their earlier loss to the Colts, but it wasn't to be as Blackbourn made a common coaching error that cost Green Bay the opportunity to win the game in the final minute. Trailing 14-10 with plenty of time to go the Pack drove to the Baltimore eight where they had first down and goal-to-go. Three plays later it was fourth and goal from the five.

Blackbourn opted to pass once more instead of kicking a three and closing the gap to one. The pass failed. and Baltimore took over on downs. The Pack got the ball again and drove into Baltimore territory. where they were forced to go for the TD instead of the field goal on fourth down. and they came up with the same result as earlier. Had Blackbourn gone for the three on the earlier possession which would have been booted from the 12, practically a PAT, his team would have had a chance at winning in the final minute, but that wasn't what happened.

The loss to the Colts (4-2) didn't cost the Packers (3-3) any ground in the division race because LA (4-2) took it on the chin from the Bears (3-3) who were suddenly in the thick of the race as was San Francisco (3-3), a winner over winless Detroit. Cleveland (5-1) continued toward their sixth straight Eastern Division title with a win over the Cardinals (2-3-1), Pittsburgh (4-2) slipped to second by losing to the slow-starting Eagles (2-3-1), and the Giants (2-4) began showing some life with a win over Washington (3-3).

Appropriately, the final stop on this three-game road trip was in Chicago. This would be the last time the Packers would play the Bears when they were under the tutelage of George Halas—at least it was the last on this tour of duty for old Papa Bear.

The Bears entered the game with a three-game winning streak, while the Packers had dropped two in a row. Green Bay had won the first contest, but the Packers hadn't swept a season series from Chicago since 1935. Art Daley wrote about the improvement in the Bears' play over the first time the two teams had met. For one thing, they were moving the ball at will now, as witnessed by the Colts, 49ers, and Rams. The Packers were no different as the Bears marched for two touchdowns in each of the first two quarters to build a half-time lead of 28-3. Another 10 points in the third quarter and an early seven in the fourth put the game out of reach, 45-3, and although the Packers gave it the old college try in the final frame by scoring four TDs of their own, the Bears went to bed that night as winners, 52-31. The total of 83 points set a new record for a Packers-Bears game, surpassing the old mark of 72, set when the Packers dumped the Bears, 44-28, in

1942. The final score could have been much worse, but the Packers intercepted five Chicago passes to halt scoring drives. And the game could have been a lot closer, but the Packers fumbled the ball away four times to stop themselves from putting points on the scoreboard. Incredibly, the Bears gained 399 yards on the ground against the Pack as Rick Casares and Bobby Watkins picked up 115 yards each. Howie Ferguson managed to pick up 120 yards of his own for Green Bay.

The loss dropped the Packers (3-4) into a tie for fourth with the 49ers, losers to first-place LA (5-2). The Bears (4-3) moved into a second-place tie with Baltimore, victims of the cellar-dwelling Lions (1-6). The Browns (6-1) continued to put ground between themselves and the rest of their division. Pittsburgh and Washington (both 4-3) were distantly in second place, the surprising Cardinals (3-3-1) in fourth, Philly (2-4-1) in fifth, and the Giants (2-5) last.

The Packers returned to Green Bay for some home cooking, and the main course on the menu was the Chicago Cardinals. Curly Lambeau had passed from the Chicago scene, and so had Jumbo Joe Stydahar. At the helm on the Chicago sideline was little known Ray Richards, and he would remain so after his tenure with the hapless Cardinals. The Packers hadn't played the Cardinals since 1947 when the Chicago eleven beat the Pack, 14-10, on their way to the division title and an NFL championship. After taking it on the chin from the Bears and their rushing attack, the Packers worried about the Cardinals' runners Ollie Matson and Johnny Olszewski doing the same thing to them. Matson had gained 130 yards on the Steelers the previous Saturday night while Olszewski and running mate Bill Mann were averaging four yards a carry in the same game. And Chicago had Lamar McHan at quarterback, the Arkansas lad who was beginning to look like the real McCoy.

The Cardinal affair was also a Packers' "homecoming" game, and the guest of honor was the team trainer Carl W. "Bud" Jorgensen who had been doing his magic on Green Bay players since 1924. As a way of saying thanks for all tape jobs he did on them, all the aches and pains he soothed in them, the Packers stormed out and thoroughly beat the Cardinals, 31-14. Rote passed to Knafelc for 25 yards and a

TD in the first quarter. Rote passed to Howton for 15 yards and a TD in the second period. Cone booted a 42-yard field goal half a minute later. Rote plunged a yard for a TD less than a minute and half after that, and the Packers went into the locker room ahead, 24-0. Rote passed to Carmichael for 15 yards and a TD early in the third stanza, then the Packers sat back and enjoyed the rest of the day, watching the scoreboard and the clock.

The win kept the Packers (4-4) in contention as the Bears (5-3) moved into a tie with LA for first in the division and the Colts slipped into a tie with Green Bay. The 49ers (3-4-1) fell to fifth, and the Lions (2-6) continued to hold up the rest of the West. Cleveland (6-2) was upset by Philadelphia (3-4-1), allowing Washington (5-3) to gain ground, but the Steelers (4-4) couldn't take advantage of the Browns' loss. New York (3-5) moved a bit closer to climbing over the Cardinals (3-4-1) and getting out of the basement.

Hope for a division crown had charged new life into the Packers as they prepared for the 49ers in Milwaukee. San Francisco was pretty much the same team as in '54. YA. Tittle at quarterback, Joe Perry at fullback. Hugh McElhenny and John Henry Johnson at halfbacks. Carroll Hardy and Billy Wilson at ends provided the offense, while Leo Nomellini and Bob St. Clair continued to lead a potent defense. The major difference in the 49ers from the year before was a new coach. Buck Shaw had been replaced by Red Strader who was more defense oriented than Shaw had been. Taking this factor into consideration, Blackbourn concentrated on the Green Bay offense during practice that week and it paid off at the right time.

Frisco scored first, taking a 7-0 lead in the opening quarter, and things might have been worse for Green Bay if not for a goal line stand late in the period. The Pack came back in the second stanza on an 11-yard pass from Rote to Howton who lateraled on the 49ers 30 to Joe Johnson who took it the rest of the way for the touchdown. Fred Cone added a field goal three minutes later, and the Packers had their first lead of the day. The 49ers scored again, and Cone booted another three before the half to make the score, 14-13, in San Francisco's favor as the teams went into the locker room. Frisco put seven more points on the board in the third period to go into the final frame leading. 21-13. Then the Packers came to life. The Packers completed a 14-play, 91-yard drive with a 34-yard scoring strike from Rote to Knafelc to bring the Packers within one point of the 49ers. Frisco came back with a pair of first downs and appeared to be unstoppable until Jerry Helluin recovered a fumble by Joe Perry on the Packers 40. Then lightning struck. Breezy Reid gained five yards up the middle. On second down, Reid took a handoff from Rote and started around right end only to be faced by four 49ers with mayhem on their minds. Reid reversed directions and lateraled to Rote who zipped down the sideline to the 49ers six where he was brought down. Howie Ferguson got the call on the next play, bowling through the middle for a TD to put the Packers on top again with 4:39 on the clock. The 49ers were in the midst of making a last minute comeback when Green Bay's defensive back Billy Bookout crashed into Frisco receiver Harry Babcock and jarred the ball loose for Val Joe Walker to recover and end the threat. Bookout hit Babcock so hard that both players had to be helped from the field. The Packers had another win, 27-21.

The Packers (5-4) had improved on their won-lost record for '54, but more important to '55, they kept pace with the Bears (6-3) for the division crown. The Rams (5-3-1) slipped a bit when they tied the Colts (4-4-1) who stayed ahead of the 49ers (3-6) and the Lions (2-7). In the Cardinals' (3-5-1) wings, 31-0, but Cleveland (7-2) remained on top by dumping Pittsburgh (4-5). New York (4-5) dumped the Eagles (3-5-1) to eliminate Philadelphia from title consideration.

Standing between the Packers and a division crown were the Lions, 49ers, and Rams—all on the road. If they should win all three, the Packers would still need help from one of the Bears' three remaining opponents the Cardinals, Lions, and Eagles. For the moment, the Bears were in the driver's seat, and as the old cliché in sports went, the Packers had to take each game one at a time.

First off, the Lions on Thanksgiving Day in Detroit. Too bad. Since beginning this holiday tradition in 1951, the Packers had been the biggest turkeys of all in the Motor City, and '55 would prove no different. The Lions were not the same team that they had been back in September in Green Bay. This Detroit squad was healthy and full of revenge. Five Packers' turnovers didn't hurt Detroit either as the Lions made off with a 24-10 win.

Green Bay (5-5) losing to Detroit (3-7) was the bad news. The good news was they were still in the division race. The Bears (6-4) were creamed, 53-14, by the Cardinals (4-5-1) in a snow storm that made the Comiskey Park turf slicker for the Northsiders than it did for the Birds. More bad news, though. The Rams (6-3-1) nipped the Eagles (3-6-1), and Baltimore (5-4-1) kicked the 49ers (3-7). In the remaining games in the East, the Giants (4-5-1) held the Browns (7-2-1) to a tie, and the Redskins (7-3) moved within a half-game of first place Cleveland by dumping Pittsburgh (4-6).

Although they were still in the chase mathematically, the Packers now had three teams to climb over for the division crown. They needed the Lions to beat the Bears the following week and the Colts to get by the Rams, while they beat the 49ers in San Francisco, a feat not yet accomplished by the Packers to date. Worse still, the Packers hadn't won a game on the West Coast since 1947 when Lambeau's squad beat the Rams, 30-10, and even if all should go according to their wishes in Week Eleven of the season, they still had to beat the Rams the following week and the Colts had to lose.

Well, the Packers did their part in making their dreams come true. They dumped the 49ers in San Francisco, 28-7, for their first win out west in eight years and their first ever victory in the other NFL city by the bay. Frisco put up the numbers everywhere except the one place where they counted most—on the scoreboard. After the 49ers took a quick 7-0 lead in the first quarter, the Packers came back with 21 points of their own in the second stanza on TDs by Rote, Len Szafaryn, and Breezy Reid. Rote plunged over from a yard out Szafaryn recovered a punt blocked by Pat O'Donahue and carried it 28 yards into the end zone. Reid's two-yard TD came three plays after Veryl Switzer returned the next 49ers' punt 38 yards to the Frisco seven. The 49ers seemed ready to make a game of it on their first drive of the second half, but Joe Perry fumbled the ball at the goal line. Val Joe Walker jumped on it for the Packers, and Frisco failed to threaten again. Rote hooked up with Reid for a 60-yard scoring pass later in the quarter, then the Green Bay defense did the rest.

The Packers (6-5) had third place all to themselves now, but they were mathematically eliminated from the division race because the Rams (7-3-1) won another close game, 20-14. Only the Bears (7-4) could catch LA now, and they could only do it if they could win their last game of the season and the Packers could defeat the Rams in LA that same day. That didn't happen as the Rams determined their own destiny with a 31-17 win over Green Bay.

The Packers (6-6) finished third behind the Bears (8-4) and Rams (8-3-1) and ahead of the Colts (5-6-1), 49ers (4-8), and Lions (3-9).

The Browns (9-2-1) won an unprecedented sixth consecutive division title in the East, then faced the Rams in the NFL Championship Game. Counting their four crowns in the old All-America Conference, the Browns appeared in 10 straight title contests, winning seven of them, including their 1955 appearance against the Rams, Otto Graham's last game, a 38-14 win on Christmas Day in Los Angeles.

The Packers watched the game on television and waited for next year.

§§§

PRETTY CROWDED BOYS..... YOU'LL HAVE TO LIMIT THE
GAME TO FIFTY YARDS....

174

When the new City Stadium, now known as Lambeau Field, was dedicated in 1957, a host of dignitaries showed up for the occasion. Left to right, Congressman John W. Byrnes, Wisconsin Governor Vernon Thomson, Miss America Marilyn Van Der Bur, Vice-President Richard M. Nixon, and Packer vice-president Dominic Olejniczak.

All-time Packer greats Babe Parilli, Tobin Rote, Tony Canadeo, and Fred Cone present a ball to young fan Larry Bero.

Tobin Rote was the Packers' leading passer and rusher from 1950 thru 1956. He was traded to Detroit before the 1957 season.

Al Carmichael came out of USC and was supposed to replace Tony Canadeo in the Packer backfield. He broke some great runs, but he never quite measured up to Canadeo. Of course, who did?

Bobby Dillon was the finest defensive back on the Green Bay roster in 1950s. He ranks among the greatest in NFL history.

The Packers have been blessed with great receivers. The first was Don Hutson, and Billy Howton, above, was the second.

Jim Ringo was one of the legacies that Gene Ronzani left for his next three successors. He's in the Green Bay Packer Hall of Fame for good reason. He was one of the all-time great centers.

Dave Hanner was the "Fridge" of the 1950s. He was the first player to have a weight clause put in his contract. He was also one of the greatest defensive tackles in Green Bay history. His nickname, "Hawg", came from the fact that he went to the U. of Arkansas whose teams are nicknamed the Razorbacks which are also knowns as "hawgs" down

Known as the "Golden Boy," Heisman Trophy winner Paul Hornung signs his first contract, a three-year deal, with the Packers as members of the executive committee look on. Left to right, Jack Vainisi, an unidentified member, Bernard "Boob"Darling, Les Kelly, Russ Bogda, and Lee Joannes.

The men in the public eye for the Packers in 1954 were, left to right standing, publicity director and former player Francis "Jug" Earpe, assistant coach Ray "Scooter" McLean, talent scout Jack Vainisi, assistant coach Tom "Red" Hearden, and, seated, general manager and business manager Verne Lewellen on the left and head coach Lisle Blackbourn on the right.

Packer head coach from 1950-53, Gene Ronzani hailed from Iron Mountain, Michigan, played college football for Marquette University in Milwaukee, played pro football for the Chicago Bears, and was an assistant coach in the Chicago organization under George Halas. He got the axe from the executive committee because he was Italian, a native of Michigan's Upper Peninsula, and an ex-Bear.

Third head coach of the Packers, 1954-57, Lisle Blackbourn was a native of Wisconsin, coached high school football in Wisconsin, and coached football at Marquette University before signing with the Packers. He got the axe from the executive committee because he told them bluntly to leave the coaching to him.

The Packers' fourth head coach, 1958 only, Ray "Scooter" McLean came from Massachusetts, attended tiny St. Anselm College, managed to have a pro career with the Chicago Bears, then became an assistant coach for Green Bay under Gene Ronzani in 1951. He survived the Ronzani massacre to serve under Lisle Blackbourn for four more years before the executive committee made the worst choice for a head coach in the team's history. Poor Scooter! He never had a clue about being a head coach. He was living proof that Leo Duroucher was right: nice guys do finish last.

12

Reverse Gear

The 1956 season began November 28, 1955, when the NFL held a preliminary Draft of college players in order to combat the Canadian Football League. For the past three years, the CFL had been raiding the NFL for players, and because the Canadian season began in the summer and ended in late November, the league to the north also got a jump on the NFL with drafting and hiring college players from the United States. Commissioner Bert Bell and the NFL owners decided the best way to keep the Canadians from signing away the best talent was to hold an early Draft, a short one of only three rounds.

The Packers, Steelers, and Cardinals were the only three teams remaining in the Bonus Pick lottery, and once again the Packers failed to win the top choice. It went to the Steelers who took Gary Glick, a quarterback out of Colorado A&M (State). Blackbourn had designs on Michigan State quarterback Earl Morrall, Ohio State halfback Howard "Hopalong" Cassady, and Mississippi halfback Art Davis, but all three were gone by the time Green Bay picked number seven. The 49ers in a coin flip with Detroit took Morrall, and the Lions chose Cassady. Pittsburgh took Davis, then the Eagles picked Maryland center Bob Pelligrini. Los Angeles, through the Giants, chose West Virginia halfback Joe Marconi, and the Cardinals took Auburn fullback Joe Childress. Finally, it was Green Bay's turn.

Blackbourn realized that pass receivers were getting faster every year, so to counter this trend, NFL defenses were looking for speedier defensive backs. The fastest man in anyone's defensive backfield was an offensive end named John Losch who attended the University of Miami, Florida. For five straight games during the '55 college season, Losch caught TD passes, none of them going for less than 43 yards. He could not only run with the ball, but he could also run without it in pursuit of opposing pass receivers, which was why Blackbourn made him his Number One pick.

Rounding out the first round, Baltimore chose Penn State's fleet halfback Lenny Moore, the Bears took Texas end Menan "Tex" Schriewer (now there's a household name!), the Rams went for Vanderbilt quarterback Charles Horton, Washington gambled on Maryland halfback Ed Vereb, and the Browns selected Arkansas halfback Preston Carpenter.

In the second round, the Packers took a tackle from SMU named Alvis Forrest Gregg, a 6'3" 235-pound mountain lion from Sulphur Springs, Texas. Green Bay had no third-round pick, having traded it to the Rams for Tom Dahms.

When the regular Draft was conducted in January 1956, the Packers were not asleep. In the fifth round, they took Bob Skoronski, a tackle out of Indiana who made the team in the fall. Round Seven, Green Bay picked up Hank Gremminger, an end from Baylor who made his mark on Packer history as a defensive back And way down in the 17th round, Blackbourn picked up an unheralded quarterback from Alabama named Bryan Bartlett Starr. The remainder of the Green Bay selections never made it past a training camp in the NFL. Of course, four of the five that did make it to the Packers' regular season roster did have an incredible impact on the Packers and the NFL in the decade-plus to come, but that was in the future.

Ideally, an NFL coach wanted four or five quality rookies every year on his team to maintain the continuity of his program, and he hoped that at least one or two would become superstar Pro Bowl types.

Blackbourn had picked five of the former such men in the '54 draft, with two—Art Hunter and Max McGee—becoming superstars; and his '55 draft produced Tom Bettis, Hank Bullough, and Nate Borden who were a cut above the average NFL player. Other collegians might have made it just as big in the NFL if not for one wild card factor: Selective Service, better known as "the draft," as in "You're in the Army now, bub." Two years away from the kind of conditioning necessary to play professional football, more often than not, meant the end of a young man's dreams of playing pro ball.

Good examples of players who were called into the service were Dick Logan and Don Barton. Both played well for the Packers in '53, but when they rejoined the team in '56, the game had left them behind. Neither man made the cut, and their careers in pro football were over.

Who could say whether some of those Packer draft choices that wound up working for Uncle Sam instead of Uncle Liz might have been that one or two players that might have made the difference between a 4-8 mark in '54 and a possible 11-1 record and a berth in the NFL championship game? Another stallion or two in the Green Bay corral in '55 might have brought home two or three more wins and a shot at the league title. Well, the horses simply weren't there, and the Packers looked to the '56 campaign as the one that would bring a winner back to Green Bay once again.

Rumors persisted in pro football circles that a move was afoot to oust long-time Commissioner Bert Bell from the NFL's top post. A few owners did want a new man sitting in the front office, but the older magnates like George Halas, Art Rooney, George Preston Marshall, and Tim Mara opposed any changes in the NFL driver's seat. Bell would stay, and the league would continue its conservative movement under his direction.

One proposal that landed on Bell's desk early in '56 was a plan for league expansion to 14 teams. The two cities that were to receive franchises under the scheme were Dallas and Buffalo. Dallas had already had a team in the NFL, but poor financial backing and inherited debt from the previous owners when the franchise was located in New York had doomed it to failure. The argument for Dallas was that a club with fresh money and no debt could succeed in the league. As for Buffalo, it had been a successful member of the late All-America Conference, and the pro-argument for putting an NFL team in that city rested on the fact that when the merger of the ACC and NFL took place the people of Buffalo had done everything asked of them to support their team but had been denied a place in the new NFL.

Bell opposed expansion at this time because he felt the new teams would be nothing more than doormats for the rest of the league for a minimum of three years and possibly four before they could even win four games in a season. Besides that, he complained about the headaches of scheduling 14 teams for a season. He proposed that the league expand to 16 teams when the time was right for expansion. Eight teams in each division would be easier to schedule, and the season could be extended two more weeks for the extra games. Bell had his way, and expansion was tabled for future consideration.

For the past year of 1955, the Green Bay Packers, Inc., made a profit of $88,578.17 before taxes, a very good year, but only a few grand better than the year before. This figure was surprising in that radio and television revenues were down from $114,350 in '54 to $35,300 for '55. Had the former amount been repeated in '55, the Packers would have made more than $150,000. The profit margin came directly from ticket sales, which were up over $51,000 with home games in Green Bay and Milwaukee accounting for $32,000 of that increase.

Business was good, but it was getting better. The corporation signed a contract with the Columbia Broadcasting System (CBS) that would pay the Packers $75,000 a year for each of the next three years for the rights to broadcast all Packer home games in Green Bay and Milwaukee. This was a real deal in '56. Three decades later CBS would sell one minute of commercial time during a Packer game for that sum.

The board of directors was expanded from 39 to 42 members that year. Elected to the board for three-year terms were Jerry Atkinson, George Whitney Calhoun, Max Cohodas, Lee Joannes, Charles Mathys, Art Mangin, John Stathas, Max Murphy, Dave Kuenzle, Frank

Birch, Fred Trowbridge, John Torinus, Albert Puelicher, Charles Egan, and Carl Mraz. Elected to fill the unexpired term of Harrison McCormick was Charles Goldberg, not to be confused with Charles "Buckets" Goldenberg, former player and also a member of the board.

When the board of directors met the following week, they reelected all the corporate officers and members of the executive committee with the exception of William P. Sullivan who was relocating from Green Bay to the West Coast for health reasons. Voted to serve the corporation for another year were Russ Bogda, president; Lee Joannes and Dominic Olejniczak, vice-presidents; John Torinus, secretary-treasurer; and Howard Bero, Bernard Darling, Les Kelly, Fred Leicht, W. Heraly MacDonald, Max Murphy, Fred Trowbridge, Bogda, Joannes, Olejniczak, and Torinus. Emil Fischer was re-elected as chairman of the board, and Dick Bourguignon was elected to replace Sullivan on the executive committee.

In one last item, Tom Miller was hired to replace Bonnie Ryan as Packer publicity director, and he was given the additional duty of sales promotions director. Miller was a native of Milton, Pennsylvania, and he attended college at Hampden-Sydney in Virginia. He played pro football for the Eagles, Redskins, and Packers, the latter in 1946.

In April, the Alumni Association began a contest to select an insignia for the Packers. Boob Darling, president, made it clear that the Alumni had no designs on changing the team's nickname. The contest was deemed necessary because the Packers were the only team in the NFL without an insignia. (If there was ever a winner, it wasn't big news in the newspapers.)

The new year of 1956 got off to a bad start when it was announced that Fred Cone retired from the pro game to take an assistant coach's position with a minor military academy in Alabama. The five-year veteran ranked fourth in career scoring for the Packers with 309 points to date and filling his spot would be a real chore for Blackbourn. Thus, in the upcoming draft, the Green Bay mentor picked four fullbacks, none of whom panned out.

More bad news two weeks later when the announcement was made that Green Bay's defensive coach Tom Hearden resigned to join the staff of new head coach Milt Bruhn at the University of Wisconsin in Madison. Hearden had improved the Packers' defense to the middle of the NFL pack in his two years with the Packers. He left the Packers for better financial security and the stability that college coaching could provide as opposed to the unsettling atmosphere of the pro ranks, especially in Green Bay where a few grumbles were already being heard about Blackbourn's tendency to make decisions without seeking the advice of the executive committee. Hearden's resignation left yet another big hole for Blackbourn to fill.

Hearden's replacement was Abe Stuber, a native of St. Joseph, Missouri. He graduated from the University of Missouri in 1927, then played two years of semi-pro ball in Ohio before becoming head football coach and track coach at Westminster College in 1929. He moved on to Southwest Missouri State in 1932 where he coached football, basketball, and track for four years. His next job was at Iowa State College where he coached the football team for seven years. His only professional experience had come the previous season when he handled the backfield chores for Jim Trimble and the Philadelphia Eagles.

As an additional aide, Blackbourn hired Earl Klapstein who would be a part-time coach, working from July 1 through the end of the year.

Klapstein was a native of Lodi, California, and he played football at the College of the Pacific, graduating in 1943. He served in the Navy for two years, then played for the Steelers one year before entering the coaching ranks. Blackbourn made him defensive line coach.

Duty in the armed forces began taking its toll on the Packers in February. Doyle Nix, the defensive back, entered the Air Force: he would never play for the Packers again. Veryl Switzer received his call to duty in March, and he went on active duty in the Air Force for the next three years, effectively ending his pro football career. Hank Bullough was called up in June, but he returned to play again in '58.

On the positive side, Blackbourn began signing free agents in April. Bill Roberts, a halfback who played college football at Dartmouth before serving in the Marine Corps for four years, inked a contract, and a week later Glenn Young, a halfback out of Purdue with three years of service in the Navy, put his signature to a Packer pact.

In late April, Blackbourn traded Green Bay's fifth-round draft choice in '57 to the Browns for tackle Don King and guard Gene Donaldson. King made the team in '56, but Donaldson never played a minute in a regular season game for the Packers.

This trade and others proved that Blackbourn was more than cognizant of a basic fact in professional sports: It is management's responsibility to the fans to do everything possible to field a winner every year, and not until the possibility of winning a championship are gone does management build for the future. Blackbourn would trade a fifth, sixth, or even a third-round draft choice for a quality player with pro experience in order to improve his team now, and he would worry about the future when the time came.

Oddly, the Packers failed to sign a single veteran from the '55 squad until Dick Deschaine, the team's punter, signed his contract in early May. Gene Knutson signed shortly thereafter, and he was followed by Gary Knafelc, Tom Bettis, Tobin Rote, Tom Dahms, and Dave Hanner also in May; Howie Ferguson in June; Buddy Brown, Joe Skibinski, Jim Ringo, Billy Bookout, Joe Johnson, Jerry Helluin, Jim Capuzzi, Jack Spinks, Al Carmichael, Breezy Reid, John Martinkovic, Nate Borden, Bobby Dillon, Bill Forester, Billy Howton, Len Szafaryn, Deral Teteak, Val Joe Walker, and Roger Zatkoff in July; and Fred Cone who surprised everybody by returning to the Packers in August. Before the first exhibition game, Blackbourn traded the Packers' sixth-round pick in the '57 draft to the Browns for six-year veteran tackle John Sandusky, and in a conditional trade with the Bears, he added center Larry Lauer to the roster.

From the opening of training camp in July with the rookies reporting first, Blackbourn was impressed by the work of one freshman player in particular. Ever since the Packers drafted Tobin Rote in 1950, the coaching staff had been searching for a back-up at quarterback. and at times. it appeared the brain trust on the sidelines was looking to replace Rote as well. Babe Parilli was the first man chosen to share the spotlight with Rote, but when he proved no better than Rote, he was traded to the Browns. The Packers continued to draft quarterbacks every year, and Blackbourn traded for passers whenever he could. None of these panned out until Blackbourn picked Bart Starr out of Alabama. Right from the start, Blackbourn remarked how Starr stood out from the handful of candidates who were vying for a position on the '56 squad. Starr's passing was a little sharper. His grasp of the offense was a little quicker. His leadership was a little stronger. His conduct on and off the field commanded a little more respect. His overall bearing suggested a little more integrity. His work ethic was a little more imbedded in a character that was beyond reproach. In Blackbourn's estimation, Starr was the perfect man for the job; all he needed was experience, and Liz intended to give him that exposure in training camp and the exhibition season. In the rookie squad game, Starr led his team to a win. In the first full intrasquad tilt, he led his team to a score in the opening drive. In both of these scrimmages, he did nothing super spectacular to draw attention to himself; he simply got the job done. All these facts set him above the rest of the men trying to make the team.

Starr received his professional baptism in the Packers first exhibition game of the '56 season. He threw four passes, completing three for 31 yards, and directed the team on two touchdown drives in the second half of the Bishop's Charity Game in Milwaukee, which the Packers won, 27-6, over the Eagles. His play wasn't flashy, but it was steady and solid as he executed the plays to perfect precision. He simply got the job done.

In the Packers next pre-season contest, Starr shone brightly again. completing four of five passes for 37 yards and scoring one touchdown on a one-yard plunge late in the third quarter. Once again, he got the job done, and the Packers won, 17-13, over the Giants in Green Bay.

Starr's light was not so bright in the third game of the practice season. He did complete three of five passes for 13 yards, but he didn't play all that much in Green Bay's 21-20 win over Cleveland. Still, he got the job done when he was in there.

The Packers dropped their next pre-season game to the Redskins, 17-10, but Starr played well enough to survive the cut of seven players

Blackbourn made after the game. Starr shared quarterbacking duties with Paul Held, Rote's back-up from the year before, and Blackbourn felt the rookie had the edge on the veteran. Starr was still getting the job done.

Starr had already earned a berth on the '56 Packers by the time the last exhibition game was played; thus, he played sparingly in the Pack's 29-21 victory over the Cardinals in Green Bay. Starr had gotten the job done again.

In the two weeks before the opening of the 1956 regular season campaign, Jack Rudolph wrote a series of articles in the *Press-Gazette*. In the first one, he started raising false hopes in Green Bay over the Packers' chances of winning the Western Division crown. As he put it, "the smart money says it isn't in the cards, but then neither were any of the others [championships]. In fact, the improbable has dominated the fantastic story of the Green Bay Packers from the very beginning." He had that last part right, but he failed to consider the times in which that statement was true and compare them to the present. If he had, he might not have been so free with his enthusiasm for the Packers' chances of winning the title.

The handicappers picked the Bears and Giants to win their respective divisions, with the Lions and Browns to be their prime challengers. Although the Packers had done well in the pre-season, the experts predicted they would finish no higher than fourth place in the West, and several writers and prognosticators placed the Packers in fifth place ahead of only the 49ers or the Colts.

Rudolph should have been exiled from the state for raising the expectations of Packer fans.

Nine days before the season began Blackbourn traded Tom Dahms to the Cardinals for Chicago's sixth-round pick in the '57 Draft. Better to trade a guy and get something for him than simply release him on waivers and get nothing.

The first four games of the Packers' schedule for '56 were exactly the same as the first four in '55. The Lions and Bears came to Green Bay, then the Packers faced the Colts and Rams in Milwaukee. Unlike the previous season, however, the outcomes of this quartet of scraps weren't the same in three instances.

The Packers had two weeks between their last pre-season encounter and their season opener against the Lions. The Detroit team that the Packers would be facing in the kickoff tilt was not the same beat up squad that visited Green Bay on opening day the year before. For one thing, Bobby Layne didn't have a sore arm in '56, and he was drinking less. For another, the Lions had revamped their defense. Detroit's NFL opponents were in for a tough time in '56, and the Packers were the first to suffer the claws of the Lions, losing, 20-16, in a game that wasn't as close as the final score would have one believe. Detroit piled up 381 yards of offense and should have scored more except that a staunch Green Bay defense rose up and stopped the Lions when they needed it the most. The Packers managed only 170 yards of offense, with nearly half of that total coming on a fourth quarter scoring drive that brought Green Bay to four down with five minutes to go. A last-minute attempt at pulling out the win ended with a Detroit interception of a Rote pass. The one major highlight for the Packers was a 59-yard punt return by rookie Jack Losch that set up their first TD.

The first game had been a sellout, and the second one was guaranteed to be the same because the foe was none other than those Monsters of the Midway who were now being coached by George Halas's long-time friend Paddy Driscoll. Halas turned over the reins to Driscoll at the beginning of the year, and the team Driscoll inherited was no worthless bunch. The Bears were loaded with talent from end-to-end on both offense and defense, and Chicago had backfields that were hard to match by anybody. The Bruin roster included such outstanding players as Ed Brown at quarterback, Rick Casares at fullback, Bobby Watkins at halfback, Harlon Hill at receiver, J.C. Caroline in the defensive secondary, Stan Jones at guard, Doug Atkinss and Ed Meadows at defensive end, Bill Bishop at defensive tackle, Joe Fortunato and Bill George at linebacker, Jim Dooley at flanker, and Bill McColl at tight end. These were not Bears to be trifled with.

The day was pleasant, and the house was packed. The Bears scored early, and the Packers carne right back when Al Carmichael ran the ensuing kickoff all the way back for 106 yards and a tying TD. The Bears added two field goals before the Packers scored again in the second quarter on a five-yard TD pass from Rote to Howton. The PAT gave Green Bay a 14-13 lead, their only advantage all afternoon. The Bears added a freak touchdown before the half ended when Watkins fumbled into the hands of Ed Brown who zipped around right end for the score, putting the Bears on top for good. Chicago added 17 more points in the second half, while the Packers could only manage one more TD on a pass from Rote to Howton again. The Bears went back to Chicago 37-21 victors over the Packers.

The Packers (0-2) were off to a lousy start, while the Lions (2-0) were roaring. The rest of the division had yet to make up their minds which they were going in '56. Surprise of surprises over in the Eastern Division, the Cardinals (2-0) won their first two games to sit on top all alone with the Redskins (0-2) on the bottom and everybody else in the middle.

A fair crowd turned out to watch the Packers play the Colts in Week Three at Milwaukee County Stadium. The Packers rolled up their highest score in four years, and they came away winners, 38-33, in an exciting contest. Green Bay took advantage of the first break in the game when Fred Cone's kickoff went untouched, and Cone recovered it on the Baltimore 11. Three plays later Rote sneaked over from the one, and the Packers were up, 7-0, with only 1:50 gone in the game. Baltimore came back with a six late in the period, but the PAT was wide to leave the lead in Green Bay's hands, 7-6, after one. Early in the next frame Rote found Knafelc for 31 yards and a TD to put Green Bay ahead, 14-6, but the Colts came right back with 14 markers of their own. The Packers charged into the lead again with a 74-yard drive that culminated with Rote plunging over from the one to put Green Bay on top, 21-20. Cone added a field goal with 15 seconds left to make the half-time margin, 24-20. The Colts' Carl Tassef took the first punt of the second half and returned it 90 yards for a go-ahead TD, but Deral Teteak blocked the PAT try to leave the score at 26-24

Baltimore. The Packers took the ensuing kickoff and marched 70 yards to regain the lead, 31-26, on a nine-yard scoring toss from Rote to Knafelc. Later in the quarter Dillon picked off a pass that had been deflected by Roger Zatkoff, and he ran it back 42 yards for the final Green Bay touchdown. Baltimore scored once more with 50 seconds remaining, but the Packers recovered the onside kick to close out the game.

Green Bay (1-2) was now in the win column, but the victory only put them in a tie with Baltimore, LA, and Frisco. Detroit (3-0) continued to ride the crest, and the Bears (2-1) won again to keep pace. In the East, those surprising Cardinals (3-0) won again to stay ahead of the Giants and Eagles (both 2-1), while the Steelers (1-2), Browns (1-2), and Redskins (0-3-0) lost.

Another decent crowd turned out at Milwaukee County Stadium to watch the Packers butt heads with the Rams the following Sunday, and Green Bay extended its winning streak at the other home field to four games. 42-1 7. The Packers totaled 498 yards of offense, and over half of it was credited to Billy Howton who hauled down seven passes for an incredible 257 yards and two touchdowns. Gary Knafelc caught two TD passes from Rote, while Rote and Cone scored the other two Packer sixes. The Green Bay defense picked off four LA passes and recovered one fumble to keep the Rams at ba-a-a-ay. (Pun intended.)

The win put the Packers (2-2) in third place all by themselves, but they still trailed the Bears (3-1) and Lions (4-0). The Rams, Colts, and 49ers (1-3) brought up the collective rear of the division. Those amazing Cardinals (4-0) dumped the Eagles (2-2) to stay ahead of the Giants (3-1), and the Redskins (1-3) upset the Browns (1-3) who were off to their worst start in their NFL history. The Steelers (1-3) also lost and gained a share of the cellar in the East.

With the season one-third over and the remaining schedule calling for six games on the road, the Packers began facing do-or-die situations. The first of these was in Baltimore, and the Colts were itching for a win after the Bears tromped on them the week before, 58-27. The good news for Green Bay was Baltimore would be without two starters: quarterback George Shaw and top defensive back and placekicker Bert Rechichar. The bad news was an unknown commodity would be replacing Shaw. This rookie signal-caller had the unusual name of Johnny Unitas. He and fellow rookie Lenny Moore put the collar on the Packers as Moore scored two TDs on runs of 72 yards and 79 yards, the latter coming in the fourth quarter and proving to be the winning marker. Unitas passed for a pair of touchdowns in his debut as a starter, and the Packers went down to defeat, 28-21. Two fumbled punts and Knafelc dropping a potential game-tying TD pass in the final stanza didn't help the Green Bay effort either.

Although the Packers (2-3) lost, they remained in third place with the Colts (2-3) but fell another game behind the (4-1) and Lions (5-0). LA and Frisco (1-4) lost again, which for all practical purposes put them out of contention for the year. The balloon finally burst for the Cardinals (4-1) as they lost to the Redskins (2-3). The Giants (4-l) beat the Eagles (2-3), but the big surprise now was the demise of the Browns (1-4), losers to the Steelers (2-3).

Speaking of those disappointing Browns, Cleveland was the next opponent for the Packers who were hoping to extend their Milwaukee County Stadium winning streak to five games. Former Packer Babe Parilli started at quarterback for the Browns, but he wasn't much of factor in the game except that he handled the ball perfectly for the Cleveland runners who gained a total of 222 yards on the ground. Parilli completed all three of his passes; two to teammates and one to the Packers. The Packers had a very balanced attack, gaining 127 yards on the ground and 168 through the air. The problem was Cleveland's defense. It scored a touchdown on a fumble recovery and allowed only one by the Packers; thus, the outcome favored the Browns, 24-7.

The loss dropped the Packers (2-4) into fourth place all by themselves. Detroit (6-0) won over Frisco (1-5) and remained on top of the division, and the Bears (5-1) beat the Rams (1-5) to keep pace. The Colts (2-3) took over third place although they were idle. In the East, the other Chicago team (5-1) beat the Eagles (2-4), and the Giants (5-1) held on to a share of the lead with a victory over the Steelers (2-4). The Browns (2-4) shared the basement again, and Washington (2-3) stayed in third because they were also idle.

With the season almost down the drain at the halfway mark, it was only appropriate that the Packers should start the second half against the Bears. Green Bay had a golden opportunity to spoil the Bears title hopes with a win in Chicago. The Monsters of the Midway were on a five-game winning streak, and in that time, they had amassed 199 points, scoring not less than 31 in any contest. The Packers had to stop this scoring machine or start talking about next year.

Someone forgot to tell the Bears that they were ripe for an upset. They rolled up 492 yards of offense; 193 on the ground and 299 through the air. The final score was a lopsided 38-14, but it could have been much worse because the Bears committed three turnovers. The Packers could have scored more, too, but they turned the ball over six times; five times on interceptions, one of which was returned 52 yards for a TD by J.C. Caroline. It was not a good day for Green Bay.

The Packers (2-5) were beginning to look forward to '57, although they still had a mathematical chance of winning the division. All the Packers had to do was win all five of their remaining games, while the Bears and Lions (both 6-1-0) beat each other once and lost the rest of their games. This was really likely to happen, right? The Colts (3-3) had a better chance at overtaking the leaders, while LA (2-5) had as much chance as the Packers and Frisco (1-6) had no chance at all. The Giants (6-1) finally took control of the Eastern Division by beating the Cardinals (5-2). Washington (3-3) stayed in the race, and Philadelphia (3-4) had a prayer left. But the Browns and Steelers (2-5) were pretty much out of it now.

Blackbourn appeared to be throwing in the towel as he put tackle Don King on waivers the week before the Bear game, then dumped Breezy Reid and Jim Capuzzi after the Chicago fiasco. The players hired to replace these guys were hardly better than warm bodies. Furthermore, Liz penciled in the name of Bart Starr as the starting quarterback for the next game, which was against the 49ers in Green Bay. He had intended to start Starr in the first Baltimore game, but when the Packers recovered the kickoff on the Colts' 11, he changed his mind and went with Rote who had his best game of the year.

The 49er game was the last regular season NFL contest played in old City Stadium, and it was George Whitney Calhoun Day. Calhoun was the man who provided press coverage for the Green Bay town teams of the second decade of the 20th Century and kept them going year-to-year until a kid named Curly Lambeau decided to quit college and play football at home. He joined Lambeau as an owner, officer, and director of the corporation that ran the 1922 Packers, and he helped form the next corporation that began operating the Packers in 1923. He served as secretary of that corporation until 1940, then gave up the post to concentrate on his duties as publicity director, a job he'd been doing since before Lambeau came into the picture and which he lost when Lambeau fired him in 1946. It was more than fitting that Calhoun should be honored at this game. Like City Stadium, his best days were behind him, but the memories—Oh, the memories! If not for Cal, the Packers would never have been anything more than a town team.

Everybody wanted the Packers to close out the old park with a win. Everybody except the last place 49ers. Starr's first possession was a miserable failure as the Packers lost seven yards, but his second ended with success when he hit Billy Howton with a 39-yard scoring strike. He had the team on the move on their next possession, but he floated a pass in the end zone that was picked off to end the threat. Cone, who missed the PAT after the TD, booted a field goal on the next drive to give Green Bay the lead, 9-0. The 49ers then scored the next 17 points. The Packers, behind Rote, carne back in the final stanza to draw within one at 17-16, but from that point on it was butter fingers, butter fingers, butter fingers for the Packers. First, Carmichael fumbled a punt with 6:11 left, and the 49ers recovered it. Second, Ferguson fumbled on the Frisco 22 with 2:12 left, and the 49ers recovered it. Then Rote fumbled away the ball with 31 seconds left on the Packer 37, and the game ended sadly for the 17,906 loyal fans who turned out for this historic occasion.

The Packers (2-6-0) were now in the cellar, and although they would win two more games, that was where they ended up in 1956. The irony of the season was that they played the Lions in Detroit on

Thanksgiving Day and slipped by them, 24-20, to drive a wooden stake into the heart of Detroit's title hopes for the year, then they did the same thing to the Cardinals in Chicago, winning, 24-21. They had a chance at breaking even again, but they played poorly on the West Coast and wound up 4-8-0, a two steps backward from the year before.

The Bears won the Western Division by a half game over the Lions, and the Giants copped the Eastern crown. The two division winners played each other during the regular season, and it ended in a tie, 17-17, setting up a rematch for the NFL championship in New York It was no contest as the Giants had everything their way, 47-7, to take the title for the last time until the '80s.

For the Packers, the '56 season brought some more talent into the nucleus that chief talent scout Jack Vainisi was building. Howton, Dillon, Teteak, and Hanner in '52; Carmichael, Forester, and Ringo in '53; McGee in '54; Bettis and Borden in '55; and Gregg, Skoronski, Gremminger, and Starr in '56. What was it Paul Christman had said about building a winner? A championship team needed 18-22 really good pros, stars, and superstars. These guys and a few others obtained in trades made up a solid nucleus. Another good draft, maybe two, and who could say what heights the Packers could scale?

§§§

13

The New City Stadium

In early 1954, a letter addressed to the Packers and the city of Green Bay from the Sullivan-Wallen American Legion Post in Green Bay and printed in the *Press-Gazette* recommended that some consideration be given to construction of a new stadium and suggested that rental fees from each game be placed in a trust fund and used to build onto the stadium in later years as the need would arise. This was the first official thought given to building a new playing facility.

Art Daley wrote a story about the need for a new stadium and what it would take to get one. He listed three things that had to happen before Green Bay could get another playground for its Packers.

(1) Winning seasons or the right kind of team.

(2) Sellout crowds at games in City Stadium.

(3) Milwaukee outdrawing Green Bay to the extent that other teams will put pressure on the Packers to play in Milwaukee rather than in Green Bay.

Thing No. 1 is an absolute must because if the Packers have a winner that will draw tremendously on the road—due to their natural small-town appeal and their power on the field... Drawing on the road would skyrocket the club's finances since it would easily wipe out the tremendous expense of traveling. Large crowds at home, drawn by that must—a good team—would thicken the stadium-building gravy.

Thing No. 2 represents the above-mentioned Joe Phan. He must demonstrate the need for a larger stadium in Green Bay. With few exceptions, the fans annually leave a number of empty seats during league games.

Last fall, for instance, only one game in City Stadium was a sellout—24,835 at the Bear go. The Detroit test drew 20,834, and Baltimore pulled in 18,713. These figures do not show a need for a new and larger stadium.

Thing No. 3 is the key ...

Every year...George Halas of the Bears puts pressure on the Packers to move his game to Milwaukee. Halas figures the Packers owe him something for the large checks they've been hauling out of Wrigley Field every fall. He wants to get a few of those checks back out of the spacious Milwaukee stadium.

Daley pointed out that other teams were also putting pressure on the Packers to move their games to Milwaukee in order to get a bigger payout from the gate and to avoid the extra expense of traveling to Green Bay. These clubs had a legitimate gripe, and the Packers knew it. Daley's article made sense, and the fans knew it. The move for a new stadium was now underway.

In June, the Green Bay city council plunked down $500 for an eight-month option on a 40-acre tract on the city's west side located between Military Avenue and Platten Street and bordered on the south by Boland Road. The owner of this land was Mrs. George Morrow who stated she was willing to accept a down payment of $30,000 and the balance of $28,000 to be paid to her over 25 years at 4% or 4.5% interest. The council's original thoughts were to offer Mrs. Morrow a $2,000 option for six months, but they opted for the longer term at less money because they wanted to give the state legislature time to pass a bill that would allow the Brown County government to become involved in the project.

Adding spice to the stadium project was the will of Dr. Clarence Delmarcelle. City Attorney Clarence Nier reported that the stadium could be financed in part by the late doctor's estate. Delmarcelle's will stated that the city was to receive the residue of his estate after all the beneficiaries were deceased and further stated that construction of a new stadium on the city's west side had to begin within one year after the demise of the last beneficiary. Nier reported that the beneficiaries ranged in age from 55 to 76 years old and that the city's share of the estate stood at $235,901.46 as of that day, June 14, 1954.

With the off-season after the '54 campaign came more talk about a new stadium for the Packers or at least a renovation of the present City Stadium. In January 1955, Russ Bogda submitted a report to the Green Bay City Park Board stating the Packers would participate in the expense of a feasibility study on the expansion of City Stadium seating to 30,000 or even 32,000. The Packers even offered to help pay for the additional seats out of ticket sales. Bogda's report pointed out how some NFL opponent's preferred playing in Milwaukee over Green Bay for two reasons: larger seating capacity at Milwaukee County Stadium and lower travel costs to the Cream City. Although the report didn't say so, George Halas wanted to play the Packers in Milwaukee instead of Green Bay because more Chicago fans could attend the game and that meant more money for both teams. Of course, the fans in Green Bay would never permit that to happen. The answer was a new stadium or at the very least a renovated old City Stadium.

The Green Bay City Council took Bogda's report under consideration, and Mayor Dominic Olejniczak, also a member of the executive committee, invited Bogda and the rest of the executive committee to attend a January 17 meeting of the council where the council intended to discuss the feasibility of replacing the wooden seats at City Stadium with steel seats and expanding capacity to 30,000-32,000. Olejniczak stated that the increased seating plan would help the Packers at the NFL scheduling meeting on January 27, meaning league opponents might be more receptive to playing in Green Bay during the coming season.

The January 17 council meeting resulted in the hiring of an architect to prepare plans and make a cost estimate of expanding the current City Stadium and replacing the old wooden benches with steel ones. Bogda told the council that renovating the old stadium was a better choice fiscally. "The big need is for added seats," he said. The reasons? "First, because we think we can fill them and, second, because it is increasingly difficult to schedule games here." His report stated City Stadium's 25,000 capacity limit compared with Milwaukee County Stadium put the club at a considerable handicap in scheduling games in Green Bay and the situation was becoming "more embarrassing as time goes by. For example, there isn't any question that 42,000 seats would be sold if the Bear game were played in Milwaukee or that the same would be true if Green Bay had that many seats."

Adding fuel to Bogda's fire, Building Inspector Al Manders said that maintenance costs of the present wooden stadium were increasing and "the time for replacing two-thirds of the stadium isn't too far off."

The only opposition to the council's action was voiced by Alderman Leonard Jahn who advocated a new stadium at the Military Avenue and Boland Road site, which the council ordered bought for a future park or arena. Jahn called the enlarging of City Stadium "near sighted" and predicted that the present stadium could never be expanded above 35,000 seats if the need should arise. He said the people of Green Bay would rather see a new stadium with plenty of parking space and asked if the Packers had considered the parking factor in their report.

Bogda replied with a lot of possibilities, such as parking on the sites of older homes in the area, constructing a foot bridge across the East River from a park on the eastern bank, and the probability that the University Extension Center might move from its present Baird Street location making it available for parking.

Alderman Robert Bittner labeled Jahn's criticism as "unfair" in the light of the complete report from the Packers which he said considered all factors. Evidently, Mr. Bittner knew where to put his lips.

The architecture firm that the city hired was Foeller, Schober, Berners, Safford, and Jahn. Ed Berners presented two plans to the

Green Bay board of education in August; one with a track running around the field and one without. The board approved the plan with the track because City Stadium was located at East High School and the young athletes of Green Bay would still need a running course for track in the spring. The new seating capacity would be increased to approximately 32,000, and this pleased the Packers, although Fred Leicht, chair of the stadium committee, said the corporation preferred the plan without the track. Leicht described the proposed new stadium as the best in professional football because of all the sideline seats, over 22,000, but he seemed to forget that the Rams played in the Los Angeles Coliseum, which had more than 40,000 seats on its sidelines.

A couple of weeks later Alderman Jahn made a report on the proposed renovation of City Stadium to the Green Bay Traffic Commission, and he received instant backing for his opposition to the project. Jahn read Green Bay's General Ordinance Number 30-54, part of which read:

No stadium, ball park, or other sports arena shall be constructed unless one parking space is provided for every five seats in the stadium. Said parking area or any portion thereof shall not be more than 800 feet to the nearest corner of the property on which the place of assembly (stadium) is located.

City attorney Clarence Nier said a determination would have to be made whether the city government's functions would be bound by the ordinance and whether the City Stadium improvement would be classified as a new structure subject to the ordinance.

The new stadium advocates countered with another part of the ordinance that supported their case. The clause provided for capacity increases in current assembly sites, stating that if parking potential should be increased by 15% the requirements of the ordinance become effective. Adding 7,000 new seats would require 1,400 new parking spaces, an increase of 28%.

Taking this into account, commission chairman Charles McFarland said:

"We should tell the council that we consider it definitely out of line to spend thousands and thousands of dollars on a new stadium at the present site when there is no chance in the world of improving the traffic and parking situation out there."

Jahn continued his salvo by pointing out all the positives for building a new stadium at the Military Avenue and Boland Road site, now called E.J. Perkins Park. He remarked on costs of construction and the accessibility of the locality to automobile traffic. He presented numbers to support the former line argument, and Lt. Harry Bultman of the Green Bay Police Department Traffic Division agreed with the latter when he offered his opinions as well as some facts on the controversy. "It goes without saying that the job of the police department would be even tougher than it is now," said Bultman.

More than a month passed before the Green Bay City Council hired architect John Somerville to do a cost study comparing the expense of renovating old City Stadium and building a new one at Perkins Park. Somerville carne up with a figure of $960,000 for a new stadium, which wasn't much more than the cost of remodeling the old stadium at East High. His study swung a majority of people to Jahn's side of the argument for a new stadium.

In January 1956, Curly Lambeau put in his two cents about the stadium situation in Green Bay. His observations made some good sense, which made them suspect by many people of the area. Born and raised on the east side of Green Bay, having attended East High School, and having played and coached the Packers in stadiums that were all located on the east side of the Fox River, it would only be natural for Lambeau to favor remodeling City Stadium, but he took the opposite stance. "That super highway is a temptation for fans in Milwaukee, south of there, and in the valley to come (here)," he said. "Same for fans coming from north and west (of here)." In other words, placing a new stadium on the west side near U.S. Highway 41 would make it more accessible to out of town fans. Practical and wise—and from Lambeau! What a shock!

In March, the ball rolling toward the construction of a new stadium was given a little more momentum with the formation of a group called "Citizens Committee for the Stadium" or CCFTS as Art Daley tagged it in the *Press-Gazette*. Heading up this bunch were Tony

Canadeo and Jerry Atkinson, and actively supporting the movement for a new stadium were Green Bay's new mayor, Otto Rachals, and former mayor and current corporation vice-president Dominic Olejniczak. At the heart of their immediate efforts was the bond issue that would be on the April 3 ballot. If approved by the voters, Green Bay—and the Packers would soon begin building a new City Stadium. They presented the argument that it would only cost each citizen of Green Bay 50 cents a year for the next 20 years to pay for the new stadium. This was based on the cost to the city of $600,000, including the interest on the bonds over that time period, divided by an average population of 60,000 over the next two decades. Put in those terms, the stadium was a real bargain.

Art Daley did his part to support the drive for a new stadium. He wrote a series of articles on the history of the Packers, and for the most part, he told the story in very general terms, hitting the highlights and avoiding the less savory moments completely. When he did get specific, he more often than not had the wrong information, such as when he perpetuated the myth that Lambeau founded the Packers all by himself. Some founder! Young Curly failed to show up at the very first organizational meeting back in 1919, a fact overlooked by Daley in his story on the so-called founding meeting. By the way, Nate Abrams, the guy who started and ran the town team the year before in 1918, did attend the first meeting of the town team in 1919 and there is reason to believe that he organized the meeting in the first place.

The outside world took notice of the upcoming election in Green Bay. *Associated Press* writer Chuck Capaldo wrote:

> The future of the Green Bay Packers' unique, 37-year relationship with this city of 50,000 hinges on a referendum on the April 3 ballot.
>
> Voters will be asked whether the city—smallest of the ten with the National Football League franchises-should float a $960,000 bond issue to finance a new stadium for use by the Packers and the city's schools.
>
> But, one fact is sure. If the question doesn't win voter approval the Packers will pull up stakes within the next few years and

move elsewhere. Possible future sites of the club include Milwaukee, Buffalo, N.Y., and Miami, Fla., and Minneapolis.

Except for the fact that the NFL was located in 11 cities, not just 10, Capaldo hit the nail on the head. No stadium, no Packers in Green Bay. That was the bottom line. Richard McFarland of *United Press International* quoted Mayor Rachals as saying:

"A victory is vital to keeping the Packers in Green Bay." [Author's italics.]

Holy flyin' footballs, Batman! This stadium thing was getting serious. More serious than many people thought in the beginning. Thus. the reason for mentioning publicly in the newspapers that Green Bay was in danger of losing the Packers if the voters turned down the bond issue. This was no scare tactic to pressure the voters. This was for real. Many NFL owners wanted the franchise moved to a bigger city with a bigger stadium, and some of them who could see past today wanted it in a bigger television market. This called for drastic measures.

A few days before the election the CCFTS called out three big guns to speak at a rally supporting the bond issue. With Tony Canadeo acting as master of ceremonies, Curly Lambeau, Johnny (Blood) McNally. and none other than George Halas spoke to an audience of nearly 1,000 people gathered at the Columbus Club in Green Bay. Each of them was quoted in the *Press-Gazette.*

> Lambeau: "The Packer franchise could be sold for a million dollars in 24 hours."

> Halas: "Buffalo is ready to double-deck its 32,000 (seat) stadium at a cost of a million dollars if it can get a franchise."

> McNally: "Minneapolis is ready, willing, and able to take over the Packer franchise. Minneapolis is just finishing a new stadium."

Translation: If you don't vote YES on Tuesday, say good-bye to the Packers on Wednesday. The day before the election Verne Lewellen addressed the local Kiwanis Club luncheon, and he made a prediction. He said:

> "I firmly believe the golden era is going to be in the 1960's."

[Author's italics.]

Now that's a real prognostication. Maybe it was only wishful thinking, but Lewellen explained his thoughts by predicting crowds of 35,000-45,000 and television audiences of 50 million and more. This was a positive attitude that hadn't been shown all that well up until this moment. Possibly, Lewellen's rosy painting of the future had an influence on the voters because when all the ballots were counted the bond issue passed by more than a two-to-one margin. Green Bay would have a new stadium, and the Packers would remain where they belonged—forever!

Now that the money was guaranteed the Packers engaged the Osborn Engineering Company of Cleveland to make a complete survey and report on the best site for a new city stadium in Green Bay. This move was not exactly within the purview of the corporation; this function belonged to the city council. Bogda stated:

> Since this new stadium is so important to the future of the Packers here, and since we are paying for half of it, we feel it is absolutely essential that all of the facts regarding the location of the stadium should be developed and studied. The Osborn company is recognized as the top authority in the nation on stadium matters, and we feel that a complete study by an independent firm of this type is a must. None of us on the executive committee are experts in this field and we want the advice of the best experts in the country when we are going to spend this kind of money.

Osborn Engineering was the same firm that had done the study and made the selection for Milwaukee County Stadium. The company's other credits included work for Notre Dame, Purdue, Indiana University, the University of Michigan, the University of Minnesota, Municipal Stadium in Cleveland, the Rubber Bowl in Akron, Yankee Stadium, Briggs Stadium in Detroit, the Polo Grounds, Griffith Stadium in Washington, and several others. In other words, their credentials were impeccable.

On July 10, 1956, the Osborn company reported to the city council that Green Bay's new stadium should be built at the southeast corner of Highland Avenue and Ridge Road, part of Ashwaubenon. This stunned just about everybody in Green Bay, especially the proponents of building the new stadium in Perkins Park. The firm also reported that parking space there would cost less than at either old City Stadium or Perkins Park. The figures also favored the new site. The cost of a new stadium with 20,000 permanent seats and 12,000 bleacher seats would be $947,000 at the Highland-Ridge location, $986,000 at Perkins Park, and $1,017,000 for rebuilding City Stadium. In addition to the cost of the stadium, the land had to be purchased and the amount necessary for parking had to be added. The land and parking at the Highland-Ridge site would be $79,500 and $50,000 for a total of $129,500. To provide enough parking at Perkins Park, another $175,000 would be needed, and the land would cost yet another $75,000. The additional land needed for sufficient parking at old City Stadium wasn't included because it was felt that renovation of the stadium was no longer a viable alternative.

Besides the dollars and cents, the report listed the advantages and disadvantages for all three sites.

City Stadium

Advantages: Land city-owned with field and track already installed; nearness for use by East High School; and convenience to downtown civic events.

Disadvantages: Poor foundation with resulting higher costs and hazardous to present high school building which adjoins the new work; extremely limited opportunity for off-street parking; restricted access from out of town because of narrow streets and few main traffic arteries; and little or no space for future stadium expansion.

Perkins Park

Advantages: Land city owned and cleared; adequate parking area could be purchased; favorable topography and foundation; and ample expansion space.

Disadvantages: Limited access to present through streets and silty soil surface requiring added costs for surfacing parking area.

Highland-Ridge Site

Advantages: Good soil; good topography; good access to major highway and through streets; no additional costs to provide parking space.

Disadvantages: Land privately owned, and all construction would be from scratch.

Only the two aldermen who represented districts near the current City Stadium raised objections to the report. Alderman Rhynie Dantinne questioned whether the Osborn report was in keeping with a location near the population center of Green Bay, and he revived the subject of building a foot bridge across the East River to be used by fans who parked on the east side of the river. Dantinne and Alderman Clarence Vandermus were clearly thinking of their own political futures rather than the future of Green Bay and the Packers.

When the city council voted on the Osborn report the following week, only seven of the 24 aldermen voted against the Highland-Ridge location. They were Tim De Wane, Eddie Bodart, Clarence Vandermus, Rhynie Dantinne, Clarence Deschamps, Robert Baye, and Don Tilleman. All of these men represented districts east of the Fox River, and all of them put their own constituencies ahead of the good of the city. This was the typical thinking of the common political hack.

Besides approving the site, the council voted the same way on four-step proposal by Mayor Rachals before construction could begin.

1. Purchase of the 53-acre site on a three-year term basis with a down payment of $26,000 to be advanced by the Packer corporation as part of its pledge to pay half the $960,000 bond issue over 20 years.

2. Directing the Board of Public Works to pick an architect to draw stadium plans with alternatives to make as certain as possible that total cost would fall within the bond issue.

3. Instructing the city attorney to start work toward sale of the $960,000 bond issue approved in the April referendum.

4. Obtaining a contract with the Packers for its half of the bond issue to pledge the corporation's assets to the fullest extent legally possible.

In October, the city council voted to pay $70,000 for the excavating that was necessary to shape the site into a bowl. This move allowed the construction of the stadium to begin before the bond issue was completed. The city Department of Public Works would do the job for much less than the lowest bid submitted by a private contractor. The earth movers began their task on October 11, 1956, and hoped to be done before the frost set in.

Although the excavating went along smoothly, the money situation didn't. The architect, John Somerville, told the stadium planning committee that his current (October 25) estimate for the stadium, after dropping alternatives from his plans, was about $995,000, a good $35, 000 over the bond issue approved in the April election. If the stadium was to be built with all the construction hoped for in the tentative drawings, the total cost would be $228,000 over the bond limit, but Somerville had come up with alternatives that would lower that amount by $193,400. The largest and most important of Somerville's alternatives was changing the seating from 24,000 permanent seats and 8,000 bleacher seats to 20,000 permanent seats and 12,000 bleacher seats as was originally proposed. The real kicker was the work and materials needed for the parking area. This cost was not included in Somerville's estimate. This was a real snag.

The city council voted to accept Somerville's proposal to cut permanent seating to 20,734 and increase the bleacher seats to approximately 12,000. Also, they chose to reduce the size of the proposed press box and make some building materials changes in the other structures which would reduce costs. By the time all these cuts were made, the total price for the new stadium stood at $939,200. With the figures now fitting the budget, target dates for the finished construction plans and the opening of bids were set. The former was December 1, and the latter was January 1, 1957.

By January 21, 1957, all the bids had been received, and much to the City Council's delight, all of them came in under the amount allotted for the construction of the new stadium. The question remained whether the new facility would have 32,026 permanent seat of steel construction or 23,490 permanent seats of concrete construction and 9,792 bleacher seats made of wood and steel.

A week later the contract to build the new stadium was awarded to George Hougard and Son, Inc., of Green Bay. The deal included a completion date of September 15, 1957, just in time for the Bears and Packers to open the '57 playing season. The final plan called for 32,026 permanent seats of concrete construction at a cost of $742,039. Each sideline would have 11,745 seats in 25 rows, while the end zones would each have 4,268 seats in 21 rows. Building all the seats with steel or making only the sideline seats permanent with concrete and the end zone seats with wood and steel would have been cheaper, but delivery of the steel needed for the job couldn't be guaranteed in time to assure the completion date of September 15. Thus, the City Council opted to go with all concrete seating. It proved to be a wise decision.

The following week the Green Bay Packers, Inc., and the City of Green Bay agreed to a 21-year lease of the new stadium that called for the Packers to pay the city $30,000 a year. This was how the Packers would pay for their half of the construction costs, and as a bonus, the Packers were given an option of continuing the lease for another 10 years under the same terms. This was a real deal for the Packers.

Now the problem of parking. The county government had the idea of making a single parking lot for the new stadium and the new arena that was being built across Oneida Street. The county gave up land to make this possible, and that more or less removed the question marks about parking space. Now all they had to do was pay for it. To do that, the city borrowed $150,000 from local banks.

With construction well begun by the fourth week of March, a dedication date of September 29 was announced by Tony Canadeo and Jerry Atkinson, designated by Mayor Rachals as co-chairmen of a citizens dedication committee. This was quite appropriate because the

Packers would be opening the '57 campaign that day against their archrival, the hated Chicago Bears.

In April, the City Council created a five-seat commission to administer the stadium. The president of this body was Clarence Nier, the city attorney, Ronald McDonald was made vice-president, and Fred Leicht from the Packer corporation was designated secretary. The other two commissioners were Jerome Quinn and Robert Baye, Green Bay aldermen.

In May, the construction moved into a new phase right on schedule. The contractor would begin erecting the steel beams that were to hold up the seats above the ground, starting with the west side of the stadium. At the same time, the team building, i.e., locker room, offices, visitors dressing room, would be started. The playing field was now dry enough to begin the laying of sod, and the sideline areas would be seeded as soon as the gridiron was completed.

Everything seemed to be going well until the carpenters went on strike when the contract between the Carpenters Local No. 1146 and the Fox River Valley Construction Association expired on the first of June. Hoping for a quick settlement, the carpenters placed no pickets around the stadium construction site, which allowed the other unions to continue their work there, but contractor George Hougard stated unequivocally that it wouldn't be long until the other workers would have to stop work as well until the carpenters returned to the job. He was right. Within two weeks, the rest of the men working on the stadium could go no further with their tasks without the carpenters.

Hougard sat squarely on the horns of a dilemma. His company was a member of the Fox River Valley Construction Association, and he could do nothing unilaterally without suffering the wrath of his fellow contractors. On the other hand, he had a deadline to meet with the construction of the stadium. To delay the job beyond the two weeks that had already lapsed would put the completion date in serious jeopardy. Fortunately, he had anticipated the strike and had set up his construction schedule to have the stadium completed by September 1 instead of the September 15 deadline as the contract stipulated. Hougard could ride with the FRVCA and risk finishing the stadium after the deadline or he could buck the system and make his own deal with the union.

Hougard did what was best for everyone involved except his fellow contractors. He signed a separate agreement with the union, agreeing to pay the carpenters 25 cents an hour more, and the carpenters went back to work on June 17. For doing the right thing, Hougard was ousted from the Green Bay Building Trades Employers Association by his fellow contractors.

The rest of the contractors settled with the union a week later, agreeing to a raise of 50 cents an hour which was spread out over three years: 20 cents the first year and 15 cents an hour for the second and third years. The deal Hougard cut with the carpenters was better for them, so he stuck to it. This was an honorable man building the new stadium.

As part of the overall change in playing venue for the Packers, a new practice facility was platted across Oneida Street from the new stadium. The Packers began practicing there on September 17, 1957, which marked the first time in the history of professional football in Green Bay, whether as the Packers or the town team that preceded them, that the local heroes practiced or played on the west side of the Fox River in Green Bay. To those people who failed to recognize how Green Bay had become a small metropolis by this time, the move was as momentous as the Brooklyn Dodgers and New York Giants moving their franchises to the West Coast later that year.

The stadium was finally completed and in time for the opening of the 1957 season. A whole celebration was planned to mark the event, and Mother Nature co-operated with near perfect early autumn weather.

A parade began at Ashland Avenue and West Walnut and proceeded to old City Stadium where television actor James Arness, who portrayed Marshal Matt Dillon in the TV series *Gunsmoke,* and Miss America, Marilyn Elaine Van Derbur, were entertaining the crowd waiting there. The procession consisted of six marching sections, each with bands, variety acts, and interspersed with 35 floats for the occasion. The ceremonies at the old stadium concluded with the lowering of the flag to mark the end of professional football there. Then a Venetian Night with spectacular fireworks and a flotilla of lighted boats on the Fox River illumined the evening. The crowds were estimated at 70,000 for the parade; 18,000 for the festivities at the old stadium; and another 15,000 for the Venetian Night.

Before the game on Sunday, Green Bay's mayor, Otto Rachals, opened the ceremonies with a dedication speech. Then he introduced members of the City Council, City Attorney Clarence Nier, City Engineer F. J. Euclide, and Roman Denissen, his 1957 mayoralty opponent and former Council president. Rachals paid tribute to the late First Ward Alderman Harold Reynolds, and he praised architect John Somerville and contractor George Hougard. Nier, as Stadium Commission president. took a turn speaking, then a brief prayer was offered by the Reverend Anselm Keefe. The Packer Band then played the National Anthem as the flag was raised over the stadium to begin a new era in Packer football history. At halftime, Wisconsin Governor Vernon W. Thomson was the first speaker. In turn, he was followed by Congressman John Byrnes, NFL Commissioner Bert Bell, George Halas, and Vice-President Richard M. Nixon. Master of ceremonies Dominic Olejniczak read a telegram from Curly Lambeau, and he introduced Gene Ronzani and Marilyn Van Derbur.

To cap off a perfect weekend, the Packers showed their appreciation for the new plant, which was considered to be the best in the NFL at the time and in decades to come. Of the 12 teams in the league in 1957, Green Bay had the only stadium that was strictly an arena for football. Every other team played in a baseball park or a stadium that was constructed for track and field events, such as the Los Angeles Coliseum. The Packers played in the smallest town in the league, but on the best field. Incredible! But that was Green Bay.

§§§

216

14

The Bonus Pick
Wasn't Enough

Finally, the Packers won the lottery for the Bonus Pick. It was
only the 11th year of the Draft gimmick.

The NFL once again began the next season while the current
season was still in progress. In order to discourage the Canadian
Football League from signing star players from the U.S., the NFL held
the first four rounds of the '57 Draft on November 26, 1956. It started
with Liz Blackbourn drawing the right slip out of Commissioner Bert
Bell's hat which gave the Bonus Pick to the Packers, and the Green
Bay coach wasted no time in saying the name of his choice: Paul
Hornung, quarterback, Notre Dame. Said Blackbourn of Hornung:

> "He has the greatest potential of all Notre Dame backs. He is
> a great natural athlete, a tremendous competitor, has great
> speed and will stand the type of punishment dealt out in the
> league. He's a good punter, kick-off man, field goal and extra
> point kicker and an outstanding defensive back. He has
> wonderful poise and we believe in one year he will become an
> excellent passer. He also is quite versatile and can be used as a

218

fullback, halfback or quarterback. Hornung is the Tobin Rote type of back and he'll fit into the Green Bay pattern nicely."

Blackbourn stopped short of saying that Hornung was the greatest all-around football player since Jim Thorpe. After the build-up Blackbourn gave Hornung, few superlatives were left for the man he chose in the regular first round of the draft, but the *Associated Press* writer found a few to describe Ron Kramer, the big, muscular end from Michigan. Kramer made every All-America team in the country. He played both offensive end as well defensive end, linebacker, fullback, and halfback. Big, fast, and strong, he had a reputation for being exceptionally rough. He was an excellent receiver and blocker.

This was a good year for finding college talent. After the Packers took Hornung, the Rams picked USC halfback Jon Arnett and the 49ers chose Stanford quarterback John Brodie. Then after Green Bay won the coin toss from Pittsburgh and Cleveland for the third slot and Blackbourn took Kramer, the Steelers tabbed Purdue quarterback Len Dawson, the Browns selected Syracuse fullback Jim Brown, the Eagles went for Michigan State halfback Clarence Peaks, the Colts picked Ohio State guard Jim Parker, the Redskins chose Miami fullback Don Bosseler, the Cardinals drafted Oklahoma linebacker Jerry Tubbs, the Giants took Baylor halfback Del Shofuer, the Lions opted for Baylor guard Bill Glass, and the Bears selected LSU tackle Earl Leggett. Every one of these players starred in the NFL or AFL, played at least eight years, and several of them are in the Pro Football Hall of Fame. It was a very good year for collegiate football talent.

As if little Green Bay wasn't paranoid enough, Daley began writing stories that gave credence to rumors that Hornung might not sign with the Packers. Every little bit of gossip that Hornung might go to Canada to play or that he might demand to be traded right away to another team in the NFL made it into the *Press-Gazette*. A story about him wanting to play for a warm weather team even surfaced. Tough trick back in '57 because the only real warm weather team was the Los Angeles Rams, although the 49ers, Colts, and Redskins played in decent weather most of the season.

Hornung repeatedly denied wishing to go anywhere else except Green Bay. He understood that only the Packers had the right to sign him to an NFL contract and if he didn't sign with them that his only alternatives were to sit out of football or sign with a Canadian team. Since Canada is colder than Wisconsin, the latter was never a real option for Hornung. The Golden Boy from Notre Dame said he would sign with the Packers, and that was that.

The Packers lost their second-round choice, Joel Wells, a halfback out of Clemson, to the Montreal Alouettes of the Canadian Football League. This was a big blow to Blackbourn's plans for '57. Green Bay needed a real halfback to run the ball, not just catch it. Jack Losch, the Number One choice in '56, was a good runner in the open field, but he wasn't a slasher or crasher at the line. Throw him the ball, and he could do just fine. Punt the ball to him and watch him go. But hit the line? He simply did not have what it takes to break through a bunch of burly defensive linemen. The halfback situation was so bad in Green Bay that Tobin Rote had been the team's best ground gainer since he joined the team in 1950. He led the club in rushing three of his seven seasons with the Packers, and he outgained every halfback in all but his first year when Billy Grimes gained more yardage than he did. Only fullbacks Breezy Reid and Howie Ferguson outrushed Rote after that, and they only did it three times out of six. Now with Wells going north of the border, Blackbourn was giving more serious thought to making Hornung into a halfback.

The Packers third-round pick was Dalton Truax, a tackle out of Tulane, and offensive line coach Lou Rymkus scouted and signed the Packers fourth-round choice, Carl Vereen, a 6'6" tackle from Georgia Tech.

True to his word, Paul Hornung signed a contract with the Packers on Tuesday, January 8, 1957, and to show him their appreciation, the Green Bay brass gave him a three-year deal. At the time of the signing. Jim Finks, a former quarterback with the Steelers and then quarterback coach for Notre Dame, had something to say about Hornung.

"Hornung can do so many more...things than other football players, that the biggest trouble Green Bay will have is deciding where he will be needed most. If he doesn't make it as a quarterback. fullback or halfback, then the pro league has surely changed."

If there was ever a man who knew talent when he saw, it was Jim Finks. This was the same Jim Finks who helped build the Vikings into a dominating team during the 1970s and the same man who did the same thing for the Bears in the 1980s. Jim Finks knew his business.

Before the regular phase of the NFL Draft, Blackbourn rehired Tom Hearden to be his backfield coach, and he let Abe Stuber go. Evidently, Hearden wasn't happy playing second fiddle to Milt Bruhn at the University of Wisconsin, and the campus life in Madison didn't suit him and his family. Hearden said:

"Pro football gets in your blood, and you just never lose your desire to get back into it. I'm happy to be back in Green Bay, which is my home and where all my friends are. It's wonderful to be back with the Packer staff that is so ably handled by Liz."

That was the good news. The bad news? Tobin Rote made the announcement that he was retiring from pro football after the Pro Bowl in Los Angeles on January 13.

"I've got a head coach down in Texas," he said, "and she says she's not going to chase back and forth to Green Bay anymore. So I'm going to stay with her."

Translation: Rote and his wife were fed up with life in Green Bay, Wisconsin. Rote had seen what the fans, directors, and executive committee had done to his first coach, Gene Ronzani, and he had seen how some players were given the same kind of treatment. He had experienced some of it himself, especially after a game like the Frisco bash in the last game in old City Stadium when he fumbled the ball on the Pack's last chance to win the game. The real truth was Rote wanted out of Green Bay, and if he couldn't be traded, then he'd quit altogether. For now, he was retired from the Game.

To cover up Rote's defection, Art Daley wrote about Bob Garrett getting out of the Air Force and rejoining the Packers in '57. Remember Garrett? He was Cleveland's Bonus Pick in '54. The Browns traded him and three other nondescripts to the Packers for Babe Parilli and Bob Fleck, both of whom were entering the service in '54. The Packers got one year out of Garrett, but nothing more. The Browns got one season out of Parilli before they traded him back to the Packers, but that was later in the year. For now, the Packers had Garrett, and Daley was touting him as Rote's replacement.

Part-time assistant coach Earl Klapstein resigned just before the Draft to become athletic director and head football coach at Cerritos Junior College in Artesia, California. This reduced the Green Bay staff to the four men who ran the team in '54 and '55: Blackbourn, Hearden, Rymkus, and Scooter McLean.

Besides Garrett, several other Packer players and prospects were due to be discharged from active duty in time for the '57 season. They included Gene White, Jim Temp, Al Barry, Norm Amundsen, Tom Pagna, Max McGee, Gib Dawson, and Charley Grant. Real players or just more practice fodder? Time would tell.

Of course, the armed forces not only returneth players, but they also taketh away Packers. Scheduled to do their patriotic duty in '57 were Forrest Gregg, Bob Skoronski, Bart Starr, Jack Losch, and Hank Bullough. Fortunately, Starr received an early discharge from the Air Force due to the recurrence of an old back injury, and he was ready to play in '57.

More bad news. Guard Buddy Brown, tackle Jack Sandusky, and linebacker Deral Teteak called it quits, and linebacker Roger Zatkoff said the same thing. Brown, Sandusky, and Teteak meant it. Zatkoff merely wanted out of Green Bay the same as Rote did, and like Rote, he would retire if that's what it took. Brown was over 30 and figured he was over the hill, while Teteak and Sandusky took college coaching jobs with the University of Wisconsin and Villanova, respectively.

At the NFL winter meeting, the Packers drafted a lot of nobodies and two players who made the team in '57. The two who survived were

Ernie Danjean, a guard from Auburn, and Jolin Symank, a defensive back from Florida, who were picked 19th and 23rd, respectively.

The highlight of the confab in Philadelphia was the picketing by the Red Rooster Sports committee, a group made up of African-American fans and former athletes. They were protesting against George Preston Marshall, principal owner of the Washington Redskins. Harry Wismer, a 20% minority owner of the Redskins, had labeled Marshall a racial bigot by his refusal to sign or even draft African-American players. John H. Young, the director of the group based in New York, promised that picketing would continue throughout the year wherever the Redskins played games until Marshall changed his stance on African-Americans. Marshall stayed true to form by not drafting any African-American players, and to add insult to injury, the other owners passed a resolution unanimously recognizing Marshall for his 25 years of service to the league. This appeared to be tacit approval of his bigotry, when they were really saying that they might not agree with him on racial issues, but that Marshall could be a bigot if he wanted to be, that it was his right to employ who he wanted, that they supported his right to freedom of thought. As the French philosopher Voltaire put it:

> "I may not agree with what you say, but I will defend to the death your right to say it."

The owners ignored the picketing and went about their business.

In matters that really counted, the league raised the player limit to 60 for training camp and 35 for the regular season, ordered all visiting teams to wear white uniforms for the sake of television (which was almost all black-and-white back then), and agreed to extend the Bonus Pick for another 12 years after the Cardinals received theirs in '58. On the bad side of the ledger, they changed the injured list rule to deny a team from hiring a substitute for a player on the list. This was dumb, of course, but it wasn't as dumb as the owners refusing to recognize the newly formed players union. Or as dumb as George Halas saying the union's request for a pension plan "was ridiculous." The owners— and the fans—would suffer for this move in time, especially in light of the fact that the Supreme Court declared a few weeks later that the NFL was subject to anti-trust laws.

With the winter meetings and the NFL Draft out of the way, Blackbourn and his staff began gadding about the country to sign the college kids, and Verne Lewellen began the job of signing the veterans. The coaches wasted a lot of time and money in pursuit of the rookies, nearly all of whom would never be much more than blocking and tackling dummies for the veterans and the few first-year men who could make it in the NFL.

At the annual meeting of the Green Bay Packers, Inc., stockholders in March, Verne Lewellen reported that the corporation made an after-taxes profit of $28,683 in '56, compared to an after-taxes profit of $47,124 in '55. This was the result of a drop in ticket sales. The good news was the Packers had $142,993 in the bank.

Stockholders elected three new directors: David B. Smith of Wausau, Kenneth W. Haagensen of Oconomowoc, and Lawrence W. Pfeiffer of Green Bay. Then they re-elected directors Howard J. Bero, Russ Bogda, Bernard Darling, Louis J. Levitas, Dominic Olejniczak, A.A. Reimer, Clarence J. Renard, Ed Schuster, Erv Bushman, Richard S. Falk, and Don Hutson.

The board of directors re-elected the same officers and executive committee members that served the previous year.

Blackbourn was faced with a real problem of building a team for '57. With the losses of Gregg, Skoronski, and Bullough to armed forces and the retirements of Rote, Zatkoff, Teteak, and Brown, he already had to find seven new replacements. After Hornung and Kramer, the draft wasn't all that strong. That meant signing free agents and re-signing those veterans returning from the service.

The first man in the fold for '57 after Hornung and Vereen was Al Barry who signed in early February. Jim Temp and Norm Amundsen signed in March. Tobin Rote changed his mind about retirement and signed in April for more than $20,000, and this cleared the way for a major trade.

Back to the Parilli trade mentioned earlier.

Blackbourn sent Bobby Garrett back to Cleveland along with the disenchanted Roger Zatkoff who came out of "retirement" for the deal. Zatkoff eventually wound up in Detroit where he wanted to go in the first place, and Garrett gave up football in training camp to go into business. In return, the Packers received six players, five of whom stuck with the Packers. The top name coming to Green Bay was Babe Parilli, the man who went to Cleveland for Garrett in the first place. The others were John Petitbon, halfback, Notre Dame; Carlton Massey, end, Texas; Sam Palumbo, linebacker, Notre Dame; and Bill Kinard, halfback, Mississippi. This appeared to be an excellent swap for the Packers and a really bad move for the Browns who were rebuilding themselves. The Packers had plenty of talent at quarterback, which made Garrett very expendable, but Zatkoff was another story. With Deral Teteak truly retired, Zatkoff's departure left the linebacking chores to Tom Bettis and Bill Forester, and although these were two extremely talented players, the continuity and unity of the linebacking corps had been seriously disrupted. Also, Kinard and Petitbon would be competing for two of the defensive back jobs that were presently held by men who had been working together for the past two seasons. This was also disruptive to the defense as a whole.

Shortly after the deal with the Browns, Daley wrote in the *Press-Gazette* that Blackbourn "quieted a raft of rumors today about deals involving Packer quarterbacks, chiefly the aforementioned Parilli." Blackbourn said:

> "We're not going to trade any one of our quarterbacks unless we're real sure we can help the team. There are no trades now that are culminated."

Famous last words. Another trade was yet to come.

Bad news. Really terrible news. Tom Hearden suffered a stroke in the middle of May. He was paralyzed on the right side initially, but within two days, his condition was beginning to show signs of improvement. The question, of course, was: Would he be able to coach when the time came? Until the question could be answered unequivocally, Blackbourn did the right thing and kept Hearden on the payroll, but he still needed a field coach. He hired one for insurance.

225

Jack Morton was head coach at University of Toledo in '56. He played defensive end of the Bears in '45, the LA Dons in the AAC in '46, and the Buffalo Bills in the AAC in '47 and '48. After pro ball, he coached the line at DePauw University for three years, 1953-55.

Back to signings. Billy Howton inked his contract in May. So did Joe Skibinski, Bart Starr, Bobby Dillon, Larry Lauer, and Dick Deschaine, Jim Ringo, Fred Cone, Jerry Helluin, Tom Bettis, Bill Forester, Nate Borden, and Joe Johnson signed in June; and Howie Ferguson, Dave Hanner, John Martinkovic, Hank Gremminger, and Al Carmichael in July.

Now about that trade that was yet to come.

Blackbourn pulled off another spectacular deal in late July when he sent Rote and Val Joe Walker to the Lions for tackles Ollie Spencer and Norm Masters, guard Jim Salsbury, and halfback Don McIlhenny. Spencer, 26, the oldest of this quartet of newcomers, attended Kansas University and played for the Lions in '53 and '56 with the years between spent in the armed forces. Salsbury, 24, played college ball at UCLA before being drafted by the Lions in '55. Masters went to Michigan State and was chosen by the Cardinals in the '56 Draft, but instead of playing for Chicago, he opted to play in the Canadian Football League that year, which prompted the Cardinals to trade their rights to him to Detroit. McIlhenny came out of SMU in '56 and gained 372 yards in 83 carries in only half a season as a rookie.

In the two blockbuster trades, the Packers gave up three starters Rote, Walker, and Zatkoff—and a backup quarterback for nine regulars—Parilli, McIlhenny, Kinard, Petitbon, Palumbo, Massey, Salsbury, Masters, and Spencer—and one guy who never played for the Pack. Green Bay didn't just get numbers in these deals. The Packers received good, sound football players, and the outlook for the coming season seemed brighter than ever when training camp opened in late July.

Training camp didn't go all that well. Joe Skibinski suffered a broken leg in the first heavy scrimmage, and the injury ended his playing career. In the same practice, Blackbourn made a painful observation that his offense was far from being a well-oiled machine.

Later Bill Lucky and his wife were injured in an automobile accident, and his playing days were over. A trade for Len Szafaryn nearly fell through when Szafaryn balked at reporting to Philadelphia, preventing Ray "Bibbles" Bawel, the player the Packers received from the Eagles, from participating in practice until the erstwhile Szafaryn did check into the Philly camp. The delay hurt Bawel's conditioning, and he never made the team. The last bit of bad luck was Fred Cone breaking his wrist which limited him to placekicking only for a while.

Blackbourn's remark about the offense lagging behind the defense became apparent in the first exhibition game when the Packers met the Cardinals in Miami, Florida. The Pack won the game, 24-16, but the defense carried the day with Bobby Dillon intercepting two passes and running them back for touchdowns. The offense managed only nine first downs, and the three quarterbacks—Starr, Parilli, and Hornung could only complete 10 of 23 passes. Furthermore, several key Chicago players missed the game with the flu. Blackbourn was forced to admit the following week that the offense was two weeks behind schedule. This was not a good sign of things to come.

The Cardinals sparred with Green Bay again the next week, only this time in Austin, Texas, and the result was almost exactly the same as the first encounter. The Packers won, 17-14. on a pass interception by Bobby Dillon that he ran back 26 yards to set up the winning touchdown. And like the first week, the offense didn't do all that much as Liz remarked that "we weren't too sharp."

The third game was a repeat of the first two except the opponent and site were different; the Eagles in Milwaukee this time. The Packers won, 16-13, and the defense provided the offense when Bill Forester recovered a Philly fumble, pitched it to Sam Palumbo, and the new linebacker ran 42 yards with it for a score. The Packers earned six first downs and gained a meager 164 yards in total offense. Again. the offense was offensive, as in insulting, and Blackbourn said so.

Blackbourn wanted Hornung to play the entire first half against the Giants in the next game, but he was so ineffective at quarterback that the coach pulled him in the second quarter and replaced him with

Starr. The steady Starr rallied the Pack to a 13-10 victory, and the fans began crowing about a championship in Green Bay for '57.

The Packers defense rose to the occasion once again in the fifth pre-season contest as Green Bay downed the Redskins at Winston-Salem, North Carolina, 20-17. The Pack picked off four Washington passes, and Starr was seven for 10 and two touchdowns passing. Unfortunately, that was the extent of the offense as Green Bay made only 11 first downs.

Blackbourn traded big John Martinkovic to the New York Giants the following week in order to get down to the player limit. The Packers received a third round draft choice for the popular defensive end and local car salesman.

In their final tune up for the regular season, the Packers once again played meekly on offense and staunchly on defense. They held the Pittsburgh Steelers to 10 points and eight first downs, but the Pack could only score 10 points of their own. Green Bay did amass over 300 total yards, but they only proved that moving the ball up and down the field is meaningless without putting points on the board.

The schedule-makers finally did something right in '57. They slated the Bears to be the Packers' first opponent in their new stadium. On paper, the Monsters of the Midway, defending champs of the Western Division, appeared stronger than they had been in '56. Paddy Driscoll had virtually the same team as he'd had in '56 with the one major addition of speedy, slashing Willie Galimore, the rookie running back from Florida A&M. Driscoll showcased Galimore throughout the exhibition season, and the flashy halfback proved he could compete in the NFL on the superstar level. Now the Packers had to worry about one more weapon in the Chicago arsenal.

After all the foofaraw surrounding the dedication of the new stadium, the Packers and Bears got down to business on the field. A sellout crowd of 32,132 fans jammed the new stadium and wildly encouraged their team to overcome the ferocious Bears.

Bart Starr started at quarterback, and he completed the first pass thrown in the new City Stadium, connecting with Gary Knafelc for 24 yards. Starr threw the first interception when rookie Vic Zucco picked off a floater in the next series. Chicago, playing without Galimore, then drove 77 yards in nine plays late in the first quarter to score the first touchdown of the game, and it appeared that the Bruins would have little trouble putting the spirited Packers in their place. Green Bay was not to be taken so lightly, however, as Babe Parilli came in for Starr to finish a Green Bay drive of 70 yards and 10 plays to tie the game early in the second frame with a 37-yard scoring strike to Billy Howton. Starting on their own 28 after the ensuing kickoff, the Bears marched right up the field again in 10 plays of their own to score on an Ed Brown to Harlon Hill pass play of 11 yards. This was Hill's first touchdown against the Packers, and it gave the Bears the lead 14-7, with 11:05 left in the half. Again, the Pack bounced right back, going 59 yards in 10 plays with Fred Cone scoring from the one and kicking the PAT to tie the Bears with 6:46 left in the stanza. What appeared to be a shoot'em up affair suddenly turned into a defensive battle from that moment on. The Bears managed a George Blanda field goal in the third quarter, but the Packers failed to put any more points on the board until the final period when Parilli found Gary Knafelc for six yards and the end zone to put Green Bay ahead. The Bears fought back and were on the move when that sneak-thief Bobby Dillon swiped a Brown pass with 3:59 to go in the game. The Packers ran off some time before the Chicago defense forced them to punt with a minute and a half left. Dick Deschaine put his leg into it, and Perry Jeter waited under it. Larry Lauer, the former Bear, raced down field. Jeter fumbled the ball. Lauer recovered it. The Packers christened their new stadium with a glorious win, 21-17, and almost all of Packerdom went absolutely nuts.

All except one man. The coach. Blackbourn kept his head. The next day at his weekly luncheon with the executive committee he thanked them for the standing ovation that they gave him upon entering the room, then he told him the bad news. The team was too high emotionally; the players were in poor psychological condition to prepare them for the next game which, unfortunately, was against Detroit, the improved Lions who missed the division championship the previous year by a half-game.

The Bears had beaten the Lions in their final meeting the year before when big Ed Meadows, Chicago's mean defensive end, slammed Bobby Layne, Detroit's quarterback, into the ground with a very late hit that the officials didn't see and which put Layne out of the game. Layne was healthy again, and he was determined to get the Lions back into the title game in December. Putting pressure on Layne was Green Bay's number one quarterback for the past seven seasons; only Tobin Rote was now playing on the same team as Layne. This gave Detroit two of the best signal-callers in the NFL.

The Lions also had a new head coach. Raymond "Buddy" Parker, the man who had manned the helm for the past seven years, taking the Lions to the title game three straight years and winning it twice, quit just before the first game of the exhibition season. He addressed the Detroit Boosters banquet and said, "This team of ours has been the worst I've ever seen in training. I don't want to get involved in another losing season, so I'm leaving Detroit. As a matter of fact, I'm leaving tonight." He walked out, and assistant coach George Wilson was handed the reins. Wilson put some spirit in the team, and Detroit won five of their six pre-season games before losing their opener to Baltimore.

The day before the Lions and Packers squared off in Green Bay on the second Sunday of the season Art Daley wrote a prophetic opener to his pre-game story:

> The Lions are due to bounce back Sunday...The Packers probably can't bounce as high as they did last Sunday!

He was only right-again. In his post-game article, he wrote:

> The Packers are human after all...They can lose a game and they can look bad doing it!

Imagine that! Daley writing negatively about the Packers. Truthful, but still negative.

Detroit mounted a 24-0 lead in the fourth quarter, then Starr engineered on a scoring drive to close the gap to 17 points. Starr directed the Packers to another seven points on their next possession, but his third attempt to rally the team ended with an interception. Green Bay wound up on the short end of a 24-14 score, and Blackbourn said it was probably for the best that they lost this one.

"It may be the best thing that ever happened to us," he said. "I was afraid with the good breaks we were getting in the exhibition season that the roof was going to fall in on us one of these days."

Well, it did.

Next up: the Colts in Milwaukee. Johnny Unitas and Lenny Moore had a year of experience under their belts now, and the Baltimore defense was becoming a formidable unit. Coach Weeb Ewbank also had L.G. Dupre and Alan Ameche at his disposal, and Unitas had Ray Berry and Jim Mutscheler for targets. This was the best Baltimore team ever, and it was getting better every week.

The Packers held their own against this powerful team for the first 30 minutes, leading at the half, 10-7, on an eight-yard scoring pass from Starr to Knafelc. The second half was an entirely different matter as Unitas and Company went to work on the Packer secondary, racking up 38 points while holding Green Bay to a meaningless last-minute TD. Because the defense had played so well throughout the exhibition season and against the Bears and Lions, the 45-17 defeat at the hands of the Colts was a little hard for the fans of Packerdom to swallow, but the campaign was only a quarter of the way complete. They continued to hold out hope for a title in '57.

The only comforting fact for the fourth place Packers (1-2) at this point was the Bears (0-3) had yet to win a game. The Colts (3-0) sat atop the division all alone, and the Lions and 49ers (both 2-1) were in second. The Rams (1-2) shared the fourth spot with the Packers. In Eastern Division, the Browns (3-0) appeared to have returned to their old winning ways behind the rushing of rookie sensation Jim Brown. The Giants (2-1) shared second with the Steelers who now had Buddy Parker at their helm. The Cards and Redskins (both 1-2) held down fourth place, and the Eagles (0-3) brought up the rear.

Reality had begun to set in for the Packers. Their defense was above average, but their offense was at best adequate. Howton and Knafelc were as fine a pair of receivers as any in the league, but Parilli and Starr were below average as passers. Between them, they had completed 38 of 79 passes (Parilli 13 of 33 and Starr 25 of 46), but worse, they had each had six passes intercepted. The running game was practically non-existent as not one Packer rusher ranked in the top 15 in the league. Bobby Dillon did have four interceptions for second place in the NFL, and Dick Deschaine was the top punter with an average of 49.2 yards per kick.

To make matters worse, Knafelc suffered a knee injury in practice and had to undergo surgery to repair it, essentially ending his season. Max McGee was given the assignment to replace him, which wasn't all that bad except that McGee was still in the Air Force and couldn't practice with the team during the week. How effective could he be was anybody's guess as the Packers prepared to face the 49ers in Milwaukee.

San Francisco had three things going for them that season. Y.A. Tittle was still a topnotch quarterback; Hugh McElhenny was a superb runner; and R.C Owens was the tallest receiver in the league. Could the Packer rush get to Tittle? Not likely. Could the Packer defense stop McElhenny? To date, he had enjoyed his best days in the NFL rushing against the Packers. Was anybody in the Green Bay secondary tall enough to keep the ball out of Owens' hands? Not even close.

The defense held up again against Frisco, keeping the entire 49ers backfield to a total of 78 yards rushing and limiting Tittle to 166 yards through the air. Green Bay's offense managed to lose the game, however. The numbers were fine everywhere except the scoreboard. Green Bay gained 194 yards on the ground and 104 through the air, and the turnovers were even at four apiece. The 49ers scored first on a field goal, but the Packers came back to take the lead on a Parilli sneak. Then the 49ers reeled off 17 straight points to take a fourth quarter lead of 24-7. With the score at 17-7, the Packers had first-and-goal on the one. Four plays later they turned the ball over on downs from the same spot. This failure to get into the end zone crushed their spirit, allowing Frisco to ice the victory with their last touchdown. Paul Hornung got into the game at quarterback for the last series of plays, and he led the Pack down the field to score a meaningless six in the final seconds, taking the ball in himself on a nine-yard bootleg for his first NFL touchdown.

The loss dropped the Packers into the cellar with the Rams and Bears (all 1-3), while the 49ers climbed into a first place tie with the Colts and Lions (all 3-1). In the East, the Browns (3-1) lost to the Eagles (1-3); the Giants (3-1) beat the Steelers (2-2); and the Cardinals (2-2) defeated the Redskins (1-3).

The flu bug hit the Packers during the following week, forcing five regulars to miss some practice. If this wasn't bad enough, their next foe was the Colts in Baltimore, and another loss would just about put an end to Packerdom's hopes for a division title. Facing a do-or-die situation, the Packers rose to the occasion.

The week before the Colts blew a 17-point lead in the fourth quarter to the Lions and lost the game, 31-27. They entered the fourth quarter of their game against the Packers leading, 14-0, and a win seemed assured, considering Green Bay owned the league's poorest offense. But, Lo! and behold! Miracles do happen!

The Green Bay comeback started in the third quarter when Hank Gremminger intercepted a Unitas pass and returned it 28 yards to the Baltimore 10. Three plays later Hornung, playing fullback, belted through the line for the final three yards and paydirt to close the gap to 14-7. On fourth and goal at the Baltimore two on the Pack's next possession, Hornung found the end zone again to tie the game. Faced with the same situation only minutes later, Blackbourn called for a field goal try, and Cone split the uprights to put the Packers ahead, 17-14.

But Baltimore had Johnny Unitas calling the signals, and Mr. Icewater directed his team to a go-ahead touchdown with one minute left in the game. With first down on their own 25 after ensuing kickoff, Parilli dropped deep, Howton raced down field and eluded his defender, Parilli threw long, Howton pulled in the pass on the Baltimore 35, and with the fans in the stadium and the fans back in Wisconsin watching the Packers on television going absolutely nuts, Howton raced for the end zone with Henry Moore of the Colts in hot pursuit. With 29 seconds left in the game, Howton juked Moore, made a dive for paydirt, landed safely, and gave the Packers a thrilling 24-21 victory over the powerful Colts.

Just when everybody was ready to give them up for dead, the Packers (2-3) found new life and climbed ahead of the Bears (1-4) to stay tied with the Rams who upset the Lions (3-2) and hold onto second with the Colts, a game behind the 49ers (4-1) whose owner, Anthony J. "Tony" Morabito, died of a heart attack in the second quarter of their game with the Bears. Cleveland (4-1) beat the Cardinals (2-3): Washington (2-3) upset the Giants (3-2); and the Steelers (3-2) bumped the Eagles (1-4).

The Packers hadn't played the New York Giants since beating them, 17-3, at the Polo Grounds in '52, and the Giants hadn't been guests at City Stadium since '51 when they beat the Packers, 31-28, in the Packers first-ever regular season home game played in Green Bay in December. New York's roster included some big names in NFL history: Kyle Rote, Roosevelt Brown, Roosevelt Grier, Ray Wietecha. Andy Robustelli, Jim Katcavage, Dick Modzelewski, Sam Huff, Emlen Tunnell, Charley Conerly, Don Heinrich, Don Chandler, Frank Gifford, Alex Webster, Bob Schnelker, Ben Agajanian, and former Packers John Martinkovic and Jack Spinks. No wonder these guys were defending NFL champions. The Packers were not in the same class as these Giants, but they were competitive. They did everything to New York that Sunday except outscore the visitors. Green Bay piled up 410 yards on offense, including 225 on the ground as Hornung and McIlhenny revived a previously lifeless running game with 112 and 88 yards. respectively. If Starr had been able to throw ball as well they ran it, the Packers might have pulled off the upset. Instead, another fizzle at the goal line cost the Packers the momentum necessary for victory, and they went down to defeat, 31-17.

With the season at the halfway mark, the Packers (2-4) had little hope of winning the division that was now led by the 49ers (5-1). The Colts and Lions (both 3-3) seemed to be fading, while the Rams and Bears (both 2-4) just couldn't get it going. In the East, the Browns (5-I) remained on top by beating Washington (2-4). The Steelers (4-2) held on to their share of second place with the Giants with their win over the Colts, and the Eagles (2-4) started the long road back with a win over the Cardinals (2-4).

The first time the Packers and Bears met that year Chicago was without the services of Willie Galimore and the Packers were higher than the proverbial kite because of their new stadium. The second meeting of these second oldest of NFL rivals in '57 was played in Chicago, and this time Galimore was healthy. However, rumors persisted that the Chicago coaching staff was at odds, and the Packers were out to sweep the Bears for the first time in 22 years. It promised to be a typical Bears-Packers brouhaha.

The Bears scored first, but the Packers struck right back with a 47-yd touchdown pass from Starr to Howton to tie the game after one quarter. Just 53 seconds into the second frame, Starr swung a pass to McIlhenny, and the fleet halfback raced into the end zone 28 yards away to give Green Bay the lead, 14-7. Art Daley blamed the Bears' next touchdown on a blocked punt, but the Zeke Bratkowski-to-Harlon Hill pass play covered 35 yards. This was merely an excuse for the failure of the secondary to prevent the score. The game remained tied until late in the game when the Packers failed to make a first down on fourth-and-a-foot at the Chicago 41. The Bears marched down the field to the Green Bay 28. With third and one, Rick Casares crashed the line and fumbled. A scramble for the ball ensued, and when the dust cleared, the Bears had the pigskin and a four-yard gain for a first down that kept the drive going to the end zone for the winning touchdown. The Packers gave it the old college try in the last minute, but no miracles on this day as the Bears eked out the victory, 21-14.

The Bears (3-4) finally got out of the Western Division cellar, and the Packers (2-5) took up sole occupancy of the basement. The Rams (3-4) upset the 49ers (5-2), while Baltimore and Detroit (both 4-3) won to close the gap between second and first. Cleveland (6-1) and New York (5-2) won their games, while the Steelers (4-3), Cardinals, Eagles, and Redskins (each 2-5) all lost.

The Packers prepared for their last home game of '57 with the intent of starting a victory streak that would give them a winning record for the year. Their opponent, the Rams, felt they had taken the first step toward a winning year the week before when they thrashed

San Francisco, 37-24, in front of 102,000 fans in LA. Also, at stake was the Packers' three-game winning skein over the Rams in Milwaukee.

Unfortunately for the Packers, history repeated itself that Sunday, but only 19,540 fans were present to witness the debacle. The Packers started out great, scoring 24 points in the first half and limiting the Rams to a mere field goal. Cone booted a 39-yard field goal to put the Packers on top early in the first quarter, and Starr hit Don McIlhenny with a 14-yard pass to raise the lead to 10-0. Starr connected on six of seven passes in the quarter for 88 yards and a touchdown. He looked just great, but his arm went haywire on him, and he had to be replaced by Parilli who padded the lead to 17-3 with a 47-yarder to Howton. That was the good news. The bad news was Starr was done for the day, and Parilli was ineffective the rest of the way. Bill Forester intercepted a pass later in the half, lateraled to Dillon at the 50, and the fleet-footed Texan raced into the end zone untouched to make the halftime score, 24-3. The aging Rams found some new life in the second half as Norm Van Brocklin and Elroy Hirsch led the counterattack LA scored three touchdowns on their first three possessions of the half, and the game was tied at 24-all when Cone booted his second field goal to give the Packers a brief lead. Then the Rams marched down the field against a Green Bay defense that appeared helpless to stop them and scored the game-winner with 1:20 on the clock Parilli made a valiant attempt to pull out a victory, but it came to nothing as the Rams went back to LA winners, 31-27.

Injuries could be blamed for this loss. Starr was lost after the first quarter. Norm Masters, Sam Palumbo, Hank Gremminger, and Jerry Helluin all had to leave the game in the first half, and none of them returned to action when they were needed so desperately in the second half. Losing that many starters would cripple any NFL team, but it hurt the Packers especially hard because they weren't that deep on the bench.

Although the Bears (3-5) lost to the Colts (5-3), the Packers (2-6) held on to last place in the division. The Rams (4-4) moved into contention because the Lions (5-3) dumped San Francisco (5-3). The Browns (6-1-1) held on to first in the East despite being tied by the Redskins (2-5-1), and the Giants (6-2) kept the heat on with a win over the Eagles (2-6).

With four weeks left to the season, any hopes of the Packers making a break-even record for the year rested with trainer Bud Jorgensen as 17 players, almost half the roster, reported to him with injuries after the LA game. The list included Gary Knafelc, Norm Amundsen, and Joe Skibinski who were out for the season. Eight players had hurts that could be treated well enough for them to play the next game, but the rest of list were doubtful, even with intensive treatment for their ailments. Masters, Helluin, Gremminger, Palumbo, Kramer, Ringo, and Borden were all pretty well banged up, and their availability for the contest with Pittsburgh was questionable.

The injuries hurt the Packers against the Rams, but not against the Steelers. Nate Borden suffered a broken arm against Pitt, and Hornung had an ankle sprained so severely that Jorgensen worried that he might miss the next game because of it. Howie Ferguson came off the bench to replace Hornung, and he had a great day, gaining 71 yards on 13 carries and scoring one touchdown on a 40-yard burst through the Pittsburgh defense. John Petitbon left the game early, but Billy Kinard filled in admirably for him at cornerback. Sam Palumbo and Norm Masters never saw any action because of injuries in the LA game, but Ernie Danjean and Carl Vereen came off the bench to fill their shoes. Jim Temp filled in for Borden and held his own. The Packers held their own as well, building a 21-3 lead in the first half, then holding on in the second half to pull off a 27-10 victory.

Winning didn't get the Packers (3-6) out of the basement, but it sure felt good in Packerdom. In other games, the Bears (4-5) beat the Lions (5-4); the Colts (6-3) took over first place with a win over the 49ers (5-4); the Rams (4-5) lost to Cleveland (7-1-1), Eastern Division leaders; the Giants (7-2) shot down the Cardinals (2-6); and the Eagles (3-6) clipped the Redskins (2-6-1).

For six years in a row, the Packers had spent Thanksgiving Day in Detroit, usually as the biggest turkey in town because the Lions had feasted on them the first five years. The Packers won in '56 to spoil Detroit's chances for a division title, and they hoped to do the same again in '57. It didn't happen. The Lions held the Packers without a touchdown and even threw them for a safety to embarrass Green Bay on national television, 18-6. The only bright spot of the Packers was the play of Starr who completed 21 of 38 passes for 247 yards.

Well, a .500 season was even out of the question now, and more than likely the cellar would belong to Green Bay (3-7) until the next campaign. Detroit (6-4) had renewed hopes of winning the division because the Colts (7-3), winners over the Rams (4-6) were headed to the coast to play first the 49ers (6-4), winners over the Giants (7-3), and then the Rams again. The Bears (4-6), losers to the Redskins (3-6-1), were now out of the picture as well. But the Lions had one serious obstacle in their way: the Browns. Cleveland (8-1-1), winners over the Cardinals (2-7), were a win away from locking up the Eastern Division crown.

The Packers were also headed to the West Coast for their annual humiliation at the hands of the 49ers and Rams. The Packers had won only two games in California since the NFL moved out there in 1946. They had beaten the Rams in '47 and the 49ers in '55. That was it. Two wins and 16 losses. The Packers thought they were playing in Death Valley instead of Los Angeles and San Francisco. The results were no different in '57. The Rams stomped all over them, 42-17, and the 49ers clipped them again, 27-20. The Packers did have an excuse against the 49ers; the Rams had beaten the stuffing out of them the week before and several key players were of the game with injuries. As it was, it took Y.A. Tittle to come off the bench in the second half to lead the 49ers from a 20-10 halftime deficit to a win and a playoff with the Lions for the Western Division title.

While the Lions were beating the 49ers for the division crown and then demolishing the Browns in the championship game, 59-14, the Packers nursed their wounds and looked ahead to the next season. Of course, they were unaware that their coach would be fired right after the New Year began, but that is another chapter in itself in the history of the Packers.

§§§

15
The Trouble With Liz

"Liz Blackbourn!"

John Torinus always said the man's name with complete disdain, disgust, disagreeableness, dis-a-lotta-things with ill-feeling. He simply did not like the man; he said so often enough. Why? Torinus often used the word *stern* in reference to Blackbourn, and he never meant it with any sort of respect.

In his book on the Packers, Torinus wrote rather kindly of Blackbourn, but in private. he stated repeatedly that Blackbourn wasn't his kind of person. "He didn't drink," said Torinus. "He didn't smoke. He didn't (do anything to relax). And he didn't tolerate any of these (vices) in others."

The first signs that something was amiss with Blackbourn's coaching methods wasn't noticed until the third year of his tenure with the Packers. Two veteran players, Dick Logan and Don Barton, walked out of training camp after the first week. Art Daley wrote that they left for "no good reasons," but he failed to state what the bad reasons were. Joining Logan and Barton in their exit was Bob Kennedy, the guard from Wisconsin who had walked out of camp in what would have been his rookie year of '53 when Ronzani was still at the helm. Kennedy stayed out of football that year, decided to attempt a go at pro football the next year, but was called into the service for two years. Like Logan and Barton, he returned to the Packers in '56 after doing his military duty, and like them, he thought Blackbourn's brand of discipline was a little too severe for civilian life.

No one noticed in Blackbourn's first two years of coaching the Packers that a lot of draftees and free agents walked out of camp without giving themselves a real chance to make it in the pro game, and worse yet, no one asked why these guys were jumping ship so early. But in Blackbourn's third year the fact that something was wrong in Packerville became evident when four of the five Green Bay draftees who played in the College All-Star game against the Browns failed to report to the Packers. Two, Cecil Morris and Bob Burris, a pair of All-Americans from Oklahoma, told Blackbourn to take a hike when he tried to talk them into coming to camp, and neither of them ever played in the NFL. Two more, Jack Losch and Bob Skoronski, cited personal problems back home for not reporting to camp, but after listening to Blackbourn over the phone, they said they would come to camp. The fifth man, Forrest Gregg, reported to the Packers when he was supposed to be there because he said he would be there, and he was a man of his word.

Besides these incidents with newcomers, Blackbourn was faced with the defections of several veteran players. In January 1957, Buddy Brown, Tobin Rote, Deral Teteak, Jack Sandusky, and Roger Zatkoff announced their "retirements." Brown, Teteak, and Sandusky really did retire. In the real world, Rote wanted more money, and Zatkoff just wanted to play for Detroit where he had an off-season teaching job. If "retiring" was the only way to get what they wanted, then that was what they would do. Besides their ulterior motives, Rote and Zatkoff wanted to be traded to a better team and a better organization, one where the local fans weren't in their faces every time something went wrong on the playing field. Blackbourn obliged both of them.

The first sign in the *Press-Gazette* that nerves were beginning to fray came in April 1957.

Roger Zatkoff had gotten his wish to be traded, but he had gone to the Cleveland Browns and not the Lions like he wanted. Tobin Rote had signed his new contract that made him the highest paid Packer in history to date. Buddy Brown had quit the pro game. A trade for Rote was still in the rumor mill. Zatkoff and Brown were the captains of the defense and offense, respectively, and Rote was the leader of the offense and essentially the team, as quarterbacks are supposed to be. Noting all this, Art Daley posed the question to Blackbourn about who would replace Zatkoff and Brown as captains for the '57 squad. Blackbourn replied:

> *"Picking captains is the least of my problems.* [Author's italics.] We'll do it during training season."

Daley went on with his column as if nothing was out of place here. He stated that pro captains were generally appointed by the coaching staff, that it wasn't a popularity contest like in college, that pro captains were picked for their "wiseness in making decisions." Blackbourn replied:

> *"And that's not tough.* [Author's italics.] The captain, if he's undecided whether to take a penalty or not, can ask the official who will explain what happens if you do this or that, and where the ball will be."

As if to slap back at Blackbourn for making him look stupid, Daley explained that defensive captains also call the signals for the defense just the same as the quarterback on offense, but in the Packers' case, Deral Teteak, also retired and known as the "Little Thinker" on the team, called the defensive signals instead of Zatkoff.

Shortly after the deal with the Browns that brought Parilli back to the Packers, Daley wrote in the *Press-Gazette* that Blackbourn "quieted a raft of rumors today about deals involving Packer quarterbacks, chiefly the aforementioned Parilli." Blackbourn said:

> "We're not going to trade any one of our quarterbacks unless we're real sure we can help the team. There are no trades now that are *culminated*." [Author's italics.]

Culminated? Now what does that mean? The dictionary defines it as "having reached the highest point." . . . no trades now that are culminated." Hm-m. Did Blackbourn mean that a trade was still in the offing but that it wasn't final? Or was he just trying to get Daley off his back by using double-speak? Or was he using double-speak to keep secret the trade he was trying to make until it was consummated?

Either Blackbourn thought the reading public was stupid or Daley did. Or maybe Blackbourn thought Daley was a fool and was treating him as such. The last was most likely. Neither Blackbourn nor Daley lacked for intelligence, but where the coach was cynical, the journalist was gullible. These last two quotes proved that Blackbourn considered Daley to be an ink slinging buffoon, a marionette for the corporation brass which was directly connected to the *Press-Gazette* via George Whitney Calhoun and John Torinus.

Blackbourn pulled off another spectacular deal in late July when he sent Rote and Val Joe Walker to the Lions for tackles Ollie Spencer and Norm Masters, guard Jim Salsbury, and halfback Don McIlhenny. In the two block-buster trades, the Packers gave up three starters— Rote, Walker, and Zatkoff—and a backup quarterback for nine regulars—Parilli, McIlhenny, Kinard, Petitbon, Palumbo, Massey, Salsbury, Masters, and Spencer—and one guy who never played for the Pack. Green Bay didn't just get numbers in these deals. The Packers received good, sound football players who were asked to jell as a unit too quickly. It takes time for an offensive line—from tackle to tackle— to learn each other's moves, especially in pass blocking; the center has to recognize when either guard has his hands full and needs help from him, the guards have to know when to help the center, the tackles have to recognize when the guards are passing an attacker to them, etc. The same applies to linemen and linebackers on defense; they have to learn how to stunt together in pairs, trios, etc. Most lines have to play together as a unit for three-to-five years under the same coaching staff and the same football system before they can perform at peak efficiency. Blackbourn didn't get the chance to work with these men for as long as he needed to work with them.

A lot of fans were upset over Rote being traded. Some showed their displeasure by hanging Jack Vainisi in effigy from a street sign at the foot of Cherry Street in downtown Green Bay in early August. Let's see. Vainisi. Isn't that an Italian name?

When Breezy Reid played for the Packers, he was one of the more popular players with the fans, with the front office, and with his teammates. When Blackbourn released him in '56, a lot of people were surprised and angry over the move. Sure, ol' Breeze was getting up in football years, but the season was already down the tubes when he was dumped. Winning those last few games wasn't going to do anything for the Packers. So why put Reid on waivers? Blackbourn's answer that the team needed new blood, younger legs, etc., wasn't good enough. Blackbourn recognized his mistake and brought Reid back as a scout for '57. This assuaged, temporarily, the ire rising in the front office and out there in Packerdom, but it was only a band-aid on a festering sore.

Blackbourn traded Jolm Martinkovic to the New York Giants two weeks before the start of the '57 season. This did not set well with one member of the executive committee. Martinkovic was a successful car salesman, and Russ Bogda owned a Chevrolet dealership and a used car business. But Bogda was not the man out to "get" Blackbourn.

The day after the Packers beat the Bears to christen the new City Stadium Blackbourn joined the executive committee for their weekly luncheon with the coach. When he entered the room, they gave him a standing ovation, then he rained on their parade by telling them that the team was in poor psychological condition for the next game. The players had gotten too high emotionally for the Bears, and when they beat Chicago, their exultation was stretched to the limit. He admitted dourly that it would be difficult to get them up for the Lions the next Sunday.

Boy, what a party pooper! Or so some members of the executive committee considered him to be at that moment.

The day after that Blackbourn dropped another hint that his team was in trouble when he was asked to compare Detroit's two quarterbacks to the pair of passers in Green Bay. He said:

> "We've got no first quarterback—we're a two-quarterback team, and we've got two good ones. We have a third one (Paul Hornung) but he's a utility man and also plays other positions.

We're not picking a No. 1 quarterback, but I guess that's what everybody (press, radio, etc.) wanted me to do Sunday night after the game. How will we play them? We'll start one of them and see how he looks, and then make our decisions accordingly. We won't play one for one half and then play the other in the other half. Yes, it is quite a change from my other years here. Tobin was pretty much in a class by himself and he had had plenty of experience, with the result that he had to be considered our No.1 quarterback."

In other words, neither Parilli or Starr was a Rote. At least not yet, although Blackbourn felt Starr would one day become a top-flight NFL quarterback.

After the debacle with the Colts in Milwaukee on October 13, the headline in the *Press-Gazette* sports section read:

Packers Collapse in Second Half, Colts Win 45-17
The sub-head read:
Bays Blow 10 to 7
Halftime Advantage

These are really negative words: *collapse* and *blow*. Three points in football is not exactly a safe lead. Especially at halftime. Neither is seven points or even eight now. To say the Packers blew such a small lead with a whole half of football left was really negative. To say they collapsed was hitting the nail on the head. When the season was over, the final stats revealed that the Packers scored only seven points in the third quarter in 12 games.

After the Packers upset the Colts in Week Five, the players gave the game ball to Blackbourn. This gesture by the players resembled the one in '53 when the Packers beat these same Colts in Baltimore and carried Gene Ronzani off the field. Looking back, this was the kiss of death to the coach. He was too popular with his players, which was counter to what the executive committee said later in the year about Blackbourn's relationship with his players.

Again, Daley used the word *blow* when the Packers lost to the Rams in Milwaukee. This time they did blow the lead, a big one of 21 points at the half, and again, they failed to do much of anything in the second half.

The first outward sign that a coaching change was being contemplated by someone on the executive committee appeared in Art Daley's *Sports Cocktails* column of November 21, 1957, and oddly, the rumor originated in Chicago.

Clark Shaughnessy and Luke Johnsos, assistant coaches with the Bears, were on the outs, and their feud was raising hell with the Monsters of the Midway. Shaughnessy had been head coach of the Rams (1948-49), and he had been an assistant to Gene Ronzani when he was taskmaster of the Packers. The rumor had Shaughnessy coming to Green Bay to replace Blackbourn who would be moved "upstairs" to become general manager, while Verne Lewellen would be only the team's business manager. Both Lewellen and corporation vice-president Dominic Olejniczak denied the rumor. Said Olejniczak:

> "The executive committee has never discussed a coaching change."

Said Lewellen:

> "It's ridiculous. I have no idea where a report like that could have started. We are not interested in contacting Shaughnessy. The report is utterly without foundation. There is absolutely nothing to it."

Said Shaughnessy:

> "I don't know any more about this than the man in the moon. Where do they get these stories?"

Good question, Clark. Where do they get those stories? Answer? Media people have sources, most of them known as the "unidentified source" in the newspapers or on television. These sources are usually someone close to the top of an organization, a "go-fer" type with ambitions of becoming the top dog but who comes up short in the leadership department, a lackey lacking in the psychological requirements necessary for accomplishing outstanding personal achievements, the office toady or witch who sneaks around behind backs stabbing them with well-placed verbal daggers. Media people recognize these social and psychological pariahs and use them to their advantage.

In the case of this story about Blackbourn being kicked upstairs and Shaughnessy becoming the new head coach of the Packers, someone close to the executive committee with a connection to someone in Chicago mentioned the discord growing in Green Bay between Blackbourn and the executive committee to this friend from the Windy City and this Chicago guy passed the dope to the sportswriter who reported the rumor about Blackbourn and Shaughnessy in his newspaper.

Who were these people who made up this rumor mill? That's hard to tell, but a story once related to this author by Jim K. Ford might be the answer.

In a conversation with Jim about Blackbourn, he spoke highly of his friendship with George Halas, Jr., better known as Mugsy Halas. He hinted that he sometimes thought Mugsy was using him to get information on the Packers for Papa Bear Halas. Could it be that Jimmy made an offhand remark to Mugsy about Blackbourn being moved out and he would be replaced by an assistant coach from another team, possibly someone with head coaching experience in the NFL? For those people who knew Jimmy as well as this author, this is not an unlikely scenario.

Rumor or not, the point back in '57 was there was smoke in Green Bay and it was coming from the office of Lisle Blackbourn.

A few days before the last game of the season against the 49ers Billy Howton was interviewed by an *Associated Press* reporter, and the story found its way back to Green Bay. It said a lot about the Packers, but for some reason, it failed to impress the right people back home.

> End Billy Howton of the Green Bay Packers blames inexperienced quarterbacking more than physical injuries for the club's poor 1957 record in the National Football League. "The heck with injuries and bad breaks," Howton said Tuesday. "You can't alibi the kind of season we've been having."

The limping Packers, preparing for their season finale against the San Francisco 49ers, have lost eight of their 11 games.

Howton said, "Don't get me wrong. Bart Starr and Babe Parilli have played their hearts out."

"But," said Howton, "with the personnel we've had this year, I believe we could have been in this thing down to the wire with an experienced quarterback."

Howton said, "I'm not saying that Starr isn't the man. I think in a year or two, he's going to be one of the best in the business. But as it is now, we'll have to rise with his improvements. That's how much he means to us."

The Packers had a shrewd quarterback in the seasoned Tobin Rote, but the club traded him to get some badly-needed linemen.

Howton, who teamed with Rote on some brilliant passes, said, "The difference between Starr and Rote is their anticipation on a pass play."

He explained that NFL teams have been shooting their linebackers at the passers so fast the quarterbacks have had scant time to spot their receivers.

"Rote could smell 'em a mile off if we got open," Howton said. "Sure, it's frustrating," he said. "But we're bound to improve."

Mr. Howton said a mouthful. He knew exactly why the Packers finished the season at 3-9, why they couldn't sustain their offense for a whole game. Blackbourn was using two quarterbacks instead of sticking with one. As soon as Starr showed any sign of stumbling in a game, in came Parilli, and as soon as Parilli bent over the center, the rhythm of the offense was mined. This might explain why the Packers were such a poor second half team in almost every game that year.

Art Daley punctuated Howton's remarks, although indirectly, in his December 17 column. Daley wrote about the difference between an experienced quarterback and a rookie when he compared Y.A. Tittle and John Brodie of the 49ers. Tittle was hurting, so Brodie was given the starting assignment against the Packers. Brodie did well in the beginning as he led Frisco to a 10-0 lead, but then things went bad for him as the Packers picked off a pair of passes and recovered two fumbles, one of which was his fault. Green Bay led, 20-10, at the half. Tittle entered the game in the second half, and the 49ers won the game, '27-20. In short, experience won the game.

Daley also wrote some wonderful words about Bart Starr:

Starr in '58?...Besides more experience, Starr picked up valuable stature that he'll need next year—real bad...Bart is just the finest guy you could ever know...on and off the field...We hope he never changes but Bart is also a wonderful guy on that field...Bart has all the tools—a good football mind, absolute coolness under fire, amazing accuracy and a strong arm...

Daley knew his football players.

That same night the corporation's board of directors held a special meeting at the Beaumont Hotel. Ostensibly, the purpose of the meeting was to discuss moving more games to Green Bay from Milwaukee, but the true reason for the conference was the resignation of Russ Bogda as president of the corporation. He was calling it quits because of his health; he had cancer and, sadly, was dying.

Another special meeting was called the next week at the Northland Hotel, and at this one, the board refused to accept Bogda's resignation as a way of saying something positive to buoy Bogda in his battle with cancer. It was a wonderful gesture on their part, if futile.

The Green Bay Packers, Inc., once again faced turmoil in the front office. Instead of accepting Bogda's resignation, they created a new post of executive vice-president and elected Dominic Olejniczak to serve in that capacity. In effect, Olejniczak would be acting-president until the annual meeting to be held March 3, 1958.

Further causing the caldron to be stirred wildly was the sudden, unexpected death of Emil Fischer on New Year's Day, 1958. Fischer and his wife had gone to Florida for their annual winter vacation, and they took in the Orange Bowl game on the first day of the year. His wife found him dead in bed from an apparent heart attack. He was 70 years old. Fischer had been a part of the Packer organization for more than two decades, serving as president for six years, 1947-53, and had been chairman of the board of directors since stepping down from the presidency. He had been part of the movement to remove Curly

Lambeau from the organization, and he had been instrumental in signing Gene Ronzani to the head coaching job, then giving Ronzani a new contract after the breakeven year of '52. The executive committee never made a move without him because he always provided such a steadying influence. He would be sorely missed.

The axe finally fell on Blackbourn January 6, 1958. He wasn't in Green Bay or even in Wisconsin when it happened. He was in Mobile, Alabama, planning to attend the Senior Bowl. Before leaving on the scouting trip, he told members of the executive committee:

> "If anything is coming up concerning me, I want to be here to defend myself. I'll send one of my assistant coaches to Mobile."

Blackbourn suspected that something might be amiss when Bogda handed in his resignation. After all, Bogda was the man who hired him, the man who wanted a college coach to take over the Packer reins, the man who chased Gene Ronzani out of town. Bogda had been his biggest supporter when things were going badly, and now that he was essentially gone the coach had no one to protect him from the hyenas waiting to tear into him.

Blackbourn left for the South with assurances that nothing but routine business was planned by the executive committee at their regular meeting. Someone either lied to him deliberately or merely misinformed him. Either way, he was double-crossed.

The first night he was in Mobile Blackbourn received a telephone call from Fred Trowbridge, the lawyer on the executive committee. "Blackbourn, would you like to resign as coach of the Packers?" he asked.

"Absolutely no," said Blackbourn. "We would still honor the terms of your contract anyway and you would get paid for next year," said Trowbridge. "No, I won't resign," said Blackbourn. "Then you're fired," said Trowbridge. The committee, at the recommendation of a specially appointed sub-committee, had reached its decision in Blackbourn's absence. Who made up the sub-committee? Lee Joannes, Fred Leicht, and Fred Trowbridge. That's the same Fred Leicht and Fred Trowbridge who were on the same committee that fired Gene

Ronzani. Hm-m. And Lee Joannes; Blackbourn had replaced his boy Ronzani back in '53.

John Torinus wrote that Blackbourn drafted Paul Hornung and Ron Kramer in '57 and that he "also acquired fullback Jim Taylor in a trade with the Pittsburgh Steelers. As it turned out, Hornung and Taylor became Blackbourn's undoing..." Sorry, John, but Taylor was taken by the Packers in the second round of the '58 NFL Draft and never played for Blackbourn. Torinus went on to state:

> Late in the 1957 season, when the Packers had won only one more game after their opening victory against the Bears, Blackbourn was questioned at an Executive Committee meeting as to why he wasn't playing Hornung and Taylor more. It had long been and still is the policy of the Executive Committee not to interfere in any way in the coaching of the football team, but the committee does retain overall supervision of the total amount of money which is allocated to the coach for player personnel. In this instance, one Committee (sic) member, Fred Leicht, felt that they were owed some explanation about why two very high-priced ballplayers were sitting on the bench. He commented to Blackbourn that the coach had asked the committee for funds over and above the normal range of player salaries to acquire Hornung and Taylor. Blackbourn retorted angrily that it was none of the Committee's (sic) business. The unfortunate part of the exchange was the fact that Leicht was probably the most respected of all the members of the committee and a very mild-mannered gentleman. The rest of the Committee (sic) took obvious umbrage at Blackbourn's handling of the situation.

Torinus was obviously confusing Taylor with Kramer who did cost the Packers more than the average draftee. But that isn't the important item here. The fact that Blackbourn had had words with Leicht is.

Trowbridge, for his part, was the corporation's hatchet man. He was just doing his job, which he was very good at doing. So, this trio—

Joannes, Leicht, and Trowbridge—recommended the dismissal of Blackbourn.

Of course, these three men were up in front of the mob after Blackbourn. Behind them were: the member who questioned Blackbourn's handling of Jack Losch, the Packers' first round draft choice the year before; the member who vowed to "get" him for trading popular defensive end John Martinkovic to the Giants; and all those fans who wanted to hang him for trading Tobin Rote to Detroit, the same Tobin Rote who led the Lions to the NFL championship.

Looking back over his final season, Blackbourn proved that he was a good judge of football talent by making Starr his starting quarterback and by moving Hornung to fullback, but he also proved that he wasn't much of a game coach when the Packers blew both games with the 49ers, the Bears' game in Chicago, and the Rams' game in Milwaukee. Those four games should have been in the win column, and if they had been, the Packers would have finished in second place with a record of 7-5. Blackbourn would have kept his job, and he would have had the chance to work with all that talent he had been assembling over his tenure.

But that's not what happened. Blackbourn was ousted, and after he was done, he had plenty to say about his stay in Green Bay. Surprisingly, it contained no bitterness.

> "It was a complete surprise to me when they called me and told me last night. They said it was for the good of the Packers and that's what I was working for. I enjoyed my association with the Packers and certainly wish them all kinds of luck. This is a wonderful break for Scooter."

In Chuck Johnson's book, he was quoted as saying:

> "I actually felt sorry for the members of the (executive) committee, the way they got crucified. They were the 'ins'-the ones on the inside of Packer football—and the rest of the town was jealous. When the team was losing, they became the object of ridicule—everything was their fault. They couldn't step outside on the street after the meeting without getting criticized. If they went to the Elks Club, everybody picked on

them there about their team. If the executive committee members had lived in a big city with their offices in different parts of town, they would have come to the meetings in a relaxed frame of mind. This way, everybody put the bee on them, on the way to the meetings and afterward, all the time. They used to show up for the luncheons all tied up tight like fiddle strings. They couldn't fight the whole world. They had to take it out on the man fixed in front of them-the coach. And they did. "

Not very sour apples there. Blackbourn took his dismissal like the gentleman that he was.

The last thing of consequence that Liz Blackbourn did for the Packers was pick five players in the first four rounds of the 1958 NFL Draft. As in the past few years, the league held part of the selection process before the end of the regular season, basing the order on the standings after 10 weeks of play. The Packers picked third behind the Cardinals who had the Bonus Pick and the first choice because they had a worse record than Green Bay.

Blackbourn took Michigan State center/linebacker Dan Currie in the first round. Currie, the third man chosen overall behind Rice quarterback King Hill and Texas A&M halfback John David Crow, said after learning that he had been picked by the Packers:

"I was really surprised when Green Bay took me first. I've heard wonderful things about Green Bay, and I'm anxious to play there."

This was a good attitude, one that would serve him well in the years to come.

In the second round, Blackbourn picked a bull of a fullback from Louisiana State named Jim Taylor. Blackbourn had a few words about Taylor: "Taylor is the kind of guy who gets the job done. He's got good weight, 205, and catches the ball well."

The Packers had two choices in Round Three because of the trade with the New York Giants in which Blackbourn sent popular John Martinkovic to Gotham. With their own pick, Blackbourn chose Dick

Christy, a halfback from North Carolina State who wound up with the Steelers in '58. With the choice from New York, Blackbourn took another fullback, this one from Illinois. This one could also play defense, linebacker, in fact. "He's also a possibility as a defensive end, but he's a bit slow for offensive," said Blackbourn. His name? Ray Nitschke.

In the fourth round, Blackbourn wanted a man who could win wars in the trenches. Did he pick a hotshot from some Big Ten team or from Notre Dame or the like? No, he went out west and found a little publicized guard at Idaho named Jerry Kramer. Actually, Blackbourn didn't find him. Former assistant coach Earl Klapstein recommended Kramer. "Earl tells us that he'll fill out like (Forrest) Gregg and he's that type," said Blackbourn.

This was another great draft by Blackbourn and his staff. They chose four future Packer Hall of Famers, two of whom would also become Pro Football Hall of Famers in those four rounds. Only the '56 Draft, when Green Bay obtained Bart Starr, Forrest Gregg, Bob Skoronski, and Hank Gremminger, compared as well. In five drafts, Blackbourn selected 10 future Packer Hall of Famers, five of whom would also become Pro Football Hall of Famers. He also signed one free agent who became a member of the Packer Hall-of-Fame. Vince Lombardi's first Green Bay roster included 18 players that Blackbourn put on the team by the draft, by trade, or as free-agent signings. Lombardi also inherited four more men who were drafted by Gene Ronzani that Blackbourn kept in Packer uniforms throughout his tenure.

One wonders what Blackbourn would have done with all this talent if he'd been given the chance to coach it. Would he have put Hornung and Taylor side-by-side in the same backfield? Would he have realized that one quarterback should be number one and the back-up man be just that, a back-up? Would he have made Nitschke his middle linebacker? No one will ever know.

Blackbourn wasn't run out of town for the same reasons that Ronzani had been, but his dismissal was handled just as poorly. The executive committee lied to him, then acted cowardly by not letting him have the chance to defend himself. Would they have done this if

Emil Fischer had lived another year and Russ Bogda had been healthy? Probably not.

To this day, the organization is still trying to hide the fact that the executive committee fired Blackbourn and Ronzani. In the "Packer Chronology" section of the team's media guide, it states that "Ronzani resigns with two games remaining..." and that "Packers post 3-9-0 mark following 4-8-0 in '56, Blackbourn resigns." Those guys back in the '50s acted shamefully, and their successors are still trying to cover up for them.

The mob got Ronzani, and it got Blackbourn, too. They would not be the last, but that's getting ahead of the story again.

§§§

16

T.I.A.R.T.A.

(The Inmates Are Running the Asylum)

Scooter McLean was a really nice guy. Everybody liked him. Everybody. He was just so nice. Too nice. Unfortunately.

As soon as Fred Trowbridge got off the telephone with Blackbourn in Mobile, the executive committee in Green Bay decided to accede to the public's demand that they hand the coaching reins of the Packers to Ray "Scooter" McLean, the man who had been an assistant under Ronzani and Blackbourn. Verne Lewellen held a press conference within the hour and said:

> The board of directors has ratified the decisions of the executive committee to buy up Liz Blackbourn's contract and to replace him as head coach by Ray McLean. Ray agreed to a one-year contract.

Scooter didn't have an agent to negotiate a better deal for him. A one-year contract? Coaches didn't get one-year contracts. Not now, not then. Especially new coaches. What were these guys thinking? Good question. What *were* they thinking? Obviously, they weren't thinking very clearly, or they were thinking very cleverly. Either they realized that Scooter was no head coach and they needed time to find a real one; or they thought Scooter could do the job with the talent on hand and once he proved them to be geniuses to put him in charge, they could reward him with a long-term contract. The answer lies somewhere between these two scenarios. Blackbourn's firing and Scooter's hiring were probably knee-jerk reactions to the pressures being put on the executive committee by the board of directors who were getting the same pressures from the stockholders and fans; and contributing to this turmoil were the death of Emil Fischer, a real executive who knew how to handle such situations, and the poor health of Russ Bogda, the typical car salesman who slashes prices when sales are off and he needs cash to keep the bank happy. Had both of these men been at that January 6, 1958 meeting and both been in good health and clear mind, most likely Blackbourn wouldn't have lost his job.

But that's not what happened. Blackbourn was fired, and McLean was hired.

But why hire Scooter? Two reasons. The first was that the only other man offered the job turned it down, and the second was that Scooter had been Blackbourn's assistant and Ronzani's assistant. Hold the phone. *Other man who was offered the job?* Lewellen divulged that Hampton Pool had been offered the head coaching job at Green Bay, but Pool said he'd rather stay in Canada where he had a reasonable chance of a future in football. Then Lewellen said they went with Scooter because the Giants had gone with Jim Lee Howell in '53 and Howell had produced four-straight winning teams and one NFL champion in '56; because the Lions handed the reins of their team to assistant George Wilson when Buddy Parker quit suddenly before the '57 campaign and Wilson's Lions won the NFL title; and because the 49ers fired Red Strader and made his assistant Frankie Albert the top man and Albert led Frisco to a tie for the Western Division title in '57. In other words, assistants who are familiar with the personnel and the organization were the answer instead of bringing in some stranger to do the job. The theory was good based on those three cases and the case of Paddy Driscoll who replaced George Halas in '56 and took the Bears to the NFL championship game. Would it work with Scooter? Lewellen and the executive committee certainly hoped that lightning would strike in the right place for them as it had for the Giants, Bears, Lions, and 49ers.

When he faced the Press for the first time as head coach, McLean answered questions with all the geniality that he was known to exude by those who knew him. He said he expected to make a change in assistant coaches, but so far, he hadn't given it any thought. He said he was satisfied with the one-year contract because it presented him with "a real challenge." Then he outlined his plans for the future:

> "One of the first things I want to do is to return the team to Green Bay for training. It will do wonders for building the morale of the team and that morale is a good 80 per cent of winning. Morale will win those close games for you. (Remember that when we get to the '58 playing season. Author's remark.)

> "The material picked up in the draft so far should be of great help to us. I'd like to develop a few more two-way players, especially in the line, so that injuries won't be so damaging.
> "We're shooting for the moon. We're going for the title. The players will be on their honor. They've set up a committee and will have their own system of fines for discipline."

Let's see. "We're shooting for the moon. We're going for the title." Hm-m. Sort of proves that Scooter was no rocket scientist. right? What else would any team have as its initial goal at the beginning of a season? "Golly, we're shooting for fifth place." A truly brilliant statement by Scooter, "We're shooting for the moon." But his decision to put the players on their honor was the epitome of gullibility. "I'm gonna leave the chickens out in the woods tonight and trust the 'coons to leave 'em be, Ma." Or: "This is the warden speaking. I'm giving all of you prisoners the keys to your cells and a key to the front gate. Now I'm trusting all of you to be in your cells when the lights go out tonight. Oh, yes, and I'm giving all the guards the week off, starting now. Have a nice day, boys." Scooter really was a nice guy.

The first change in the Packers after McLean became head coach was the resignation of Lou Rymkus. McLean accepted it with regret, but Rymkus had a better offer from the Rams and Sid Gillman, a real head coach. Rymkus knew that McLean was a nice guy, but why go down with a sinking ship when you can take a cruise on the love boat? What did Rymkus give for a reason for leaving?

> "I resigned primarily because I feel that Scooter should have a completely free hand in selecting his staff and my voluntary dropping out of the scene will eliminate any embarrassment to him in that respect. I have the highest admiration and respect for Scooter and his ability. I wish him all the success in the world, and I wish the fans and the many friends of Green Bay among whom I have spent some very enjoyable years the best of luck in the future."

Translation: Scooter McLean a head coach? You've got to be kidding. Fans and friends in Green Bay? I can't wait to get out of town. Those people deserve each other.

Jack Morton, desperate for a job, chose to stay with the Packers and McLean. Scooter said he would hire no more assistants until after the NFL Draft in late January, and he kept his word. He signed Nick Skorich as his line coach in early February, recently fired Cardinals' head coach Ray Richards three days later as his defensive coach, and former Packer player and scout Breezy Reid as backfield coach a week after that.

Skorich had played under Jock Sutherland at Pittsburgh, then returned as an assistant under Walt Kiesling and Buddy Parker. Richards had 20 years of coaching experience as an assistant and head mentor on the college and pro levels, including stints at UCLA and Pepperdine College, the LA Rams, Baltimore Colts, and Cardinals. His head coaching stops were at Pepperdine and the Cardinals, and his records at both places were nothing to brag about.

Jack Vainisi remained on board as talent scout, assistant coach, and executive assistant.

Scooter was a popular fellow in Green Bay with the executive committee, the board of directors, the stockholders, the players, and the fans, and like most popular fellows, he did the popular thing all the time. He even did it in the Draft. After choosing Oregon State quarterback Joe Francis in the fifth round, he completed the first 10 rounds with Ken Gray, a tackle from Howard Payne; Doug Maison, a quarterback from Hillsdale; Mike Bill, a center from Syracuse; Norm Jarock, a hometown halfback from St. Norbert; and Carl Johnson, a tackle from Illinois picked as a future.

Howard Payne? Hillsdale? St. Norbert? Where the heck were these colleges? Who ever heard of them? Evidently, Scooter had. Or if he hadn't, he soon learned that Howard Payne College was located in Brownwood, Texas, and Texas has always been a hotbed of football talent. Although Gray never played for the Packers, he did play 13 seasons in the NFL, mostly with the Cardinals. Hillsdale was a small school in Hillsdale, Michigan, and in the mid-'50s, Hillsdale was a powerhouse among smaller schools because of Maison. However, the NFL was a far cry from the lower levels of college ball. And St. Norbert was in Green Bay's back yard in De Pere, Wisconsin. Of course, Scooter knew where it was, and he knew how popular Jarock was with the fans of Green Bay and St. Norbert. He drafted Jarock, who had very little chance of beating Paul Hornung and Don McIlhenny out of their jobs, because it was the popular thing to do. Unfortunately, history will never know if Jarock would have made it or not; he broke a leg during the first few days of training camp and never made it back.

Joe Francis managed to survive the Turk for three years, but none of the others ever made it past training camp. The same was true of the other 20 men picked by McLean and staff in '58.

In league news, the NFL dropped the Bonus Pick from the Draft. The reason? It was termed as being something of a lottery by Congress at its hearings investigating the NFL for anti-trust violations. In other words, it touched on being a form of gambling, and of course, gambling was—and still is—a real no-no with professional sports. The Bonus Pick was the brainstorm of Curly Lambeau who believed every team should have the chance at the top player in the country. It was a good idea as far as it went.

To further appease Congress and get the government off their backs, the NFL magnates added a wrinkle to the Draft. If a player was dissatisfied with the team that drafted him, he could ask the league to change him to another team, if he had a good reason. Of course, no one explained what a good reason might be, so the rule had no teeth in it. Still, it appeased Congress, which proved what kind of wizards were running the country back in 1958.

On February 22, 1958, Russell W. Bogda passed away from cancer. He was only 46. Although he handled the situation with Gene Ronzani poorly and his plan for expanding old City Stadium instead of building a new playing facility showed a lack of foresight and imagination, he should be remembered for making Verne Lewellen the corporation's business manager and for hiring Lisle Blackbourn. Those were his only achievements as president of the Green Bay Packers, Inc.. It was Lewellen who did the most to put the Packers on firm financial ground in the '50s, and it was Blackbourn who built a majority of the team that Vince Lombardi took to so many titles in the next decade.

In front office news at the annual stockholders meeting, business manager Verne Lewellen reported a gross profit for the corporation of $50,130.92 for 1957 as both income and expenses increased for the year. An increase of $62,000 in ticket sales was due directly to the new stadium, but pre-season expenses, such as the extra game that was played in Miami and having to pay players $50 per game, canceled the gain from attendance. Lewellen pointed out that the Packers were taking in $20,000 more for road games than they were paying out for home games. The Packers received an average of $51,000 for each of their six away tilts but paid out only $31,000 to opponents who came calling to Green Bay and Milwaukee. The only way the Packers could increase revenues at this time was either to raise ticket prices or to move at least one of the Milwaukee games to Green Bay. A committee headed by Jerry Atkinson recommended to the board of directors that they do the latter. Said Atkinson:

"The committee felt that the people of our area deserve more than three games in their new stadium. We made a complete study of the situation, including an IBM sales analysis, population trends of Green Bay and Milwaukee, driving times to and from the two cities, season ticket sales in outside communities, and promotion expenses and other phases. We found no risk about this being financially sound. Our crowds of 32,000 are nice but we must look forward to the day when we must count on crowds of 40 to 45,000. The stadium was constructed so that it can be easily enlarged."

The board supported the committee's recommendation, and a fourth game was added to the Green Bay slate, leaving Milwaukee with two games. This led to a rebellion of stockholders and directors from the Milwaukee area when they met again in April to elect officers. Buckets Goldenberg led the charge by presenting a three-point ultimatum.

1. That the Packers must return a third game to Milwaukee this fall.

2. That Curly Lambeau must be "considered" for the general manager's post, now held by Verne Lewellen.

3. That a secret-ballot be held for president of the corporation when the election of officers takes place...

4. That the downstate group be represented on the executive committee.

Goldenberg and his supporters, which included Don Hutson, planned to nominate Max Murphy or Dr. Robert L. Cowles as their candidate to fill the vacancy at the top. Murphy was a member of the executive committee, but he said that he planned to resign from that post. As spokesman for the group, Goldenberg said:

"Milwaukee is a good pro football town, and if the Packers don't want anything to do with Milwaukee, you can bet there will be some negotiating for a pro franchise."

When asked if that might mean the shift of the Chicago Cardinals who were looking for a new home, Goldenberg answered with a firm yes.

When push carne to shove at the annual election meeting, Goldenberg backed down and said that he was misquoted by the Milwaukee newspapers. He said: "Everything's fine; I'm satisfied." And he pledged to continue to support the Packers in Milwaukee.

Not one of the Milwaukee group's demands was met, although Don Hutson was offered a spot on the executive committee, which he turned down because his business was in Racine and he would be unable to attend the weekly meetings on a regular basis.

What was really behind this move by the Milwaukee group? Maybe the question should be: Who was really behind this move by the Milwaukee group?

Answer: Curly Lambeau. The previous fall when the rumors began spreading that Blackbourn was in trouble with the executive committee and that Verne Lewellen would be relieved of his duties as general manager Lambeau applied for Lewellen's job, at least the general manager part of it. When his application seemed to be going nowhere, Lambeau looked for the weakest link in the Packer organization, and he found it in Goldenberg and Murphy. Lambeau saw himself coming back to the Packers just like George Halas returning to the sidelines with the Bears. Halas had done it back in the '30s, in the '40s after World War II, and he was doing it again '58. Lambeau figured, if Halas could make three comebacks, then he would make at least one. He figured wrong as he so often did.

The members of the executive committee flatly told Goldenberg that Lambeau was history and he would remain history as long as he lived; they weren't about to let the fox back into the chicken coop again.

Realizing that he was out of his league with these businessmen, Goldenberg backed off his demands and returned to the herd.

At the March meeting, the stockholders re-elected Tony Canadeo, Dick Bourguignon, Fred Cobb, Ed Fritsch, Buckets Goldenberg, Les Kelly, Fred Leicht, Ed Liebmann, Heraly MacDonald, Herbert Mount,

Herb Olson, A.C. Witteborg, and Charley Goldberg to the board of directors. To fill the vacancy created by the death of Emil Fischer, the board elected John S. Stiles of De Pere.

A month later the board of directors elected Dominic Olejniczak to replace the late Russ Bogda as president of the corporation, reelected Lee Joannes as one vice-president, elected Dick Bourguignon as the other vice-president, and re-elected John Torinus as secretary-treasurer. Tony Canadeo, Jerry Atkinson, and Carl Mraz were elected to fill the executive committee vacancies left by the deaths of Bogda and Emil Fischer and the resignation of Max Murphy. Re-elected to the executive committee were Fred Trowbridge, Healy MacDonald, Fred Leicht, Howard Bero, Bernard Darling, and Les Kelly. Dr. Cowles was elected to the board of directors to complete Bogda's term. On a final note, Lewellen announced that the Packers had $170,426.92 in the bank and that as of April 28 they had sold 20,382 season tickets the '58 season in Green Bay.

Once McLean had his coaching staff in place the Packer brass began the task of signing veteran players for the '58 season.

First into the fold for '58 was offensive tackle Forrest Gregg who would be released from the Army in time for the exhibition season. They also signed their top six draft choices as well as others in January and February.

First out of the fold was defensive back John Petitbon who had come to the Packers from the Browns before the '57 season in the trade for Roger Zatkoff. Petitbon wanted out of Green Bay, and if retiring was the only way, then he would retire. McLean managed to swing a trade for Petitbon and defensive back Doyle Nix who was coming out of the service later that year. He sent the rights to both of them to Washington for halfback Steve Meilinger and defensive tackle J.D. Kimmel. Petitbon never played again, and Nix played two years for Washington before playing in the AFL for a few years.

McLean made other trades before training camp that summer. In April, he gave a draft choice for defensive tackle Ray Krouse of Detroit on condition Krouse made the team; he never played for the Packers, nullifying the trade by demanding to play for a team in the East because he lived in Washington and his wife was ill and his demand was upheld by NFL Commissioner Bert Bell. In May, he gave the Browns a draft choice for defensive end Len Ford on condition Ford made the team; he did.

In March, McLean lined up his quarterback for '58 by signing Bart Starr to a contract. Starr had some good stats in '57: 117 completions out of 215 attempts for 1,489 yards with only 10 interceptions and eight touchdowns. He was followed by Max McGee who was finally through with the Air Force and Tom Bettis in April: Babe Parilli, Jim Temp, Gary Knafelc, Jim Ringo, Hank Bullough, and Billy Howton in May: Billy Kinard, Carlton Massey, Dick Deschaine, and Norm Masters in June; Al Romine, Nate Borden, Al Carmichael, Bobby Dillon, Howie Ferguson, Bill Forester, Hank Gremminger, Dave Hanner, Joe Johnson, Don McIlhenny, Jim Salsbury, Ollie Spencer, and John Symank in July. Paul Hornung was already under contract, having sign a three-year pact in '57. Ron Kramer was also under contract, but the leg he'd broken in the second Ram game of '57 had yet to come back to playing condition.

McLean started the training season by having the quarterbacks, all five of them, report early for a little classroom work on the play book. The rest of the squad reported a week later.

Right from the beginning, the Packers appeared to be in a state of confusion. McLean tried to buck the trends in professional football by turning back the clock to the two-way player era. Whereas other head coaches had recognized years before that quarterbacks should only be quarterbacks and players at other positions performed best if they played only one position. McLean had his players working at two positions—one offense, one defense—in an effort to build bench strength. The coach succeeded only in taking precious practice time away from his players, and some of the men, such as Jerry Helluin, suffered injuries while playing that extra position McLean wanted them to learn.

The Packers opened the pre-season in a downpour, an omen of what was to come the rest of the year. Their opponent, besides the weather, for the Shrine Game in Milwaukee was Buddy Parker's Pittsburgh Steelers, and for 59:58 it was the most boring game in history as neither team could put a single point on the board or even threaten to score. The Steelers finally got close enough to the goal posts, thanks to a pass interception, to boot a field goal with one second left. McLean called the game "a complete waste of time and effort." He was only right.

The Eagles came to Green Bay for Labor Day, and they were good guests, bowing to the Packers, 20-17. This was the first ever pre-season game played in the new City Stadium. The contest was memorable in that it featured a host of future NFL stars for both teams.

Buoyed by the win over Philadelphia, McLean bragged a little about his coaching methods, claiming that having the team practice on both sides of the ball was making them better players. His boast found support when the Packers traveled to Boston to meet the Giants for Green Bay's third pre-season match. The Pack trailed at the half, 20-13, then the Giants fell apart in the second half, throwing three interceptions that the Packers turned into touchdowns against New York's second-string defense. The final, 41-20, made the Packers look like a real threat to take the division title, or so the fans thought. Not so Scooter. He warned:

> "Don't let the people get the idea that it's (the defense) that good. We made quite a few little mistakes and we've got to correct them."

Sure, Scooter, sure. You're just joking, right? We know the defense is that good. Such was the thinking in Packerdom. No one wanted to take Scooter seriously; leastways, not this early in the season.

The next week the Packers flew down to North Carolina to face the Redskins at Winston-Salem. McLean's boys did not play very well in a 23-14 loss.

> "The Redskins pointed out better than I possibly could in a lecture that we have a lot of work to do on offensive blocking assignments when different defensive maneuvers are made. We were real sluggish on offense. Just awful. I don't know just what it was. We've been going along pretty good."

No one in Green Bay could see yet that poor Scooter didn't have a clue about being a head coach, but they didn't care because

Scooter was such a nice guy.

The Chicago Cardinals had a new coach for '58. His name was Pop Ivy, and he had coached in Canada the year before. The Canadian game was played with 12 men on each side, the extra man being an eligible receiver, and passing was emphasized. Ivy brought his offense with him from north of the border, and it promised to open-up the American game. Ivy pioneered what later became recognized as the "pro set" where the two running backs line up behind the tackles instead of just outside the guards. The third back is flanked outside, either beyond the tight end or in the slot between the split end and the tackle.

The Green Bay coaching staff made fun of Ivy's offense as they prepared to play the Cardinals in Minneapolis for the final pre-season game for both teams. They made remarks about the Cardinals needing a 12th man to beat the Packers, or that Chicago's backs would have trouble getting through the line because of where they lined up. Their snickers must have been heard in the Windy City because the Cardinals piled up 382 yards of offense on the Packers and won the game, 31-24. The Cardinals took their turn laughing all the way back to Chicago.

The Packers started "Bear Week" by getting down to the player limit. McLean traded Dick Deschaine to Cleveland and Dick Christy to Pittsburgh, and he placed Ron Kramer on the military list. He released Sam Palumbo and rookie Ken Gray who caught on with the Cardinals. Deschaine had been the best punter in the NFL over the past three seasons, but McLean didn't believe in carrying a specialist on the squad. The punting chores were given to Max McGee.

One last move that seemed insignificant at the time was the addition of Jesse Whittenton to the Packers. Whittenton had played two years with the Rams, then was traded to the Bears for Kline Gilbert in the summer of '58. He came down with pleurisy during training camp and had to be hospitalized for two weeks, so when cutdown time came, Halas was forced to put him on waivers. The Packers picked him off the waiver wire.

As always, the tilt with the Bears was sold out long before game day. Papa Bear George Halas had declared early on that the Bears were 20% better this year than they had been in '57. Chicago had won only five games the year before. Did he mean that the Bears would win six games in '58? Who knew with Halas? Whatever he meant, Halas intended to beat the Packers twice, starting with the opener in Green Bay.

Halas mixed 10 rookies into a veteran roster to roll through the exhibition season undefeated in six games. The likes of Ed Brown, Harlon Hill, Bill McColl, Rick Casares, Bill Bishop, Willie Galimore, Stan Jones, Joe Fortunato, J.C. Caroline, Vic Zucco, Henn Lee, Larry Strickland, Doug Atkins, Bill George, and George Blanda were joined by newcomers Erich Barnes, Bob Kilcullen, Bob Jewett, Johnny Morris, Merrill Douglas, Ralph Anderson, Bill Roehnelt, Ed Cooke, and Dick Klein. None of the new Bears played in key positions, such as quarterback or running back, but they contributed to the overall quality of the team.

The Packers got off on the right foot when Bobby Dillon picked off an Ed Brown pass 1:17 into the game and returned it 37 yards for a touchdown to give Green Bay the early lead, 7-0. The Packers stifled the Bears in three plays and forced a punt, but returner John Symank fumbled the kick, the Bears recovering it on the Green Bay 32. Five plays later Willie Galimore crossed the goal line from a yard out, and George Blanda converted the PAT to tie the game. Hornung put the Packers ahead with a 23-yard field goal with five minutes to go in the first quarter. That was the last lead for Green Bay. Galimore scored on an eight-yard run in the second quarter to put Chicago ahead for good. 14-10; then Brown found the end zone on a two-yard sneak to put the Bears up, 21-10. Hornung added another field goal before the half ended. Galimore scored his third six of the day in the third period when Brown hooked up with him on a 79-yard pass play. Brown connected with Hill for 13 yards and a touchdown in the fourth quarter to put the Bears up, 34-13. Hornung scored a meaningless touchdown with just under three minutes to go to give him 14 points on the day, but the Bears won handily, 34-20.

The game wasn't as close as the score indicated. The Chicago defense mauled the Green Bay offense for all but the closing drive when the outcome of the game had already been decided, and the Green Bay defense could only stop the Bears occasionally as Halas chose to run the ball 40 times and attempt only 15 passes. Always full of himself and false statements, Halas said after the game that the Bears would only go six and six on the season and "the Packers will do better than that. I'm not being fooled by all this... "Yeah, right, George. He also said, "the Packers are the most improved team in our division. They are going to give a lot of people terrific headaches this season, beginning next Sunday." Ah, yes, Mr. Halas.

The Lions were the reigning champions of the NFL in '58, and they hadn't lost one bit of their power in the off-season. Sure, they'd been beaten by Baltimore the first week of the season, but the breaks just hadn't gone their way in that one. They were playing the Packers in Week Two, and they wouldn't need the breaks to beat this bunch of kids. Or so they thought when the oddsmakers put them up as 10-point favorites.

The Packers upset the Lions, if a tie could be called an upset. Art Daley wrote:

> Worse things have happened to the Packers in the last few years...And this knot—the first played by the Bays since a 21-up show against the Bears in Chicago in 1953—indicated that there's nothing wrong with the Packers *but what some quarterbacking won't cure.* [Author's italics.]

This was Daley doing his job again. Covering up for the Packers so the public wouldn't suspect anything was wrong. Quarterbacking the problem with the Packers? Not hardly. Starr played the game on one good leg and went 19 for 31 with a touchdown and 196 yards. He was intercepted twice, but those two miscues were not the difference in the game. If anything, the Lions should have won the contest, but their kicker missed two second half field goal tries, one from only 15 yards away.

No, Daley was covering up for the executive committee and the coaching staff. Those guys in the board room didn't want the fans to know what some members of the committee were beginning to suspect already: they'd made a mistake giving Scooter the head coaching job. The tell-tale sign? No points in the third quarter; just like '57. A little deeper than that, no offense in the second half, no adjustments at halftime by the coaching staff; same as '57. Daley did hint at the problem in column, but he didn't delve into any reasons behind the failure of the offense in the second half. He simply asked the question: "How can the Packers score some points in the second half?" He didn't elaborate beyond mentioning how the offense had only crossed the 50-yard line three times in the second half of the two games so far in '58, and their results: two missed field goals and a meaningless touchdown against the Bears in the closing minutes after the game's outcome had been decided.

Of course, it was too early for the fans to see that the Packers had problems in '58. As far as they were concerned, their Packers had won a moral victory over the league champions, and they just might be able to beat the Colts in Milwaukee the following Sunday. Fat chance of that happening.

The Colts had started the season by clubbing the Lions, 28-15, then winning a wild one from the Bears, 51-38. Baltimore's defense might be a little loose, but their offense more than made up for it. Daley tried to soften the loss to the Colts by writing that the "Packers deserved a better fate" than they received at the hands of the division leaders, but once again he was only doing a cover job for the coaching staff. Same story. Packers built a 17-0 lead in the first half, then watched it slowly evaporate to lose, 24-17. No scoring in the second half. Why? Bad coaching. Fourth and inches on the Baltimore 11 early in the fourth quarter with Green Bay still ahead, 17-14. Field goal attempt from the 18, almost a sure thing, to go up, 20-14? No, try to sneak it against a defensive line that had shut down the Packers all afternoon. Result: turnover. Bigger result: another Green Bay loss.

The evidence was already beginning to point at the same glaring deficiency in Green Bay that had been there in '57. Daley again asked the question in his column:

Why is it so tough for the Packers to score-much less move the ball in the second half?

Answer: He didn't have one, at least not one in print. He didn't write that no one on the coaching staff was able to make any adjustments to the other team's play of the first half in the second half. Once word of this spread around the league it spelled curtains for the Packers.

Already two and a half games out of first place and with only three home games left, the season was essentially over for the Packers; they had only two chances of making a run at the Western Division crown: slim and none. McLean was already looking to do something just to save his job. But what? Win! How?

Maybe start with the Redskins in Washington the following week. The Skins featured the shortest quarterback in the NFL, five-foot nothin' Eddie LeBaron. What he lacked in height, LeBaron made up for with heart, stamina, and brains. When the Packers invaded Griffith Stadium, he was the leading passer in the league. When they headed home again, he was still on top of the league. LeBaron only threw nine passes, but he completed five of them for 89 yards and two touchdowns. He didn't have to throw much because the Washington running game was fast and furious as four backs gained 292 yards on 49 carries. The Redskins ran up a 34-0 lead through three quarters before the Packers got into the game. The final was 37-21. The Packers were pathetic.

The season was now a third over, and the Packers (0-3-1) were dead last with the Lions. The Colts (4-0) were cruising a game ahead of the Bears (3-1) and two games ahead of LA and Frisco (both 2-2). In the Eastern Division, the Browns (4-0) were in their usual spot. followed by the Giants, Redskins, and Cardinals (all 2-2), with the Eagles and Steelers (both 1-3) bringing up the rear.

Speaking of the Eagles, they were the next foe to come to Green Bay. These Eagles had Buck Shaw as their head coach and Stormin'

Norman Van Brocklin as their quarterback Shaw coached the 49ers for nine years; best record 12-2 in 1948, worst record 3-9 in 1950—his only losing season. He never won a division crown, and that's why he was dumped by Frisco owner Anthony Morabito. Van Brocklin was still the "Flyin' Dutchman" on the field, but he was a little too argumentative for Sid Gillman off the gridiron, thus the reason he was in Philly.

Scooter had been furious with his team after being blown out by the Redskins, and his anger carried over during the week. The players practiced hard for the first time since the final roster was set just before the Bear game. Scooter made changes in the starting lineups for the game, the biggest of them being Parilli replacing the injured Bart Starr at quarterback.

Neither team seemed to be interested in the contest during the first quarter as the Packers put up the only points, a field goal by Hornung after Dave Hanner recovered an Eagle fumble. Green Bay finally came to life in the second period when Parilli found McGee down the middle for a 35-yard scoring pass to put the Pack up, 10-0. The Eagles bounced back on their next possession, but the Packers responded after an exchange of punts with a 52-yard drive that was capped off by Howie Ferguson plowing in from two yards out. Philly scored before the half, and the two teams rested with the score at 17-14 Packers. The Eagles took the second half kick and headed for the end zone until Bobby Dillon picked off a Van Brocklin pass and returned it to the Philly 38. Six plays later Parilli hit Al Carmichael under the goal posts from 14 yards out to put the Packers further ahead, 24-14. Tom Bettis recovered another fumble by the Eagles on their very next play, and Parilli moved the Packers 33 yards for another score, this one on a 10-yard pass to Gary Knafelc to make the lead 31-14. After forcing Van Brocklin to punt, the Packers took over on their own 44. Seven plays later Parilli hit McGee for 25 yards and Green Bay's final score of the day to increase the margin to 38-14. The joint was really rockin' now, and the fans wanted more. Unfortunately, they didn't get it from the Packers. They did get some excitement from the Eagles who scored 21 points in the final period, their last touchdown coming with :56 on the clock to make the score read 38-35 Packers. Dick Bielski tried an onside kick, but rookie Ray Nitschke covered it for the Packers on their own 49. Out of timeouts, the Eagles could only watch the Packers run a single play as time expired to the great relief of the 31,043 in the stands.

All right! The Packers (1-3-1) had their first win of the season. So, did Detroit, so Green Bay was still in the cellar of the Western Division behind the Colts (5-0), Bears (4-1), Rams (2-3), and 49ers (2-3). But it was still a win, and Green Bay no longer had the worst record in the NFL. The Eagles and Steelers (both 1-4) did, and they trailed Cleveland (5-0), Giants (3-2), Cardinals (2-3), and Redskins (2-3).

The Packers won, right? You'd never have known it in Green Bay the week after. Art Daley gave a serious clue to the trouble that was beginning to brew in Bay City:

> What's this letdown business? The Packers were supposed to be hungry for a victory; they're leading the Eagles 38-14 and then almost collapse with joy while the Phillies are scoring 21...Why? Coach McLean says "we got too conservative and we got lax"...Maybe it's human nature to let up —the equivalent of a boxer easing off when the other guy is groggy...The Redskins did the very same thing in Washington the previous Sunday...Remember? They were leading the Pack 34-0 and the Bays whipped off 21 points in the last quarter. Washington's letdown wasn't quite as complete as the Packers because the Skins added a vital three points. Let this be a lesson, men!

Daley wasted his words on these Packers. Next up for Green Bay was a trip to Baltimore to face the highest scoring team in the NFL. Daley pointed this out three days before the game with the Colts:

> The Packers gave up 72 points in the last two games...That's a shame!
> Green Bay's defense isn't that bad, you say? But it happened, the Redskins getting 3 7...and the Eagles getting 35...
> Worse yet, the Redskins and Eagles aren't necessarily high scoring teams...Both scored less than the Packers who counted 109 in five games—the Eagles with 103, Redskins 95.

And that reminds us of two items.

(1) The Packers play the Colts in Baltimore Sunday and

(2) those Colts happen to be the hottest and highest scoring team in the league with 178 points. Horrors!...

Maybe we should stay home?

Mr. Daley, you were only right. So very right. The Packers should have stayed home. In fact, they should have folded up their tents and gone fishin' for the rest of the season. The Colts annihilated the Packers, 56-0, in the worst beating any Packer team had taken to that date, November 2, 1958; and the worst beating since then through the writing of this volume of their history. At the time, it was Baltimore's first ever shutout of anybody, it was the Packers' first shutout loss since 1954, and it was the most points a Packer team had ever given up in their history.

The question here: Were the Colts that good or were the Packers that bad? The answer: Both. The Packers were charged with eight penalties, seven of which gave the Colts first downs. The Packers threw five interceptions and completed only five of 26 passes. The Colts gained 220 yards on the ground and 170 through the air. The Packers did everything wrong in the game, while the Colts could hardly do anything less than perfect. Oh, yes, it rained the whole game. Funny, but it rained the week before in Green Bay when the Packers were taking it to the Eagles. The weather was no excuse. These Packers were simply an embarrassment to themselves, to their coaches, to their fans, to the NFL.

The season was at the halfway mark, and the Packers (1-4-1) were no longer a viable contender for anything except the cellar. So were the Lions (1-4-l), losers to the 49ers (3-3). The Rams (3-3) upset the Bears (4-2) that week, and the Colts (6-0) looked like one of the greatest teams of all time. In the East, the Eagles (1-4-1) managed to tie the Cardinals (2-3-1), while the Steelers (2-4) began playing good ball by upsetting the Redskins (2-4). The Giants (4-2) stopped the division leading Browns (5-1) to keep one race alive in the NFL.

Needless to say, morale in Green Bay was at an all-time low. Scooter pointed a finger at seven or eight veteran players who had a defeatist attitude, and he said that he would do something about it in the near future. He also admitted publicly that the players were taking advantage of him, meaning his genial nature. This problem had begun in training camp, but McLean refused to do anything about it then, telling the executive committee that he didn't want to disclose to the press, and thus the public, that he was levying fines on the culprits. John Torinus disagreed with him and advised him to go public with the problem, but McLean refused to do so. The problem only grew.

As if matters in Green Bay weren't bad enough, the Packers had to travel to Chicago the following week to face the angry Bears. Halas had no morale problems. He could only shake his head when he heard what McLean was saying up in Green Bay. Get up for the Bears? They asked Scooter. He replied:

> "That'll be a matter for each individual player. We've just got to get up and come out fighting."

Poor Scooter! He didn't have a clue. The Packers were pathetic, and he blamed the players for their lackadaisical play. Morale and attitude have always been the responsibility of the head coach, no matter what the sport. Scooter didn't understand this rule of coaching. Proof of that was the presence of Dominic Olejniczak at a team meeting in which the Packer president gave the squad a pep-talk about the glorious past of the Packers. Afterward, McLean delivered his ultimatum to shape up or ship out. Very few players took him seriously.

The local radio personalities and the Milwaukee papers pointed their collective fingers at the executive committee for the problems the Packers were having. Art Daley used his column to defend the men who guided the business fortunes of the Packers. He had to. One of his bosses was John Torinus. He pointed out that not one of the executive committee members was in uniform in Baltimore, and he restated the accomplishments of this group over the years. What he failed to address was the fact that they also hired and fired coaches. They hired Ronzani, and he moved the team in the right direction and built a solid talent base. Then they fired him because he was Italian, hailed from the Upper Peninsula of Michigan, and was an ex-Bear. They hired Liz Blackbourn who inherited and continued to build on the foundation that Ronzani had left for him. Blackbourn solidified the organization of the team and was on the verge of greatness when the executive committee succumbed to public pressure for a winner and dumped him. As John Torinus put it:

> "The people of Green Bay demanded that we give Scooter a chance. He was such a nice guy."

But he was a lousy coach, and finally, the fans were coming to this realization. Even so, they hoped he might turn things around in the second half of the season, starting with the Bears.

The Packers bounced back against Chicago, showing some of the old fire that had characterized Packer teams of old. Green Bay came out smokin' and put three points on the board in the first quarter on a field goal by Hornung. Of course, this was after missing three earlier chances at scoring on the sagging Bears. Encouraged by the fact that they only trailed by three points after 15 minutes of play, the Bears took the initiative and ran off 24 points over the next 36:35, while the Packers could muster nothing on offense, not even a first down. The Packers did make a brief attempt to make the game respectable by scoring midway through the final stanza on a Jim Taylor plunge, but that was the extent of their effort as they lost, 24-10.

Said Scooter after the game:

> "There were 35 boys out there trying. I was satisfied with their effort."

Nobody was released that week.

The Packers (1-5-1) finally had the basement all to themselves as the Lions (2-4-1) upset Cleveland (5-2). The Giants (5-2) moved into a tie with the Browns by upsetting the powerful Colts (6-1) who still held an edge on the Bears (5-2) and the oncoming Rams (4-3), big-time victors, 56-7, over the 49ers (3-4). Buddy Parker and Bobby Layne had the Steelers (3-4) looking like champions as they kept the struggling Eagles (1-5-1) in the Eastern cellar, while the Cardinals (2-4-1) and Redskins (3-4) were playing out the string.

The Packers sold only 28,051 tickets for the game with the Rams in Green Bay. This was the only time in the history of the new City Stadium that Packers played before less than 30,000 fans. The final score of this affair was 20-7 Rams, but the game was hardly that close. LA ran up 504 yards of offense. Two interceptions, a lost fumble, and 89 yards in penalties kept the Rams from scoring at will. The same could be said for the Packers as the Rams picked off four of Parilli aerials and recovered one fumble to stop Green Bay scoring drives. Although the Packers lost, one young fan, Jeff Everson of Clintonville, Wisconsin, then only a lad of seven, experienced the greatest day of his life as he witnessed his first ever Packer game in person.

Overall, the Packers (1-6-1) looked better against the Rams (5-3) than they had against the Bears (5-3) and Colts (7-1), but they were still looking up at the Lions (3-4-1) and the 49ers (3-5). The Browns (6-2) resumed sole possession of first in the East because the Giants (5-3) took it on the chin from Buddy Parker's improving Steelers (4-4). Philadelphia (2-5-1) beat the Cardinals (2-5-1), and the Redskins (3-5) continued to fade.

The 49ers filled the bill for the Packers' final home tilt of the season in Milwaukee. Once again, the final score failed to tell the real tale of the game. Frisco ended up on top, 33-12, but if not for some good defense at the right times, it would have been a lot worse. Kicker Gordy Soltau had two field goal attempts blocked, and two others missed. The 49ers amassed 539 yards in offense, but they suffered 75 yards in penalties. The Packers helped the visitors with four turnovers and another poor performance by Babe Parilli who was six for 19 passing.

The loss buried the Packers (1-7-1) deeper in the cellar of the Western Division behind the Colts (8-1), Bears (6-3), Rams (5-4), 49ers (4-5), and Lions (3-5-1). The Browns (7-2) stayed ahead of the Giants (6-3), the oncoming Steelers (5-4), Redskins (3-6), Eagles (2-6-1), and Cardinals (2-6-1).

The Packers began the fourth quarter of the season with their annual trip to Detroit to be feasted on by the Lions. Unlike the past four weeks when they were being handed their lunch by opponents, the Packers actually put up a good fight in this one. The two teams traded fumbles deep in their own territories, resulting in touchdowns for each and 7-7 tie in the first quarter. A bad snap from center forced Max McGee to run instead of punting minutes later, and the result was a field goal by the Lions to put them up at the half, 10-7. The Packers drove 74 yards in the third quarter to take the lead, 14-10, but Detroit came right back with a march of 87 yards to regain the lead, 17-14. With 3:55 left in the game, McGee took off on a run instead of punting, failed to find a hole, and passed incomplete, giving the Lions the ball deep in Green Bay turf. Detroit converted the break into seven points and put the game away, 24-10. The Packers actually gained more yards than Detroit, 232-198, but those were not the numbers that counted.

On Monday morning, December 1, 1958, the standings of the National Football League had Baltimore (9-1) on top of the Western Division. The Browns (8-2) sat atop the Eastern Division. Behind the Colts were the Rams (6-4), Bears (6-4), Lions (4-5-1), 49ers (4-6). and Packers (1-8-1). Coming after Cleveland were the Giants (7-3), Steelers (6-4), Redskins (3-7), Eagles (2-7-1), and Cardinals (2-7-1) The Colts had clinched their division and had to wait for the Browns and Giants to decide who would meet them in the title game. But more important to the Packers was the fact that they had the worst record in the NFL and this was the day of the NFL's College Draft. Green Bay had first choice.

Scooter took Randy Duncan, a quarterback from Iowa, as Green Bay's first choice. Duncan had done well in the Big Ten, leading Iowa to the conference title and a berth in the Rose Bowl. He washed out as a pro.

In the second round, Scooter chose Alex Hawkins, a speedy halfback from South Carolina. Hawkins never played for the Packers, but he did have a good career with the Colts and Falcons in the NFL that lasted 10 years.

Scooter made one really solid choice for the Packers. With the team's third pick, he chose a fellow who led his team in both passing and pass receiving. His name was Boyd Dowler, and he could fly, running the 100-yard dash in 9.9 seconds. He played quarterback at

Colorado when the team lined up in a T-formation, and he played end when the team ran from the single-wing.

The Packers had no fourth-round pick because Scooter had traded it to Cleveland for Len Ford who retired after the season.

As much as he wanted to avoid having the worst season in Green Bay history, Scooter McLean couldn't prevent it from happening. The Packers lost their last two games on the West Coast. The 49ers rocked them, 48-21, and the Rams put them away, 34-20. The Frisco game was never close, and LA only toyed with the Packers for the first half.

Nice guy that he was, Scooter McLean saved the executive committee the trouble of firing him. He resigned as head coach of the Packers on December 17, 1958 and took a job as backfield coach of the Lions the same day.

The Packers finished 1-10-1 for the worst record in franchise history to date. This was the *piece de resistance* to his year at the helm of the Packers. It topped his other accomplishments of being the coach of the team that suffered the worst defeat in Packer history, of being the first head coach to really resign from the Packers, and of being the head coach of the Packers for the only game that ever drew less than 30,000 fans to the new City Stadium.

Poor Scooter! He was such a nice guy. Too nice. Maybe Leo Durocher had Scooter in mind when he made his famous quote. You know the one.

"Nice guys finish last."

Well, Scooter was the nicest guy of them all, and his record proved it.

Poor Scooter. He deserved better.

§§§

Summary

Curly Lambeau was born in Green Bay. He grew up there. He continued to live there the rest of his life, although some of his adventures did take him elsewhere for months at a time. He was the hometown boy who never really left home.

Lambeau helped organize the town football team in 1919, and because he had always been the leader on the playground, his teammates elected him to be their captain. Working with real coaches on the sidelines, he directed the fortunes of the Packers on the field. Working with businessmen, he directed the team's fortunes off the field. He was quite successful at both, and in time, he became the kingpin of the Green Bay Packers.

Throughout the '20s, '30s, and '40s, Lambeau produced winners on the field, and this resulted in the Packers being winners off the field as well. As long as Lambeau produced, the other men in the organization let him do just about anything he pleased. When he abused this freedom and matters turned sour for the Packers on the field as well as off, these men, the executive committee, tried tightening the reins on Lambeau, but he had been the king for too long to allow this to happen. He fought back, and they fought back. Something had to give, and it was Lambeau. He moved on to coach the Chicago Cardinals.

The executive committee of the Green Bay Packers felt they had learned a valuable lesson from Lambeau, which was never again to allow any single man to have the authority that Lambeau had exercised over the years. With that thought in mind, they hired Gene Ronzani to replace Lambeau as the head coach of the Packers in 1950. Although he was given the same titles as Lambeau, i.e., head coach, general manager, and vice-president, Ronzani was never given the same authority as Lambeau. He could draw up all the plays he wanted to run, make his players practice as hard as he wanted them to practice, discipline them when they needed it, etc. But he couldn't spend any of the corporation's money without prior approval from the executive committee. Ronzani was all right with this control over him; he was a football coach, not a businessman; the executive committee could watch the bottom line all they wanted; he would watch the goal lines.

The executive committee was all right with the fiscal control that they held over Ronzani; he was a football coach, and they were businessmen; he could watch the lines on the field, and they would watch the lines on the ledger. They worked in complete harmony with Ronzani for three years, and because he was showing them a steady improvement in the team, they rewarded him with a new contract.

Then came 1953 and this working relationship between Ronzani and the executive committee went to Hell in a hand basket. Why?

The only major change in the structure of this relationship was at the head of the organization. Emil Fischer stepped down as president of the corporation, and Russ Bogda was elected to replace him. Fischer was the president of a large business that did not live and breathe by the whims of the purchasing public; he understood the terms steady growth and continuity. Bogda headed up an automobile dealership that sold both new and used cars; the terms steady growth and continuity were foreign to him; he was accustomed to getting results today no matter what it took. Fischer had directed the fortunes of the Green Bay Packers, Inc., according to the sound business principles that had worked so well for him with his company. Bogda applied the same theory when he took over; i.e., he tried to run the Packers by the same methods he used in his business; he treated the Packers like a car dealership. Fischer weeded out the problems of the organization when he forced the resignation of Curly Lambeau, then he rebuilt the Green Bay Packers, Inc., from the ground up. When he stepped down as president, the Packers were in better shape than when he was given the leadership reins. Bogda took a well-oiled ship and tinkered with it until it began springing leaks, and the first thing he did was exactly what all sales manager's do when sales fall off: he pointed the finger of blame and started firing people.

History of sports franchises has shown that organizations with strong continuity produce the most winners over the long run. The Packers were a prime example of this fact. For nearly three decades with Lambeau at the helm, the Packers were the most successful team in the National Football League. Two factors caused their demise under Lambeau, and both were money related. Lambeau was misusing the corporation's funds for his own purposes, and the Packers could not earn enough money to compete with the teams of the All-America Conference for the high salaried players when the AAC and NFL were at war in the second half of the '40s. If the AAC had never come into existence, Lambeau probably would have stayed at the helm of the Packers until he either died or was too incapacitated to coach. He would have continued to misuse funds for himself, but the executive committee would have kept that under control.

To support this hypothesis that continuity is the secret to success in professional sports, let's look at the Dodgers of baseball. From 1954 through this writing, the Dodgers have been owned by one family and have had only two field managers, and over that time span, whether in Brooklyn or Los Angeles, the Dodgers have the best record in all of baseball. Other teams have had spurts of success, such as the Oakland A's of the '70s and the Atlanta Braves of the '90s, but no others have had the success of the Dodgers. The New York Yankees? The Yankees lost their continuity when Yogi Berra was fired as manager, and it took them a decade to regain what they had in the '50s and early '60s, but they lost that when owner George Steinbrenner began playing musical managers in the '80s.

Further support comes from the Dallas Cowboys who had only one head coach for almost three decades. Tom Landry built a sound team from scratch, then kept it on or near the top for 20 years. Only his last few seasons could be termed off years because the Cowboys had finally exhausted the talent pool and had to rebuild. Landry never got the chance to do that, just the same as Lambeau, because of a change in ownership.

In 1953, Russ Bogda fell into the trap of making changes when overly high expectations are not met. He thought the Packers were no different than the salesmen at his car dealership; when sales were off, something had to be wrong with the salesmen; find out what it was and fix it and get them back on track; if that didn't work, fire a few and scare the rest into producing better; after all, salesmen are a dime a dozen; and if that doesn't work, then fire the sales manager. Substitute players for salesmen and head coach for sales manager, and *voila!* you have what happened to Gene Ronzani and Packers in 1953.

Of course, after you fire the sales manager, you have to hire a new one, one who fits your style a little more. Bogda did just that when Lisle Blackbourn was hired to coach the Packers. Bogda got a man of his own ilk, and sales picked up again and the team was once again headed in the right direction. For three years, the team was headed in the right direction. Then expectations got high again, and the sales force failed to meet the goals set for them by the public.

This is simplifying the situation a little too much. It was more complicated than that. But the bottom line was still win, win, win, win! Or hit the road, Jack!

John Torinus wrote that it was the executive committee's practice to let the coach do his job and not to interfere with the operation of the team. How did he put it exactly?

> Late in the 1957 season, when the Packers had won only one more game after their opening victory against the Bears, Blackbourn was questioned at an Executive Committee meeting as to why he wasn't playing Hornung and Taylor more. It had long been and still is the policy of the Executive Committee not to interfere in any way in the coaching of the

football team, [Author's italics.] but the committee does retain overall supervision of the total amount of money which is allocated to the coach for player personnel. In this instance, one Committee member, Fred Leicht, felt that they were owed some explanation about why two very high-priced ballplayers were sitting on the bench. He commented to Blackbourn that the coach had asked the committee for funds over and above the normal range of player salaries to acquire Hornung and Taylor. Blackbourn retorted angrily that it was none of the Committee's business. The unfortunate part of the exchange was the fact that Leicht was probably the most respected of all the members of the committee and a very mild-mannered gentleman. The rest of the Committee took obvious umbrage at Blackbourn's handling of the situation.

First off, Torinus was confused about the players being Hornung and Taylor when Taylor never played under Blackbourn. [See Chapter 15 for more about this episode.] But never mind that. The point is Torinus stated *the executive committee never interfered with the coaching of the team,* [Author's italics] then he turned around and stated except when it came to playing high-priced players because of their fiscal responsibility to the corporation. Sorry, that doesn't wash. The simple truth is the executive committee was trying to tell Blackbourn how to run his team. Their reason for doing so had no bearing whatsoever on the fact that they did it after agreeing not to do it. No wonder Blackbourn was angry. Torinus excusing the executive committee for breaking the rules which they established is the same as the homeowner who accidentally sets his house on fire then blames the firemen for not putting out the fire correctly and saving his house. If Leicht had never posed the question to Blackbourn, the coach might not have replied angrily. Ever have some stranger tell you how to deal with your child in a grocery store? Most people give angry replies at such interference in a family matter. Blackbourn was merely doing the same thing.

Torinus went on to state that Blackbourn lacked the ability to communicate and motivate the modern professional player. This was probably true, but the interference of the executive committee with the team, as Bob Forte stated when Ronzani was fired, might have had something to do with that. It appears that the executive committee was undermining Blackbourn's authority over the players by dealing with them on the side as Forte related to Chuck Johnson. It's no wonder that Blackbourn flew off the handle at Leicht and now caught with their hands in the coach's cookie jar, the executive committee responded by firing Blackbourn.

There is also the possibility that the executive committee wasn't thinking too clearly as a group when they fired Blackbourn. Consider the two sad facts that Emil Fischer had died only five days before they made their decision and that Russ Bogda was dying of cancer. At such times, people do act irrationally. This could explain why they fired Blackbourn; not so much out of anger with him but because they were distraught over the loss of one good friend and the impending demise of another.

This could also explain why they gave the head coaching job to Ray McLean. Those men of the executive committee, when in a proper state of mind, must have known that Scooter was not head coaching material. He was no authority figure, and he certainly didn't have the intelligence to be a head coach. Being a great guy is not the sole qualification for being a head coach in the NFL or a manager in the Majors. If it was, my boyhood hero, Ernie Banks, would have been manager of the Chicago Cubs ever since his playing days were over. As anyone who knows anything about Ernie Banks will tell you, Ernie is a saint, but he is no rocket scientist. Neither was Scooter, but the executive committee didn't want to admit that they had made a mistake while they still had time to correct their error. Instead, they let poor Scooter make a fool of himself through the '58 season.

This was the final shameful act of the executive committee for this decade. It was the cherry on their chocolate sundae of shameful acts in the '50s. Firing Ronzani was the ice cream and dumping on Blackbourn the way they did was the chocolate sauce. The really shameful part of all this was these cowardly acts soiled their two greatest achievements: They built a fine, new football facility in City Stadium, and they preserved the franchise for the city of Green Bay and the fans in Wisconsin and Upper Michigan. They accomplished both of these feats against incredible odds. It's just a shame that their finest hours had to be tainted by their lowest.

As 1959 began, the Green Bay Packers were in total confusion. They couldn't find a coach, and no one was sure where to look for one. To paraphrase Bette Davis, what a mess!

Then a miracle happened, as it always seems to with the Packers.

When he addressed the executive committee for the first time after being hired as head coach and general manager of the Green Bay Packers, Vince Lombardi slammed his hand on the table and said:

"I want it understood that I am in complete command here."

Lombardi got their attention, and... well, the rest comes in future volumes of this history of the Green Bay Packers.

§§§

Bibliography

BOOKS

The Baseball Encyclopedia, Sixth Edition, Revised, Updated & Expanded, edited by Joseph L. Reichler, Macmillan Publishing Co., Inc., 1985

George Halas and the Chicago Bears, George Vass, Henry Regnery Company, 1971

The Green Bay Packers, Pro Football's Pioneer Team, Chuck Johnson, Thomas Nelson & Sons, 1961.

The Green Bay Packers, The Story of Professional Football, Arch Ward, G.P. Putnam's Sons, 1946.

Halas on Halas, George Halas with Gwen Morgan and Arthur Veysey, McGraw-Hill Book Co., 1979

This Day In Packer History, Jeff Everson, Angel Press of WI, 1998

History of American Football, Allison Danzig, Prentice-Hall, Inc., 1956.

The NFL's Official Encyclopedic History of Professional Football, Macmillan Publishing Co., Inc., 1973

Official 1985 National Football League Record & Fact Book.

The Packer Legend: An Inside Look, John B. Torinus, Sr., Laranmark Press, 1982

The Pro Football Digest, edited by Robert Billings, Digest Books, Inc., 1978

The Scrapbook History of Pro Football, Richard M. Cohen, Jordan A. Deutsch, Roland T. Johnson, and David S. Neft, The Bobbs-Merrill Company, 1977.

NEWSPAPERS

Chicago Sun, The
Chicago Daily News, The
Chicago Herald-Examiner, The
Chicago Tribune, The
Daily Georgian and Sunday American
Green Bay Gazette
Green Bay Press-Gazette, The
Iron Mountain News, The
The Los Angeles Examiner, The
Los Angeles Times, The
Milwaukee Journal, The
Milwaukee Sentinel, The
New York Daily News, The
New York Times, The
Packer Report, The
The South Bend Tribune, The

PERIODICALS

Collier's
Time
Sport Magazine
Sports Illustrated
Touchback, The

Green Bay Packers Media Guide, 1986 Green Bay Packers Media Guide, 1987 Green Bay Packers Media Guide, 1988 Green Bay Packers Media Guide, 1989 Green Bay Packers Media Guide, 1990 Green Bay Packers Media Guide, 1991 Green Bay Packers Media Guide, 1992 Green Bay Packers Media Guide, 1993 Green Bay Packers Media Guide, 1994 Green Bay Packers Yearbook

§§§

ABOUT THE AUTHOR

Larry Names has had 44 titles published to date, 28 novels, and the remainder non-fiction all dealing with sports teams or sports figures. He is a recognized authority on the Green Bay Packers, Chicago Cubs and Chicago White Sox.

He resides in central Wisconsin with his wife Peg on a family farm that has been in his wife's family since 1854. They have a son, Torry and a daughter, Tegan, a klepto-cat - Cleo, an escape-artist palomino named Lucky Moondancer, an Arabian mare named Amerrah, a Tennessee Walker named Windy and an award-winning Arabian stud colt named Micah.

Larry has four children from his first marriage: daughter Sigrid, an author in her own rite; son Paul; daughter Kristin, an award-winning screenwriter; and daughter Sonje. He also has 17 grandchildren and two great-grandchildren.

The author was born in Mishawaka, Indiana and has lived in nine different states during his life and went to eleven schools growing up and three colleges after serving his country in the Navy. He is an avid researcher, genealogist, and traveler.

For more information about Larry Names and his books, go to www.larrynames.com

"Like" Larry Names on his Facebook Fan page at: https://www.facebook.com/LarryNames/

Larry Names Book List

Oswald Reflection, The, Books-in-Motion
Shaman's Secret, The, Books-in-Motion
Bose, Books-in-Motion
Boomtown, Books-in-Motion
Amazon Kindle Editions
Creed #1: A Texas Creed
Creed #2: Texas Payback
Creed #3: Texas Powderkeg
Creed #4: Kentucky Pride
Creed #5: Missouri Guns
Creed #6: Texan's Honor
Creed #7: Texas Freedom
Creed #8: Colorado Prey
Creed #9: Cheyenne Justice
Creed #10: Arkansas Raiders
Creed #11: Boston Mountain Renegades
Prospecting For Murder
The Oswald Reflection
Tegan O'Malley – A Traveler in Time
Tegan O'Malley – Stowaway on Titanic
Maisy Malone – Starring Mabel Normand & Mack Sennett -A Two Reel Murder
Non-Fiction—Hardcover
Dear Pete: The life of Pete Rose
The History of the Green Bay Packers, The Lambeau Years, Part One
The History of the Green Bay Packers, The Lambeau Years, Part Two
The History of the Green Bay Packers, The Lambeau Years, Part Three
The History of the Green Bay Packers, The Lambeau Years, The Shameful Years
Bury My Heart At Wrigley Field: The History of the Chicago Cubs
-When the Cubs Were the White Stockings, Part One
Green Bay Packers Facts & Trivia, 1st Edition
Green Bay Packers Facts & Trivia, 2nd Edition
Green Bay Packers Facts & Trivia, 3rd Edition
Green Bay Packers Facts & Trivia, 4t Edition
Chicago White Sox Facts & Trivia
Out at Home by Milt Pappas, Wayne Mausser and Larry Names
Home Plate by Steve Trout, Dave Campbell and Larry Names
Non-Fiction – Trade Paperback
Green Bay Packers Facts & Trivia, 1st Edition
Green Bay Packers Facts & Trivia, 2nd Edition
Green Bay Packers Facts & Trivia, 3rd Edition
Green Bay Packers Facts & Trivia, 4t Edition
Chicago White Sox Facts & Trivia
The Lambeau Years, Part One - The History of the Green Bay Packers, Vol. 1
The Lambeau Years, Part Two - The History of the Green Bay Packers, Vol. 2
The Lambeau Years, Part Three - The History of the Green Bay Packers, Vol. 3
The Shameful Years - The History of the Green Bay Packers, Vol. 4
Bury My Heart At Wrigley Field: The History of the Chicago Cubs
-When the Cubs Were the White Stockings, Part One
Non-Fiction – Kindle
The Lambeau Years, Part One - The History of the Green Bay Packers, Vol. 1
The Lambeau Years, Part Two - The History of the Green Bay Packers, Vol. 2
The Lambeau Years, Part Three - The History of the Green Bay Packers, Vol. 3
The Shameful Years - The History of the Green Bay Packers, Vol. 4
Bury My Heart At Wrigley Field: The History of the Chicago Cubs
-When the Cubs Were the White Stockings, Part One

§§§

Index

Made in the USA
Coppell, TX
14 November 2022

86354701R00177